American Society for Training &

I N A C T I O N

Effective Leadership Programs

TWELVE

CASE STUDIES

FROM THE

REAL WORLD

OF TRAINING

JACK J. PHILLIPS
SERIES EDITOR

FRANKLIN C. ASHBY
EDITOR

ASTD

Ordering information: Books published by the American Society for Training & Development can be ordered by calling 800.628.2783 or 703.683.8100.

Library of Congress Catalog Card Number: 99-73473
ISBN: 1-56286-119-0

Table of Contents

Introduction to the
In Action Series

L ike most professionals, the people involved in human resource development (HRD) are eager to see practical applications of models, techniques, theories, strategies, and issues relevant to their field. In recent years, practitioners have developed an intense desire to learn about the first-hand experiences of organizations implementing HRD programs. To fill this critical void, the Publishing Review Committee of the American Society for Training & Development established the *In Action* casebook series. Covering a variety of topics in HRD, the series significantly adds to the current literature in the field.

The objectives of the *In Action* series are:

- *To provide real-world examples of HRD program application and implementation.* Each case describes significant issues, events, actions, and activities. When possible, actual names of organizations and individuals are used. Where names are disguised, the events are factual.

- *To focus on challenging and difficult issues confronting the HRD field.* These cases explore areas where it is difficult to find information or where processes or techniques are not standardized or fully developed. Emerging issues critical to success are also explored.

- *To recognize the work of professionals in the HRD field by presenting best practices.* Each casebook represents the most effective examples available. Issue editors are experienced professionals, and topics are carefully selected to ensure that they represent important and timely issues. Cases are written by highly respected HRD practitioners, authors, researchers, and consultants. The authors focus on many high-profile organizations—names you will quickly recognize.

- *To serve as a self-teaching tool for people learning about the HRD field.* As a stand-alone reference, each volume is a practical learning tool which fully explores numerous topics and issues.

- *To present a medium for teaching groups about the practical aspects of HRD.* Each book is a useful supplement to general and specialized HRD textbooks and serves as a discussion guide to enhance learning in formal and informal settings.

These cases will challenge and motivate you. The new insights you gain will serve as an impetus for positive change in your organization. If you have a case that might serve the same purpose for other HRD professionals, please contact me. New casebooks are being developed. If you have suggestions on ways to improve the *In Action* series, your input is welcomed.

Jack J. Phillips, Ph.D.
Series Editor
Performance Resources Organization
Box 380637
Birmingham, AL 35238-0637

Preface

The world of work has changed radically during the past decade and it continues to change faster than at any time since the industrial revolution. Now, in the computer age, managers have immediate and continuous access to new information, revolutionizing their ability to make decisions. In truth, new managers today are faced with a culture bearing little resemblance to that of past generations.

Gone, too, in most companies, is the old hierarchical structure in which top management made all the decisions and filtered them down through a series of layers to the rank-and-file. Today things are more collaborative, more team-based, more cross-functional. People at most every level are expected to know about, and often contribute to, multiple aspects of their organizations' activities.

This has led to a new challenge for leaders of today's organizations. Managers can no longer rely on the authority of their positions to command results, but must now—more than ever—elicit not just the willing cooperation, but the active participation of all members of their staffs to achieve their goals.

So how have they responded? In many cases, by rethinking the attitudes and perceptions that dominate their organizational cultures, embracing the inevitability of change, and retooling the processes and systems they use to run their businesses. Old philosophies are clearly being replaced by new and better approaches that take into consideration the sweeping changes that have already occurred, and those that promise to continue occurring in corporate America well into the new century.

Here is just a sample of some of the more notable.

The Ever-changing, Advancing Technologies

Research clearly suggests that tomorrow's leaders will not, and *cannot,* be satisfied with the status quo. The focus will be on finding better ways of doing things, continually pushing innovation forward, prompting newer, ever more amazing technology-driven solutions.

Diversity in the Workforce

According to a study issued by the Hudson Institute, by the year 2000, only 15 percent of those entering the workforce will be American-born white males. This has enormous implications for the future of American industry, and it's imperative that steps be taken to recognize the value and capitalize on the benefits that this increasingly diverse population can bring to organizations. In addition, more women are working in positions previously dominated by men, and more women and members of minority groups are moving up the ladder into leadership positions. Training programs must be provided to help managers understand, appreciate, and deal with these changes.

A Continued Focus on Teams

Thousands of organizations throughout the world have embraced the idea of team-based work groups. Many have restructured, replacing the traditional *boss-subordinate* management model with empowered teams and other collaborative groups who work with team leaders in making major decisions and carrying them out.

The Continued *Flattening* of Organizational Structures

Despite increased hiring in recent years due to a booming economy, the trend toward flatter, less middle-heavy organizations continues. In truth, and in large part as a result of the influence of quality gurus like Edwards Deming and Joseph Juran, a great many middle-level positions have been eliminated throughout corporate America in the past 10 years. This has created a good deal of added pressure on those who remain, and, in some ways, many organizations are still struggling with ways to stay competitive while doing "more with less."

A Continuing Focus on Cost-Reduction and Cost-Containment

Surveys continue to show that senior-level executives in most every industry still view the reduction of expenses and the containing of costs central to the long-term performance and profitability of their firms. Corporate spending has taken a much more conservative tack in the past 10 years, and the likelihood is, despite continuing good economic news, the trend will continue.

A Continued Emphasis on Creativity and Innovation

Managers have long recognized and, indeed, much appreciated the importance of constantly seeking new, better ways of doing things. This trend will also continue and accelerate as we move into the new

millennium. The key drivers? The relentless search for bigger profits, wider margins, and better standards of living.

The Manager as Coach

The best business leaders of tomorrow will have among their competencies the ability to coach others to maximum performance. Gone
will be the dictators, the tyrants, and the distant "command-and-con-
trol freaks." Replacing them will be more enlightened, more approachable
and respectful leaders, still with high expectations, but now with a
much more skilled and reasonable approach to working with diverse
cultures, motivating Gen-Xers, and creating high levels of morale and
motivation.

The Need for Continuous Self-Development

Although studies have shown that most outstanding leaders view
themselves as perpetual "works-in-progress," it seems clear that a similar attitude and increased access to sound, relevant training and educational opportunities will soon be expected from, and by, most every
American worker.

To meet the demands of leadership in the new century, top management must give its full support to leadership training programs
that hone the skills of promising managers and team leaders at every
level of the organization. Such programs must demonstrate a practical, results-oriented approach to new habit development and be designed in ways that maximize participant involvement and motivation.
This book contains case histories of unusually successful leadership
interventions that satisfy those criteria. Each offers an explanation
of the strategies, techniques, and methodologies used to identify and
address the leadership-related issues faced by the organizations involved. And each also provides insights into how similar approaches might be used by others.

Target Audience

This book should interest leaders and managers at all levels. It can
be a valuable tool for newly appointed supervisors and managers eager to learn more about leadership training. It will also serve as a means
of exposing experienced senior managers to the latest techniques in
executive coaching and leadership development. And it can be used
by team leaders as a guide to developing and leading their teams.

Human resources managers and training and development specialists will find information in this book that will help them strength-

en the leadership development programs currently a part of their organizations. Senior executives and business owners will find it helpful in broadening their understanding of the solutions available to them when confronted with a leadership-related problem or crisis.

College and university professors should find this book extremely useful; they can use the cases as illustrations and examples of real life leadership challenges and as meaningful learning examples. This casebook can also be used as a supplement to a standard text in management or adult and continuing education and as a reference source for term papers, theses, or dissertations.

The Cases

The most challenging part of developing a publication of this sort is selecting the appropriate cases. Each had to meet specific guidelines and offer methodologies that proved unusually successful. From the many cases submitted, we selected those that we considered both the most compelling and the most useful to those looking to this book for guidance.

Because each author's method of presentation is individual, the style and content of the cases are not all structured in the same manner. It is important for the reader to experience each intervention as it is developed and to identify the issues involved in each setting and situation. The result is a variety of presentations with a variety of styles.

There was no attempt to restrict cases to any particular type of methodology. It is helpful to readers to be exposed to a wide range of approaches. We have also resisted the temptation to pass judgment on the various solutions, preferring to let the reader evaluate the different techniques and their appropriateness for each particular setting.

In some cases, the name of the organization is identified, as are the individuals who are involved. In others, the name of the organization, and those involved, is disguised at the request of the case author.

Case Authors

It would be difficult to find a more impressive group of contributors to an HRD publication than those contained in this book. Each is an experienced, knowledgeable professional at the leading edge of their field.

Collectively, they represent practitioners, consultants, researchers, and professors. Individually, they represent a cross-section of those involved in the HRD field today. A few are well-known speakers and writers who have made a substantial contribution to their field and have taken the opportunity to provide an example of their top-quality work. Others have made their mark quietly, making great contributions to their organizations and the lives of others, but with a lower profile.

It has been a great pleasure and a genuine privilege working with them all.

Suggestions

We welcome your input. If you have ideas or recommendations regarding the presentation of the cases in this book, the case selection, or the quality of the cases, please send them to Performance Resources Organization, Box 380637, Birmingham, Alabama 35238-0637. All letters will be appreciated and acknowledged. Your opinions about this volume will help improve others in this series.

Acknowledgments

Although this casebook is a collective work of many individuals, the first acknowledgment must go to the case authors. Each did a superb job and was a pleasure to work with. I also want to acknowledge the organizations that have allowed the use of their names and programs for publication. I trust the final product has portrayed them as the progressive organizations they are; firms interested in their people, and in the developing of leadership talent.

Don Milazzo and Terry Cantrell from The Performance Resources Organization have served as the chief architects and directors of the effort to identify the most qualified authors and the best cases. Without them this publication could not have been developed or delivered within a reasonable time frame. They made a difficult job look easy.

My wife, Rita, and son, Danny, also deserve a special thanks for their understanding and patience, and for giving up weekend after weekend of fun while I worked on this manuscript.

Franklin C. Ashby, Editor
Smithtown, New York

September 1999

How to Use This Casebook

These cases present a variety of approaches to developing leadership potential. Most focus on training interventions, whereas others deal with executive coaching and individual mentoring strategies. Collectively, they offer a wide range of settings, methods, techniques, strategies, and approaches, representing manufacturing, service, government, and educational organizations and institutions.

Target groups for the programs range from senior-level executives to supervisory and nonmanagement personnel, well established professionals to youths at risk. As a group, these cases represent a rich source of information about the strategies of some of the best practitioners, consultants, educators, and researchers in the field. Table 1 provides an overview of the cases in this book.

Each case does not necessarily represent the ideal approach for the specific situation. In every case it is also possible to identify areas that could benefit from refinement or improvement. That is part of the learning process—to build on the work of other people.

Using the Cases

There are several ways to use this book. It will surely be helpful to anyone interested in the topic of leadership or leadership development. Specifically, four uses are recommended:

1. The book will be useful to HRD professionals as a basic reference of practical applications of leadership training and leadership development strategies. A reader can analyze and dissect each of the cases to develop an understanding of the issues, approaches, and, most of all, refinements or improvements that could be made.

2. This book will be useful in group discussions, where interested individuals can react to the material, offer different perspectives, and draw conclusions about approaches and techniques.

3. This book will serve as an excellent supplement to other management and training and development textbooks. It provides the extra dimension of real-life cases that show the outcomes of leadership training and executive coaching interventions.

Table 1. Overview of the case studies.

Case	Industry	Key Features	Target Audience
Allstate Insurance Company	Insurance/United States	Senior executive development, leadership development strategies, 360° feedback, measurement surveys	Executive coaches, program designers, HRD professionals, trainers, senior executives
Dr Pepper/Seven Up, Inc.	Food Processing/United States	Contingency leadership principles, internal partnering, customer service assessments	HRD staff, program designers, trainers, consultants, assessment specialists
Michigan's Family Independence Agency	Public Service/United States	Fast-track leadership development, teaching organization model	Counselors, HRD managers, HRD supervisors, trainers, consultants
E.G. Verlander & Associates	Consulting/United States	Executive coaching strategies, senior level leadership development, trends in leadership coaching and development	HRD staff, consultants, trainers, executive coaches, managers
Affiliated Capital Corporation Prudential Burnet Realty Valuation Management Consultants, Inc.	Real Estate/United States	Competencies, assessments, leadership development strategies	Business managers, supervisors, executive coaches, HRD staff
Sandia National Laboratories	Defense/United States	Mentoring, pretesting, posttesting, satisfaction testing, skill transfers via mentoring	Government managers, HRD professionals, consultants, trainers, executive coaches

Organization	Industry/Country	Focus	Audience
Haywood Insurance	Insurance/United States	Executive coaching, leadership development, transformational coaching	HRD staff, consultants, mentors, senior executives, trainers, managers, executive coaches
Ohio State University	Higher Education/United States	Leadership development strategies, purpose and mission, quality improvement strategies	University officials, HRD professionals, education consultants, trainers, university department heads
University of North Carolina Health Care	Health Care/United States	360° Assessments, internal partnering, mentoring, leadership development modeling	HRD staff, consultants, health care administrators, trainers, managers
Camp RYLA, Rotary International	At-Risk Youth/United States	Motivating of young people, behavior transformations, leadership modeling for young adults	Counselors, HRD staff, trainers, social psychologists, consultants, managers
Northern States Power Company	Utility/United States	Executive and management coaching, program design, evaluation systems, management support systems	HRD staff, trainers, consultants, managers, executive coaches
Mobil Oil's North America Marketing and Refining Division	Petroleum/United States	Assessments, self-awareness, simulations, leadership competencies, action learning	Consultants, trainers, HRD staff, assessment specialists

4. Finally, this book will be extremely valuable to managers and executives who do not have primary training responsibility. These managers provide support and assistance to the HRD staff, and it is helpful to them to understand the methodologies HRD professionals use, and the results their programs can yield.

Follow-Up

Space limitations have required that some cases be shorter than the author and editor would have liked. Some information concerning background, assumptions, strategies, and results had to be omitted. If additional information on a case is needed or desired, please contact either the lead author or Performance Resources Organization, Box 380637, Birmingham, Alabama 35238-0637; tel: 205.678.9700. In most instances, the address of the lead author is provided in the biographical information offered by each person at the beginning of his or her case.

The Past, Present, and Future of Leadership Development

Franklin C. Ashby

As the dynamics of organizational cultures have changed over the past decades, so too has the function of the leader. Influenced by technological innovations, the ease and speed of communications and, most important, the attitudes of the men and women who staff organizations, the role of the leader has shifted from control by power to coordination and collaboration through persuasion and motivation.

The Changing Power Structure

Robert L. Dilenschneider (1992) describes the changes discussed above (Table 1). Dilenschneider emphasizes that to succeed in their changing role, leaders must create a strong vision, articulate a clear course, and motivate their organizations toward action.

From Vision to Reality

Boyett and Conn, in their best-selling book, *Workplace 2000,* add that in order to communicate a lofty vision, future leaders must earn the trust of subordinates. This involves:
- building confidence by providing opportunities for a series of increasingly larger successes
- reinforcing all successes through meaningful rewards, recognition, and praise
- making work fun
- coaching for ongoing improvement.

According to Boyett and Conn, good leaders make sure staff members have the training and resources they need. They make themselves available for advice and counsel, then step back and let team mem-

Table 1. The evolution of power.

1950s and 1960s	1970s and 1980s	1990s
Power as administration	*Power as management*	*Power as leadership*
Conformist	Exception driven	Visionary
Chain of command	Ad hoc	Instant
Stable	Turbulent	Sustaining
Introspective	Market driven	Positioning
Apprenticeship	Mentoring	Collegial

bers take action. If trouble develops, they're available to offer the support necessary.

The new role of the leader can be summarized in what I refer to as the "Four Cs of Contemporary Leadership": *Collegiality, Cooperation, Collaboration, and Coaching.*

But Does the "Four C" Model Work?

According to a recent study by the University of Southern California's (USC) Marshall School of Business, using data supplied by 216 Fortune 1000 companies, researchers rated organizations on the prevalence of employee involvement practices. They then compared the companies' rates of return on a range of financial indicators. On every one of the indicators—including sales, equity, assets, and stockholder investment—researchers found significantly better returns for companies that were high users of employee involvement.

For instance, in fiscal year 1996 the average return on stockholder investment (stock price appreciation minus dividends) was 44 percent among high users of employee involvement efforts, compared with 21 percent among low users. "The difference represents billions of dollars of returns to investors," said study lead researcher Edward Lawler, a professor of management and organization at USC's Marshall School. Lawler noted that employee involvement programs tend to make workers more satisfied with their jobs and less likely to leave them. That's an important finding because many companies are now scrambling to find skilled workers and retain the ones they have.

The Challenge of Developing Leaders for the Future

The much reported challenge of locating and retaining top management talent has been exacerbated in recent years by a continued shrinking pool of experienced managers, escalating costs in recruiting outside talent, and a startling lack of attention to developing leaders from within. James K. Schwab, CEO of Manchester Partners International, a global human resources consulting firm headquartered in Philadelphia, says the avoidance of succession planning is a serious factor that cannot be ignored. Schwab contends the leadership gap is pervasive and will bedevil the corporate world for decades to come. A corresponding survey of 200 *Fortune* 500 companies indicated that the average company expects 30 percent turnover at the executive ranks in the next five years, with one-third of human resources executives believing they'll have significant difficulty finding suitable replacements. It is estimated that first-year costs of filling an executive vacancy is approximately $750,000, which includes finding the replacement, training and development, and the opportunity cost involved in getting the new hire up to speed.

Three-quarters of corporate officers surveyed for a study by McKinsey and Company, an international management consulting firm based in New York, said their companies had insufficient talent or were chronically talent-short across the board. This shortage is intensified by the changes in the type of characteristics one seeks in managers today. Leadership is becoming more focused on the psychological needs of human beings. Don Clifton, chairman of the Gallup Organisation in London, commented: "We've done more than a million surveys and have found that the old dictator-type leadership style doesn't work nearly as well as a more caring one. Workers who believe their supervisors care for them perform better, and financial results bear this out." Cindy Hartley, vice president of human resources at Sunoco, concurs. "Today's workforce requires a different kind of leader than 10 years ago, leaders who can inspire people and lead teams are essential. Because of these requirements, the bar has been raised in terms of what we expect."

The 12 Qualities of Truly Great Leaders

During my research for this book and other projects, I've found that although much of the counsel and advice on leadership dispensed by the management "gurus" of the 1980s and 1990s is good, there is a tendency to overstate and overcomplicate.

Although it seems fair to say that most outstanding leaders have probably faced and overcome a multitude of diverse problems and challenges in their lives, I've found they also exhibit many similar characteristics and behavior patterns. I've come to call these patterns "The 12 Qualities of Truly Great Leaders," described in the following paragraphs. Truly great leaders:

1. **Have enthusiastic followers.** Often people in positions of authority can compel subordinates to follow orders by virtue of the power of their jobs. But such people are not true leaders. Yes, the orders will be followed, but in many cases that's all that will happen. True leaders develop confidence, trust, and enthusiasm in their associates (note that they think of them as associates—not subordinates). This engenders a desire not only to follow the lead of the manager, but to initiate, innovate, and implement ideas that move the organization closer to its goals.

2. **Take a constructively discontented view of the world.** Good leaders aren't complacent. They're constantly on the alert for innovations that will improve the way work is done, assure continuing customer satisfaction, and increase the profitability of the organization. Their minds are open to new ideas. They welcome suggestions. And even after changes and improvements are made, they keep looking for even better ways to accomplish their goals. Leaders like this are never fully satisfied. They review practices and procedures on a regular basis to fine-tune them. They don't get enamored with their own ideas, but are instead forever open to constructive criticism. They want what's best. And they know the way to assure it is to be constantly on the look-out for better ways of doing things.

3. **Consider themselves a work-in-progress.** Just as effective leaders are constructively discontent about their work, they are never entirely satisfied with themselves. They attend seminars and self-improvement programs, purchase and listen to motivational tapes, and read books and periodicals to keep up not only with the latest in their fields, but to improve their knowledge and understanding in a variety of areas. I've found most great leaders don't limit their talents to their jobs. They take active roles in professional and trade associations to keep in touch with new developments and share ideas with colleagues from other organizations. They attend and participate in conventions and conferences and develop networks of people to whom they can turn for knowledge and advice.

4. **Excel when the stakes are high.** We've all heard the adage "Leaders are made not born," and, like most adages, there is a great deal

of truth in this one. However, some people do seem to be born leaders. From early childhood, they take the lead in playing games, take risks, are selected as team captains, are elected to student offices, and take charge of everything in which they are involved. In some ways (at least according to their proud parents), they always seemed destined for big things in life.

Many of the greatest leaders were not born to greatness, however, but developed it when placed or forced into leadership positions. History is replete with stories of ordinary men and women who rose to the heights at critical moments when leadership was needed. Lech Walesa is, of course, a good, much publicized example of this. As we know, in 1980 when the workers at the Lenin Shipyard in Gdansk, Poland, went on strike for better working conditions, the communist government cracked down on them. Walesa was an electrician in the shipyard and one of the leaders of Solidarity, an independent trade union. He had little education and had never considered himself anything more than an artisan. But when leadership was needed, he stepped out to speak up for the workers in defying the authorities. Despite several arrests and imprisonments, his leadership of the strike inspired the Polish people to work to overthrow the communist regime. In 1983, he was awarded the Nobel Peace Price and in 1990 was elected president of Poland.

5. **Demonstrate a good understanding of the "affective domain."** Great leaders understand people—what causes them to act and react the way they do. They recognize the importance of being a motivating factor for people—appealing to the drives and the feelings of others.

They also take a genuine interest in the people with whom they interact. As Dale Carnegie succinctly pointed out: "You can make more friends in two months by becoming genuinely interested in others than you can in two years by trying to get others interested in you."

6. **Expect more from *themselves* than they do others.** The best leaders I know set high standards for themselves and then work hard to exceed them. They know they're "visible," and they take seriously their responsibilities as role models.

However, like everyone, they also make mistakes; and when they do, they view them as learning opportunities. Truly great leaders strive hard to be the best they can be at everything they do, but they also understand and appreciate their own human frailties, enabling them to react with grace and dignity when they occasionally falter.

One well reported but still excellent example of this was demonstrated several years ago by Coca-Cola's late CEO, Roberto Goizueta.

As we know, when Goizueta made the decision to change the long-time formula of Coca-Cola, the public reaction shocked the company. Despite their market research, consumers did not like the taste of "New Coke" and wanted the old formula back. A man with less integrity would have stuck to his decision and poured advertising dollars into saving his idea, but Goizueta swallowed his pride and brought back the old product under the new name, "Classic Coke." His decision was right. In a short time "New Coke" disappeared from the market as Classic Coke resumed its long-established first-place position.

7. **Rely on some fixed, unwavering set of convictions or beliefs that serve as their "guiding light."** Sir John Templeton, the founder of the Templeton Fund, one of the most profitable mutual funds, has a philosophy of business that the most successful people are often the most ethically motivated. He says that such people are likely to have the keenest understanding of the importance of morality in business and can be trusted to give full measure and not cheat their customers.

But the most ethical principles, Templeton insists, come from what goes on in the mind. "If you're filling your mind with kind, loving and helpful thoughts, then your decisions and actions will be ethical."

Hard work, combined with honesty and perseverance, is key in the Templeton philosophy. "Individuals who have learned to invest themselves in their work are successful. They have earned what they have. More than simply knowing the value of money, they know their own value."

8. **Have both a "tough hide" and an ability to laugh at themselves.** According to a number of recent studies, it does seem that many, if not most, strong leaders throughout history have had both a developed wit and the ability to avoid taking themselves too seriously. One good recent example of this is Victor Kiam, now owner and CEO of the Remington Shaver Company. Kiam reportedly often entertains clients and co-workers with self-deprecating stories about his past mistakes, including the time when he was a salesman selling Playtex girdles. He came up with what he thought was a great marketing gimmick. Knowing that girdles frequently were hard to clean, he offered a special promotion: women who brought in their old, worn-out girdles could buy a new Playtex model at a discount. But according to Kiam, the plan worked a little too well. So many dirty girdles were turned in at a New York department store, he said, that he was "nearly arrested for violating the city health codes."

9. **Are not deterred by disappointment, failure, or rejection. They have strong views yet maintain a "visceral equilibrium."** One well known and well reported example of this quality is Tom Monaghan, who nev-

er let failure get him down. Monaghan created and grew Domino's Pizzas from a one-store pizza parlor to a chain of several thousand home-delivery outlets over a period of about 30 years. In 1989, he decided to sell his hugely successful company to concentrate instead on doing philanthropic work. His plan, however, did not work out. After two and a half years, the company that purchased the chain failed to maintain the momentum that Monaghan had built; to save the company, he was forced to come back. It took much work and persistence to first rebuild and then expand the organization. The dogged determination that enabled Monaghan to rise from a childhood of poverty and deprivation to become a great entrepreneur enabled him to not only return Domino's to its original prominence, but to expand it to 6,000 stores—of which 1,100 are in countries other than the United States.

10. **Accentuate the positive.** Research has shown time and time again that a positive, optimistic demeanor often dramatically improves personal effectiveness. It puts the mind in a position to succeed. It sharpens the faculties, makes concentrating easier, and drives out doubt, fear, and uncertainty.

A good example is Michael Jordan, widely regarded as the greatest basketball player of all time, who attributes much of his remarkable talent and success to positive thinking. In basketball, as in all aspects of life, it is easy to become discouraged when things are not going well. Jordan writes: "Some people get frozen by fear of failure— by thinking about the possibility of a negative result. They might be afraid of looking bad or being embarrassed. I realized that if I was going to achieve anything in life, I had to be aggressive. I had to get out there and go for it. I don't believe you can achieve anything by being passive. I know fear is an obstacle for some people, but to me it's an illusion. Once I'm in the game, I'm not thinking about anything except what I'm trying to accomplish."

11. **Place a high premium on focus, discipline, and the ability to get things done.** We've all come across people in management positions who appear to have all the attributes of a good leader, but somehow never quite succeed. Somewhere along the line, they've missed the boat.

A few years ago I had the opportunity to study this first hand. One of my clients had hired a regional sales manager, about whom they were extremely enthusiastic. He had come to them highly recommended. During the selection process, he had impressed the interviewers with his thorough knowledge of their markets, his innovative ideas on how to increase business, and his charming personality. During the first several months on the job, he developed a creative and comprehensive marketing program. He spent weeks fine-tuning it, writing materials, creating graphics, and making presentations to management and to his sales force. But unfortunately that's where it ended. The plan was never implemented; the real work never began. Why? Because for one reason or another, other work and other distractions took priority. The manager lost focus. Got intrigued with other things. Forgot why he was hired. The result? Within seven months he was replaced and forced to move on to another company.

The problem in this case had little to do with skills, and everything to do with habits. The best managers I know clearly understand that follow-through, the ability to be a self-starter, and careful attention to the details are three of the most important characteristics of both great workers and great leaders.

12. **Understand the power of the informal organization.** One of the most powerful forces within most organizations today is its network of *unofficial leaders,* lower-level managers and nonmanagers who exert great influence over the opinions and morale of their fellow workers. A recent example: Barbara Wilson (not her real name), the manager of a department of 15 computer programmers, was commended by her boss for running a highly productive unit. At a staff meeting, her boss commented that her department was always the first to accept new ideas, adapt to changes in operation methods, and seemed to exhibit the highest morale. He asked Barbara to share with the other managers her "secret of success." Her response was one word: "Rachel." Rachel, she explained was one of her best data processors. She'd been with the company for 13 years and was a mother figure to the younger people in the department. They brought her their problems and accepted her advice on matters both job-related and personal. When Barbara took over the manager's job a few years ago, she recognized the important role Rachel played and carefully moved to gain her support. Over the years she discussed with Rachel problems she had with workers and important changes that were to be made in the work. The result was a long-term, smooth, and successfully run department.

This is one of dozens of recent examples I've witnessed of managers who understand the importance of the informal organization and the informal leaders who often exercise great control over the organizational mood and spirit. Effective executives work within this structure instead of trying to defy or overcome it. They understand and appreciate the power of the informal leaders within their organizations, and work hard to cultivate their support.

Innovations in Leadership Development

The challenge of providing leaders for the future is both quantitative and qualitative. There is an urgent need to be ready to fill vacancies that will inevitably occur, but more important, to select men and women with the personalities and characteristics that adapt easily to an endless onslaught of change and innovation and the often vastly different perceptions and thinking styles of younger people.

In January 1998, the American Society for Training & Development (ASTD), together with the American Productivity and Quality Center; James Kouzes, chairman of TPG Learning Systems; and Professor Robert M. Fulmer of the College of William and Mary, conducted a study to identify and examine innovations and key areas in present-day leadership development. They made an in-depth study of 35 organizations recognized as having strong, innovative leadership development processes. Here's a look at some of the key findings of their study:

- Leadership development does not stand alone. It must be aligned to the overall strategy of the organization.
- Senior-level executives with extensive line experience must be involved in the design of the leadership development program. By combining their experience with the expertise of those in human resources, corporate education, and academe, a business and educational mix is created.
- A model of leadership competencies is developed which is consistent throughout the organization and reflects the values of the organization.
- Best-practice organizations develop their own leaders rather than recruit them from other companies.
- Action, not knowledge, is the goal of best-practice leadership development. The program not only provides leaders with knowledge and information, but equips them with the necessary skills, qualities, and techniques to apply their knowledge in a variety of situations. By having participants solve actual business problems, the learning experience is tailored to the organization's and the learner's development.
- The leadership development process is linked to the organization's succession planning. Leadership development becomes important in maintaining a steady flow of information throughout the organization to ensure that its top talent is tracked and continues to grow.
- The leadership development process is a symbiotic tool of effective leadership. To succeed it requires top-level support. In turn, the success of the program engenders continued high-level support.

- Successful programs are continuously assessed. Although the study showed companies used a variety of assessment methods, all assessed results on a regular basis, reflected on the results, made adaptations, and kept listening and learning.

The Cases

The cases outlined in this book reflect how specific organizations are developing and implementing training programs to meet the changing needs of management today. They are drawn from a variety of organizations including financial institutions, manufacturing companies, public utilities, government agencies, hospitals, and universities. Some of the areas covered are:

- leadership development as a business strategy
- developing effective supervisors
- using executive coaching for ongoing leadership growth
- strategies and competencies to enhance leaders for the new millennium
- transformational coaching—a new paradigm for executive development
- creating a learning environment for continuous leadership development.

There are also many more examples of how progressive firms are meeting the challenges resulting from a changing organizational environment.

The authors are experts who have had many years of hands-on experience in training and development. The cases are current, real-life situations to which training and development specialists can readily relate and from which readers can obtain valuable ideas to apply in their own organization.

References

Boyett, J., and H. Conn. (1992). *Workplace 2000*. New York: Penguin.

Dilenschneider, R. (1992). *A Briefing for Leaders*. New York: HarperBusiness.

Additional Readings

Fulmer, R., and S. Wagner. (1999, March). "Leadership Lessons From The Best." *Training & Development*.

Miccio, L. (1999, April). "Empowering Employees Pays Off." SHRM, HR News on Line.

Pell, A. (1994). *The Supervisor's Infobank*. New York: McGraw-Hill.

Watkins, K., and V. Marsick. (1996). *Creating The Learning Organization*. Alexandria, VA: ASTD.

Leadership Development as a Business Strategy

Allstate Insurance Company

Trina Stephens

The Senior Management Team at Allstate Insurance Company, the nation's largest publicly held personal lines insurance company, with a net income of $3.29 billion, laid the groundwork in 1996 to maximize business results through the creation and implementation of a long-term, systemic leadership development process. The process was built in-house and consists of a four-phase cycle of Assessment, Feedback, Development Planning, and Development. A 360-degree feedback instrument was created and became the core of assessment and development efforts for all leaders in the company. The preliminary results as to the success of the program were compiled by correlating data from the 360-degree feedback instrument with an existing tool, the Quarterly Leadership Measurement Survey. The findings indicate there is a relationship between leadership behavior and superior business results and that certain behaviors create more impact than others. Allstate is using this data to more aggressively develop its near-term and future leaders.

Organizational Profile

The Allstate Corporation is the parent of Allstate Insurance Company, the nation's largest publicly held personal lines insurance company with more than 20 million customers. As the second largest personal, property, and casualty insurer in the United States, Allstate's 29 million policies in force corner 12.4 percent of the market share for automobiles and 11.7 percent of homeowners' products. Allstate is also the nation's largest writer of nonstandard auto insurance, which serves

This case was prepared to serve as a basis for discussion rather than to illustrate either effective or ineffective administrative and management practices.

customers with higher-than-average risk profiles due to lack of prior coverage, poor driving records, or car type. The company earned a record net income in 1998: $3.29 billion (a 10.7 percent increase over 1997) on revenues of $25.8 billion.

Allstate is headquartered in Northbrook, Illinois. Its 52,000 employees work at the home office, 17 regional offices, eight regional commercial centers, seven operations, processing, and support centers, as well as in several countries outside the United States. The Allstate brand name is widely known, and the company states that Allstate is the number one company that comes to mind for auto insurance in the U.S. markets it serves. The company also has been cited numerous times as being an exemplary employer, particularly for women and minorities.

Background

Allstate, previously a subsidiary of Sears, finalized a spin-off in 1995, and the senior leaders of the nascent company realized the need for capable leadership to actualize the company's goal of becoming "the premiere insurance company in the world." Additionally, these senior leaders were cognizant of the tenuous nature of leadership supply and demand across all corporations and believed that leadership is a valuable, although intangible, asset for competitive advantage. Therefore, in 1995, Allstate's Senior Management Team (SMT), consisting of 14 officers led by CEO Jerry Choate, laid the groundwork to maximize near-term and future business results through a systemic, long-term leadership process. Although recently retired, Choate's theory on leadership is infused in the company culture. He states, "Power is not bestowed by the title you hold, but by the people you lead. . . . Leadership is really painting a picture of the future—allowing all of our people to understand what the future looks like—a future of trust and integrity, with leaders doing the right thing" (1998).

To establish a common framework throughout the organization, the SMT first defined "leadership" as achieving results and creating a supportive work environment. Next, the SMT conducted focus groups, interviews with other leaders, and benchmark comparisons of best practices to determine the leadership factors necessary to enable the corporation to achieve its key business strategies. Based on the resulting information, the SMT established 14 leadership competencies, designated as the Leadership Critical Success Factors (LCSFs) (table 1). The Leadership Critical Success Factors were then incorporated into a four-phase Leadership Development Model consisting of Assessment, Feedback, Development Planning, and Development. Allstate CEO Jerry Choate and President Ed Liddy subsequently introduced the definition of leadership and the Leadership Development Process to the company's 200 officers at the 1996 Leadership Conference.

Also introduced at the 1996 Leadership Conference was the Allstate Partnership, a declaration of mutual expectations between the company and its employees. This document augments the definition of leadership by specifying behaviors inherent in a "supportive work environment." The partnership provides Allstate employees with a clear understanding of what they can expect from their leaders and also lists expectations the company has of its employees. Table 2 details the mutual expectations of the Allstate Partnership.

The vision and commitment of the Senior Management Team to develop leaders at Allstate, supported and clarified by the declarations in the Allstate Partnership, provide the foundation for the development and subsequent success of Allstate's Leadership Development Process. This case will explain how the Leadership Development Process, as a business strategy, has affected Allstate Insurance Company since 1996.

Table 1. The 14 Leadership Critical Success Factors.

1. Thinks conceptually/strategically	8. Inspires others to share vision/ direction
2. Plans and implements	9. Communicates effectively
3. Is hardworking and performance oriented	10. Practices teamwork and networking
4. Consistently achieves business results	11. Manages careers and performance
5. Has breadth and depth of business, insurance, and technical knowledge	12. Copes with demands and stresses
6. Has experience in start-up, turnaround, and/or adversarial business situations	13. Establishes a supportive/caring work environment that promotes balance, integrity, and trust
7. Sets and inspires behavior consistent with direction	14. Through self-awareness, engages in self-improvement and constant learning

Source: Used with permission of Allstate Insurance Company.

Table 2. Expectations of the Allstate Partnership.

Expectations of the Employees from the Company	Expectations of the Company from the Employees
• Offer work that is meaningful and challenging.	• Perform at levels that significantly increase our ability to outperform the competition.
• Promote an environment that encourages open and constructive dialogue.	• Take on assignments critical to meeting business objectives.
• Recognize you for your accomplishments.	• Continually develop needed skills.
• Provide competitive pay and rewards based on your performance.	• Willingly listen to and act on feedback.
• Advise you on your performance through regular feedback.	• Demonstrate a high level of commitment to achieving company goals.
• Create learning opportunities through education and job assignments.	• Exhibit no bias in interactions with colleagues and customers.
• Support you in defining career goals.	• Behave consistently with Allstate's ethical standards.
• Provide you with information and resources to perform successfully.	• Take personal responsibility for each transaction with our customers and for fostering their support.
• Promote an environment that is inclusive and free from bias.	• Continually improve processes to address customers' needs.
• Foster dignity and respect in all interactions.	
• Establish an environment that promotes a balance of work and personal life.	

Source: Used with permission of Allstate Insurance Company.

Key Issues and Events

After the Leadership Development Process was introduced at the 1996 Leadership Conference, the responsibility for developing and implementing the process was handed off—in 1997—to the Performance Development Team. The Performance Development Team is part of the Performance Solutions Team—the HRD division of the human resource department. Instead of immediately "developing a program," Performance Development first grounded the process in a four-phase leadership development model—Assessment, Feedback, Development Planning, and Development. A 360-degree feedback instrument was created as the centerpiece of the Assessment phase of the model. The instrument was designed to provide feedback to leaders from their peers, direct reports, and immediate managers regarding perceived demonstration of leadership behaviors—specifically, the Leadership Critical Success Factors. In addition to identifying individual strengths and development needs of the participant, the tool also provides the means to measure the strengths and development needs of the entire Leadership Team on an aggregate basis. Performance Development decided to have the 78-question instrument processed by an external vendor who would in turn generate both individual and aggregate reports.

Early in the process, the team decided to use the 360-degree feedback for developmental purposes only and not link it to the individual's performance appraisal. Each leader would have the option to share results with his or her immediate manager; however, it was requisite for all participants to incorporate their feedback into an individual development plan.

Two resources were created to support the Feedback and Development Planning phases of the model, the *Feedback Interpretation Guide* and the *Leadership Development Resource Guide*. The purpose of the *Feedback Interpretation Guide* is to assist the participants in better understanding their results on the 360-degree instrument. Individual participants receive a copy of the guide during a debriefing session after the 360-degree instrument has been completed and processed. The participants are also encouraged to identify an internal coach for further help in analyzing the results and creating a development plan. All of the Allstate leaders who participate in the 360-degree feedback process also receive a *Leadership Development Resource Guide*. This guide was produced to assist participants in identifying development options to address specific needs. During the debriefing session, the participant is introduced to a variety of intervention options that support long-term development or behavior change.

To further assist company leaders in creating a supportive work environment, a "Coaches Workshop" was developed. A network of 150 coaches countrywide was identified and trained in a train-the-trainer format to assist leaders in further developing this necessary competency.

Target Population

The Leadership Development Process was first implemented in 1997, to an audience consisting of 200 officers of the company. The required process involves all leaders completing the 360-degree instrument, a development plan, and demonstrating commitment to the leadership development process. To provide consistency across the organization, later in 1997 and throughout 1998, the process was extended to front-line leaders as well. Currently, participation in the process is open to all leaders in the company.

Action Items

Although Performance Solutions (human resources) is currently the primary process owner of the Leadership Development Process, implementation involved the cooperation of all departments. In 1998, as part of Allstate's Performance Management process, a leadership major responsibility/performance goal was established as a requirement in the performance appraisals of all leaders throughout the corporation. The focus of this performance goal is on leadership development, development of direct reports, and living the Allstate Partnership by creating a supportive work environment. This requirement, coupled with other subprocesses needed to support the 14 Leadership Critical Success Factors, led to the implementation of several additional action items.

To provide guidance to the Leadership Development Process, a Leadership Council was established in 1998, and a benchmark study was completed. The mandate of the Leadership Council is to instill the Leadership Development Process throughout the corporation. Rob Maple, chair of the council and vice president of the human resource Performance Solutions Team, sees the council as being critical to the long-term success of leadership development at Allstate. He states, "Meeting regularly with leaders in other business units to guide the Leadership Development Process has forged a strong, internal partnership that has allowed us to better leverage the process. I think the input and direction the Leadership Council provides is crucial to developing leaders committed to Allstate's continued success." To gain a better understanding of leadership development best practices, Allstate participated in a benchmarking study conducted by ASTD/American Productivity & Quality Center (APQC). This study provided insight into leadership development practices of other corporations and identified some next steps for Allstate's Leadership Development Process.

Several development options were also created to support the process. Allstate partnered with the MenTTium Corporation to create a process of matching high potential female leaders with a mentor from another participating corporation in the Chicago area. As part of the mentoring partnership with MenTTium, Allstate is committed to dedicating senior leaders to serve as mentors to mentees in other corporations. Allstate plans to use a similar mentoring format for women at various levels of leadership throughout the company. Another development option is the "Leader to Leader" speaker series conducted on a quarterly basis for Allstate leaders. Sessions in the speaker series involve leaders from various external business organizations sharing their expertise on topics related to current business issues or strategies identified by senior leaders at Allstate.

Models and Techniques

The model used in the Leadership Development Process consists of Assessment, Feedback, Development Planning, and Development (figure 1). Assessment and Feedback are provided through the 360-degree instrument as well as on an ongoing basis through the company's performance management process. Development Planning focuses on leveraging this feedback by creating a specific, individual development plan to address any deficiencies. From a development perspective, the company is moving from a skills- and competency-based model to a curriculum-based model with a strong emphasis on application of learning in the actual work setting. Development also includes development options beyond the required curriculum, such as job experiences and assignments, mentoring, coaching, the "Leader to Leader"

Figure 1. The Leadership Development Process.

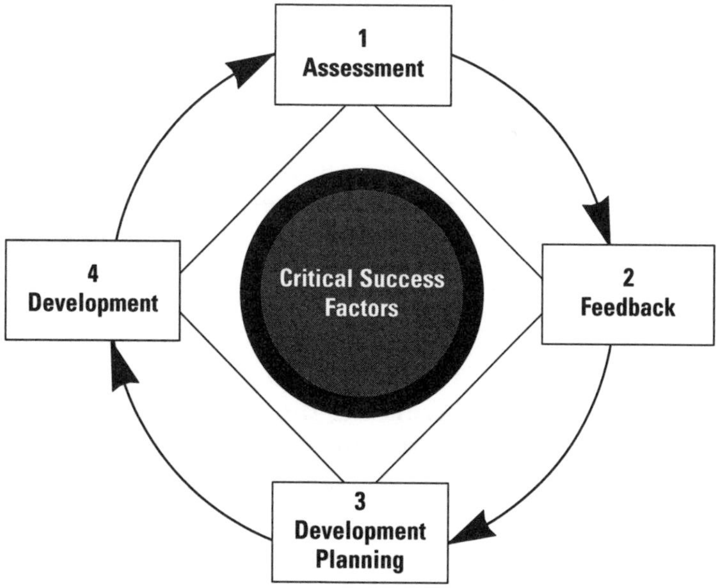

Source: Used with permission of Allstate Insurance Company.

speaker series, an executive MBA program, and professional and supplemental education.

HRD Program Description and Delivery

Although the Performance Development Team is responsible for leadership development, the Education Design and Delivery Team worked closely with them throughout the process. To support the development of all leaders, and based on the initial aggregate results of the 360-degree feedback instrument, a required leadership curriculum, with separate tracks for the Leadership Team (officers, directors, and bonus managers) and front-line leaders was developed. The Leadership Development Curriculum is central to the Development phase of the Leadership Development Process model.

Education Design and Delivery created the Leadership Development Curriculum by combining a variety of learning experiences to support the development of the Leadership Critical Success Factors and to fulfill development needs identified through the 360-degree instrument. The curriculum was also tailored to further the vision, culture, and business strategies of Allstate. The leadership curriculum is based on six factors—the five clusters of the Leadership Critical Success Factors and a policy and practice area concentrating on the issue of integrity. The required Leadership Development Curriculum is shown in table 3.

Criteria for including courses in the curriculum involve aligning them with Allstate's business strategies, the Leadership Critical Success Factors, and an understanding that all courses must instill a common knowledge, values, and culture before they can be included in the leadership curriculum. Courses are continuously reviewed and new courses are added if they meet the criteria and address the development needs of the Leadership Team. All new leaders must complete the required courses within 24 months. Table 4 details the current courses being offered.

Costs

Although specifics concerning the costs of the program are proprietary, areas involving cost, other than salaries, will be discussed. The initial expenditures for the Leadership Development Process involved the design and implementation of the 360-degree feedback instrument, and charges are ongoing for the processing of the instrument. Other significant expenses were related to specific development options such as mentoring, coaching, the on-site MBA, and the "Leader to Leader" speaker series.

Table 3. Leadership Development Process—required curriculum map.

	Other Managers	Bonus Managers and Directors	Officers
Vision			Leadership Conference
Performance	Managing Performance Improvement / Maximizing Agency Performance		Aligning Strategy and Vision
Knowledge	Managing the Business		Strategic Overview
Leading People	Transitions	TBD	TBD
	Coaching... Lost Art of Leadership		
Learning	360-degree Assessment and Feedback		
Policy and Practice	Orientation to Management		New Officer Orientation
	Behavior Descriptive Interviewing		
Audience	**Other Managers**	**Bonus Managers and Directors**	**Officers**

Source: Used with permission of Allstate Insurance Company.

Another expense was the development and ongoing delivery of courses in the leadership curriculum. However, because the decision was made to eliminate any courses that were not directly linked to the 14 Leadership Critical Success Factors, the available course offerings were reduced from 47 to 20. This decision actually reduced expenses from previous levels. Although most of the initial courses were developed in-house, Johnny Shumate, human resource director of Education Design and Delivery, opted to purchase generic courses when it made business sense to do so. If an off-the-shelf generic course met the requirements of the curriculum, in-house resources were not used to develop a similar course. However, courses for topics such as "Orientation to Management" had to be developed within Allstate, because the need was for a company-specific course.

Table 4. Leadership development curriculum—course map.

Cluster	Audience	Course title/length/objectives
Vision	Officers	*Leadership Conference* (3 days) Objectives: • align top company leadership with corporate goals and strategies • strengthen teamwork among officers *Aligning Strategy and Vision* (1 day) Objectives: • align organization for customer focus • lead company change initiatives • develop action plans to achieve strategic goals
Performance	Bonus managers/managers	*Managing Performance Improvement/Maximize Agency Performance* (2 days) Objectives: • candidly discuss performance issues • adapt a personal style for effectiveness • develop action plan for improvement
Knowledge	Directors/bonus managers/managers	*Managing the Business* (2 days) Objectives: • understand key financial principles • understand key organizations • identify consumer issues

Leading people	Officers (all new officers)	*Strategic Overview* (1 day) Objectives: • presentations by senior leaders in key strategies • broad exposure to company priorities • changing agenda due to current priorities
	Managers	*Transitions* (5 days) Objectives: • deliver and receive feedback • create a mission statement • improve listening and questioning skills • improve relationship building and influencing skills • learn coaching model
		Coaching (1 day) Objectives: • learn coaching model to improve performance • help others explore options and set goals • use questions to coach others
	Bonus managers/directors	*Leading for Results* • series of workshops designed to teach leadership skills
	Officers	TBD
Learning	Officers/directors/ bonus managers/ managers	360-degree assessment and feedback

continued on page 22

Table 4. Leadership development curriculum—course map (continued).

Cluster	Audience	Course title/length/objectives
Policy and practice	Directors/bonus managers/managers	*Behavior Description Interviewing* (2 days) Objectives: • use process to apply past behavior as indicator of future performance • understand basic legal requirements
	Managers	*Orientation to Management* (3 days) Objectives: • understand basic policy and procedure knowledge • use job aids and tools as guides to resolve human resource issues
	Officers	*New Officer Orientation* (individual activities scheduled over six months) Objectives: • introduce key contracts • recommend structure for activities • attend business unit overviews

Source: Used with permission of Allstate Insurance Company.

Another strategy used to reduce costs involved course delivery. A train-the-trainer format was utilized for many of the courses in the curriculum. This decentralized approach helped to reduce travel and related expenditures by making it possible to deliver the course in field locations.

Data Analysis and Results

The Allstate Research and Planning Center (ARPC) in Menlo Park, California, became an important partner in measuring the success of the Leadership Development Process. This arm of the company performs the function of an internal business consultant, particularly in the area of conducting and analyzing research. Using internal resources such as the ARPC also contributed to cost control and strengthened intradepartmental relations. Data was collected and analyzed to show performance results on individual leaders, and a correlation analysis was completed to reveal broader impact. An individual case study will be examined first to highlight the initial effect of the Leadership Development Process on an individual officer's performance.

Data was compiled on the results of one officer of the company with more than 25 years of service at Allstate. This individual had been exposed to numerous assignments in multiple functions and was respected and recognized for achieving key business results. The results of the first feedback cycle from the 360-degree instrument in 1997 are shown in figure 2. They identify two clusters, Knowledge and Leading People, as being below the norm for the officer peer group, and several items were targeted for improvement. (See figure 3.) A short-term action plan (figure 4) was drafted, and developmental tasks were subsequently completed. Improvements made during the second feedback cycle are indicated in figure 5. The individual progressed in every area specifically targeted for improvement.

To measure organizational impact, a correlation analysis was conducted to determine if a relationship existed between leadership behaviors and the achievement of business results. Results from the 360-degree feedback instrument were correlated with business results as evidenced by Allstate's proprietary internal measurement tool, the Quarterly Leadership Measurement Survey (QLMS). The findings indicate there is a relationship between leadership behavior and superior business results and that certain behaviors have more impact than others. The behaviors that differentiate the top one-third of leaders at Allstate are as follows:

- keeps up to date on developments within area of expertise
- effectively manages performance

Figure 2. Leadership Development Process—individual case study.

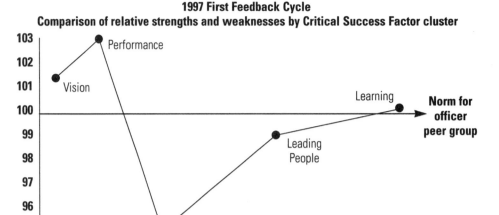

Source: Used with permission of Allstate Insurance Company.

- deals with behavior that undermines teamwork
- provides regular feedback to improve performance
- deals with underperforming employees
- involves others in plans and decisions
- uses external networks for information and "best practices"
- seeks feedback to enhance performance.

The research center is partnering with Performance Solutions to identify job-related assignments that will specifically develop these behaviors as well as other competencies inherent in the Leadership Critical Success Factors.

Conclusions and Recommendations

The implementation of the Leadership Development Process at Allstate emanated from the Senior Management Team down to all leaders throughout the organization, thus ensuring a link with other business strategies. A key issue addressed through the process is the availability of leaders for both the near-term and the future. Preliminary results of the Leadership Development Process indicate areas of success, opportunities for improvement, and a strategy for the future.

Quantitative and qualitative data illustrate that the program is a success. The correlation between leadership behavior and superior business results is significant and has led to an increased empha-

Figure 3. Leadership Development Process—individual case study.

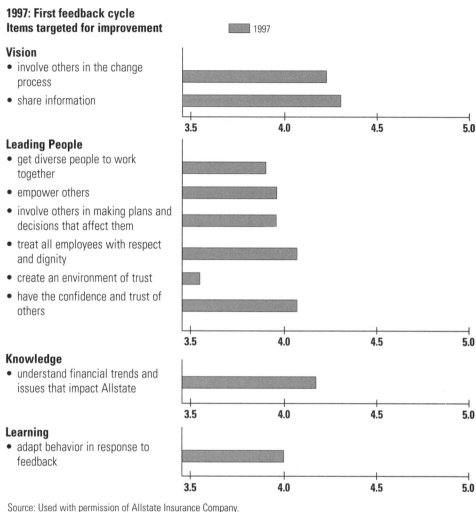

1997: First feedback cycle
Items targeted for improvement   ▨ 1997

Vision
- involve others in the change process
- share information

(scale: 3.5, 4.0, 4.5, 5.0)

Leading People
- get diverse people to work together
- empower others
- involve others in making plans and decisions that affect them
- treat all employees with respect and dignity
- create an environment of trust
- have the confidence and trust of others

(scale: 3.5, 4.0, 4.5, 5.0)

Knowledge
- understand financial trends and issues that impact Allstate

(scale: 3.5, 4.0, 4.5, 5.0)

Learning
- adapt behavior in response to feedback

(scale: 3.5, 4.0, 4.5, 5.0)

Source: Used with permission of Allstate Insurance Company.

sis and urgency for leadership development. Initial results showing individual improvement after targeted development efforts are also encouraging. Another qualitative result is the positive way education is perceived and practiced at Allstate.

The Performance Solutions Team is continually improving the 360-degree feedback instrument and the leadership curriculum. The 360-degree feedback instrument has been shortened and focused more closely on the most important leadership behaviors. The courses in the leadership curriculum have been assessed for applicability; how-

Figure 4. Leadership Development Process—individual case study.

1997 Development Plan
Short-Term Action Plan

Need	Action Plan	Measure
1. Encouraging differing views	I will work with senior staff and request feedback on listening skills.	Talk time versus listen time
2. Seeking input	I will open myself up to more feedback… open-ended questions.	Survey senior staff and others two times per year
3. Establish supportive work environment	Spend additional time with diversity team.	Quarterly feedback conversations
4. Breadth and depth of business knowledge	Attend professional education seminar	Complete program
	Serve on an industry committee	Complete task force project

Source: Used with permission of Allstate Insurance Company.

ever, other developmental courses need to be updated and formally aligned with company vision, strategy, and culture. Because cost is an increasingly important factor, courses that have the most organizational impact will be emphasized, and other learning technologies are being investigated for use.

For the future, Allstate is focusing on development options that will have the greatest impact on the next generation of leaders. One area of focus is enhancement of the linkage between leadership development and the succession management process. Allstate is upgrading the existing functionality of *BluePrint,* the centralized database used for succession management, by creating areas to track ongoing development plans of key leaders. This will enable the placement of key leaders in developmental assignments across the organization. The on-site MBA program is also being enhanced to include a structured mentoring process as well as action learning experiences. These improvements will allow leaders to apply key lessons to critical business issues within the organization.

A final development option will ensure that existing leadership possesses the necessary skills, experience, and knowledge to achieve future business results. By leveraging the 360-degree feedback aggregate

Figure 5. Leadership Development Process—individual case study.

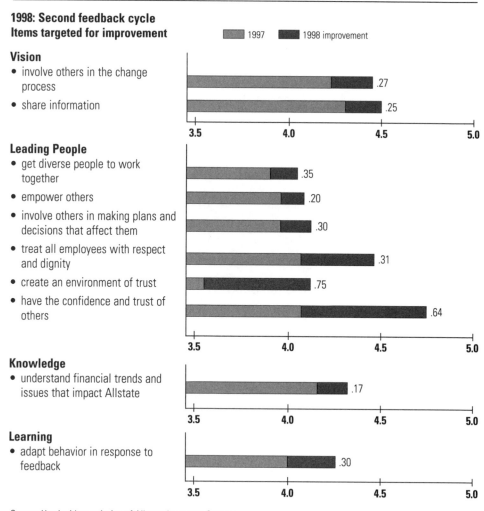

**1998: Second feedback cycle
Items targeted for improvement**

Legend: 1997 | 1998 improvement

Vision
- involve others in the change process — .27
- share information — .25

(scale: 3.5, 4.0, 4.5, 5.0)

Leading People
- get diverse people to work together — .35
- empower others — .20
- involve others in making plans and decisions that affect them — .30
- treat all employees with respect and dignity — .31
- create an environment of trust — .75
- have the confidence and trust of others — .64

(scale: 3.5, 4.0, 4.5, 5.0)

Knowledge
- understand financial trends and issues that impact Allstate — .17

(scale: 3.5, 4.0, 4.5, 5.0)

Learning
- adapt behavior in response to feedback — .30

(scale: 3.5, 4.0, 4.5, 5.0)

Source: Used with permission of Allstate Insurance Company.

reports, the Leadership Development Team will be able to ensure enhanced development assignments and development options to address gaps in the Leadership Critical Success Factors. The existing Leadership Critical Success Factors are being reviewed to ensure they are aligned with and support new business strategies. Allstate will also focus on the accelerated development of a pool of individuals possessing high leadership talent as identified through the succession planning process. The development of these individuals will be accelerated by placing them in key assignments based on need. The intent is for individuals within this pool to be developed cross-functionally and to have increased exposure to the Senior Management Team and possibly the board of directors. The emphasis will be on *"What development does the person need?"* versus *"Who do we have who can do the job?"* Enhanced coaching and mentoring, using both internal and external resources, will provide the means to accelerate the development of individuals demonstrating leadership potential and will further build the coaching skills of senior leaders.

Allstate plans to continue to explore and quantify the links between exceptional leadership skills and superior business results. As a business strategy, the Leadership Development Process is proving to be an effective tool for developing the calibre of leaders the company needs to maximize its business results. As the company succeeds in developing its leadership, shareholders, customers, and employees alike truly will be "in good hands" at Allstate for a long time to come.

Questions for Discussion

1. Allstate made the decision to "build" versus "buy" their future leadership. What are some of the possible consequences, both positive and negative, of this decision?
2. Define leadership in your own words. Discuss how you would actualize your definition in a large organization such as Allstate.
3. Employee development is a vital part of Allstate's Leadership Development Process. What are some additional methodologies, particularly technology-based, that the company could use to develop its leaders?
4. Measuring the impact of an HRD initiative such as leadership development is a challenging task. What other measures would be appropriate and beneficial for Allstate to undertake in determining the efficacy of its Leadership Development Process?

Acknowledgment

The author gratefully acknowledges the helpful comments from Pam Murphy, senior manager of the human resource Performance Solutions Team at Allstate Insurance Company, Northbrook, Illinois.

The Author

Trina Stephens is president of Human Resource Dynamics, Inc., located in Boiling Springs, North Carolina. The primary focus of her company is to assist small to mid-sized businesses with maximizing human resource development processes to achieve organizational goals and objectives.

Stephens co-authored *Putting Corporate CLEP to Work for You and Your Employees,* published by the College Board, as well as numerous articles for business publications. She is the past president of the Valleys of Virginia Chapter of the American Society for Training & Development. She received her M.A. in career counseling and her Ph.D. in adult and continuing education/human resource development from Virginia Polytechnic Institute and State University.

Reference

Choate, J. (1998). Allstate Leadership Conference proceedings. Northbrook, IL: Allstate Corporate Relations, video.

A Customer Service Trifecta: Situational Leadership, Quality, and Satisfaction

Dr Pepper/Seven Up, Inc.

Karl J. Krayer

This case provides details about a successful and effective leadership program that focused on an intervention for a corporation's customer service unit based on contingency leadership principles. The objective of the intervention was to improve quality, reduce costs, and increase customer satisfaction. The case illustrates a partnership undertaken in 1997 between a customer service unit's manager and myself, a training manager, to bring about desired results. The case reports actual events and data, although I have changed the names of the participants.

The Organization

The focus of this case is on the customer service unit within the purchasing department of Dr Pepper/Seven Up, Inc., located in Dallas, Texas. Dr Pepper/Seven Up, Inc., is the third-largest soft drink company in the United States, and is wholly owned by Cadbury Schweppes, PLC, of London, England. The customer service unit consisted of a manager, who reported to a corporate director of purchasing within the marketing services wing of the corporation and five customer service representatives. The customer service representatives varied in experience in their position between nine months and 10 years. The manager, Mandy, had been in her job for only four months at the time that we began working together.

At that time, I was a training manager for the corporation, with responsibility for providing interventions in the marketing and mar-

This case was prepared to serve as a basis for discussion rather than to illustrate either effective or ineffective administrative and management practices.

keting services divisions. These two divisions consisted of the largest number of employees at the corporate headquarters facility, and were outranked in quantity by only the corporate field sales force. I had more than 10 years experience with the corporation at the time that these events took place, but had undertaken work with these two divisions for less than two months.

The basic job of the customer service representative involved taking orders over the telephone or via fax or email from franchised bottlers who held licenses to produce, promote, distribute, and sell the various soft drinks owned by the corporation. These bottlers were the actual customers of the corporation. In some cases, the department took calls from field sales representatives who represented various brands, inquiring about or placing an order on behalf of a bottler. Most of the calls were for stock items containing the trademark logo of one of the drinks owned by the corporation. Sample items included golf balls, T-shirts, jackets, paperweights, pens, beach umbrellas, snow skis, caps, and so forth. Most of the orders were for large quantities, as the bottlers used these items in retail outlets for give-aways, drawings, or employee incentives. Generally, a different customer service representative took responsibility for each brand of drinks (Dr Pepper, 7 UP, A&W, IBC) or segment of business (grocery, convenience store, club).

These stock items appeared in large catalogs that each customer representative could easily access at his or her desk. In addition, the customer representatives could access a growing number of items on a merchandise CD-ROM that they kept available in their computer throughout the day. The catalogs contained specs such as stock number, warehouse location, unit price, estimated freight costs, and a brief description of each item. For some items, customers had the option of selecting certain colors, a variety of sizes, or type of material.

Although the customer representatives' primary input for ordering these items was from telephone calls, they also received a good number of order forms by fax and email during the day. These orders were generated from the company's extensive mailing and distribution of quarterly national promotions, many of which included requests for a large number of these items. For example, a holiday promotion usually offered availability for logo-identified tree ornaments, chocolate candy boxes, or other seasonal items.

The customer service representatives completed a standardized order form while taking calls. The form allowed them to record the item numbers, desired quantities, essential shipping information, and other relevant data. Because the company did not maintain its own warehouse, but rather outsourced the inventory and distribution of products to various suppliers, the customer service representative had to forward the order by fax, mail, or, with certain suppliers, electronically. The representatives frequently used email to send memos concerning details about various orders to others within the company.

In some cases, the bottlers or field sales representatives wanted to order custom products containing the name and dates of specific commemorative events. A good example of this was a logo-identified golf towel for a particular tournament held on certain days. Another example was miniature footballs with a brand logo, containing the two teams, stadium, and date for an important contest.

Because a customer service representative could not look these items up in a book or on a CD-ROM, he or she had to be very careful to record the exact information the customer desired and then talk with one of the corporate buyers who purchase custom merchandise.

Problems and Symptoms

As manager of the department, Mandy became extremely concerned about a lack of overall quality in the daily operations. For example, in the two months immediately preceding the intervention, various customer service representatives:

- gave incorrect purchase order numbers
- failed to enter certain items on orders
- incorrectly entered item numbers on orders
- misfiled orders
- incorrectly entered quantities on orders
- billed the wrong person or firm
- forwarded duplicate orders
- shipped orders via regular delivery instead of priority
- failed to obtain essential information while the customer was on the phone
- agreed to ship items past the deadline date
- sold a quantity of items not available in inventory at the warehouse.
  These actions resulted in:
- One out of every five orders contained some kind of error, which caused a representative, at minimum, to locate and contact the customer, and, at maximum, reorder or reship. Because the company was responsible for all freight costs when the error was theirs, the cost for these mistakes was astronomical.
- Some customer service representatives became frustrated when holding an order because they could not locate the customer to ask a follow-up question or to obtain information that they did not receive during the first call. In some cases, the customer service rep-

resentative simply guessed what the customer wanted, and, in those cases where he or she was wrong, the company had to reship. To meet customer deadlines, the products often shipped at overnight and priority rates.

- Field sales representatives expressed disgust with the department due to lack of quality, poor follow-up, escalating costs, and failure to meet deadlines.
- Some customer service representatives expressed discomfort in referring customers to each other. Even though each person had responsibility for a certain brand or promotion, the customer service representatives felt as if the "person who takes the call should deal with it to completion."

Leadership Analysis

As part of her duties as a manager, Mandy completed the corporate training program in Leadership Development. Although not everyone who takes the course is serious about implementing its principles, Mandy kept her work situation "top-of-mind" as she participated in the program exercises and simulations. Her participation reinforced the importance of providing leadership for her direct reports and installing quality for her department.

The program began with a review of "management versus leadership" and challenges faced by managers who want to become leaders. The course then covered four different approaches to leadership—trait, styles: one best way, styles: contingency, and motivational. For each approach, the participants learn the basic assumptions, focus, and required behaviors, and then practice various skills associated with the approach.

This situation in the customer service department was one that clearly called for emphasizing leadership rather than management. No amount of time that Mandy might have spent reviewing and enforcing policies and procedures from a company manual would improve the situation and give her, the department, and the company its desired results. This situation would improve only by Mandy behaving as a leader: through expressing a vision, taking risks, solving problems on a person-by-person basis, and doing "right things" even though she may not do "things right."

Further, because of the wide variance among the customer service representatives in their background, experience in their position, and performance level, Mandy decided that she should not take a "one best way" approach and address problems held by her direct reports in exactly the same way. In addition, because the problems presented by different customer needs and different suppliers varied widely, she concluded that no single set of principles or procedures would apply to all her customer service representatives. Despite her limited training in leadership principles, Mandy believed that she should proceed from a contingency approach.

The challenge was to coordinate a leadership effort and quality initiative simultaneously. Further, not all of the customer service representatives shared the same enthusiasm for improving the situation in their department.

After consulting with me, Mandy decided that the first step was to obtain management endorsement of the plan. Mandy would likely be unsuccessful in this effort if she did not receive solid backing from her immediate manager (a director) and the manager at the next level (a vice president). Mandy issued invitations to both of these managers to attend the "kickoff" meeting where she would explain the role of the quality initiative and teach her direct reports some of the basic principles of leadership that she intended to implement. The director in the purchasing department accepted her invitation and attended the meeting.

Methodology

The first step in the intervention was for Mandy to experience and obtain a complete understanding of exactly how each direct report in the department worked. In her first three weeks as the department manager, Mandy spent a half day sitting with and observing each of her direct reports doing his or her job. Two important components that Mandy needed to thoroughly understand before we could begin to attack quality were 1) the steps, tasks, or activities that each direct report performed and 2) the skills each of them had to exhibit to conduct these tasks and achieve expected outcomes.

To solidify that understanding, we asked each of the direct reports to meet with us to contribute any suggestions that he or she had for improving his or her own quality and productivity and to gain insight on how each direct report did his or her job. Each customer service representative responded to these questions:

- Give us some examples of instances where you made an error or had to initiate a "re-do."
- Give us some examples of lengthy execution time in filling an order.
- Explain how relying upon other sources within the company help or hinder your job.

- What does a "good job" look like to you or your customer?
- What kinds of complaints do you receive from your customers?
- What effect does your work have on others, inside or outside the company?

The second step was to talk directly with some of the customers who interact directly with the representatives. Mandy arranged for several field salespersons to meet with her department in Dallas during one of the national meetings. In her invitation to this event, she informed them that the customer service representative department was participating in a quality initiative, allowing it to reduce errors, save time, improve accuracy, satisfy customers, and streamline processes. She noted that if the department was to improve its service to them, the department must know exactly what their expectations and needs were. The discussion questions included:

- What services can our department provide your organization that would be truly "added value"?
- When we provide you service, what actions or behaviors do you expect us to perform in order to make the experience satisfying for you?
- What kinds of needs do you have (or do you foresee) that we can provide for you to help you do your job better?
- What input do you have concerning the processes by which we serve your organization?

The meeting was revealing. The most candid, yet astonishing, finding was that these salespeople believed that the customer service representatives' bureaucracy was so deep and prices were so high that they would rather search out another source. In many cases, their bottlers would even prefer to pay higher prices for a more accommodating local source.

These meetings allowed us to make decisions about what methods to use to provide leadership to each of Mandy's direct reports. We had several objectives. First, we wanted each employee to adopt a personal fulfilling and challenging vision for performing his or her work in a quality manner. Second, we wanted to inspire each of them to think about quality as a new way of doing work, and, even better, as the way "to do work." Third, we wanted to instill a value for personal responsibility and risk-taking. Fourth, and most important, we wanted to lower error rates, cut the costs associated with orders placed through customer service representatives, and improve customer satisfaction.

The meetings revealed that each of Mandy's direct reports had different strengths, abilities, and opportunities for improvement. Because they were clearly at different levels of development, any attempt to use the same leadership behaviors for all members of the team would likely fail. Mandy made the decision to use Situational Leadership principles.

Situational Leadership was developed and popularized by Ken Blanchard more than 25 years ago.[1] The major assumption of Situational Leadership is that a leader must adapt the amount of direction and support that he or she provides to a direct report, based upon that direct report's levels of competence and commitment on a specific task. Situational Leadership begins by assessing a direct report's knowledge, skills, motivation, and confidence on a specific task. This assessment provides a development level for each direct report, ranging from D1 (least) to D4 (most). The next step requires a leader to match that direct report's development level with the appropriate amount of direction and support. The program uses two anchor lines: "different strokes for different folks," and "different strokes for the same folk—depending on the task."

Mandy completed an assessment form with Situational Leadership principles for all of her direct reports on each of the key tasks and responsibilities required for the job. We made the decision that we would concentrate exclusively on those skills that Mandy rated as "low," indicating that the direct report experienced a significant problem or difficulty with the skill.

In general, three major problems surfaced among the customer service representatives:
1. The customer service representatives did not get all the information they needed the first time they had the customer on the telephone. This was because the form containing questions was not conducive to recording and because the customer service representatives were not skilled at asking questions to get the information.
2. Even when they had the customer on the telephone, they did not ask the right questions in the right manner to get the information they needed.
3. The customer service representatives' skill in constructing and replying to emails was inadequate, often perpetuating or exacerbating problems, rather than solving them.

Intervention

Having identified specific development levels for the major tasks, the next decision that Mandy had to make was to select an appropriate intervention method to facilitate improvement. With my consultation, Mandy suggested that we undertake several steps:

1. She thought that it was senseless to develop her customer service representatives' fact-finding and questioning skills if the instrument from which they asked queries and recorded answers was unsuitable. In Mandy's view, the first step was to provide the customer service representatives with a revised template form to record the answers from customers on the telephone in a quality manner. The form needed to provide the representatives with a set of questions to ask customers in chronological order. The form also needed to provide spaces for options in order to record a variety of potential answers.

2. The second step was to work with each customer service representative on specific fact-finding skills. Depending upon which person was the focus of the training, the specific drills and activities differed.

3. The third step was to improve each customer service representative's skill in writing memos and recap letters through email.

The first task was to construct and carefully pilot test a template for the order form that the customer representatives could use when taking phone orders. Although we desired to keep the form to one page, the more important issue was that the form contained the questions that the representatives needed to ask, in the proper sequence, and provided space for all the necessary information the representatives needed to take from customers. Over a period of three weeks, Mandy held several staff meetings to discuss versions of the form and receive feedback about different revisions.

After each customer service representative expressed agreement about the format, Mandy asked them to use the form in the telephone calls that they would take for one full day and return an evaluation. She continued to upgrade the form and pilot test each version until the group expressed a consensus decision as to its quality and usefulness.

Mandy's analysis of three of her direct reports revealed low knowledge, skill, and confidence in using appropriate fact-finding questions when talking with customers over the telephone. According to Situational Leadership principles, for this task, these representatives were at the D1 level, requiring Mandy to use a directing style—high direction and low support. Fact-finding involves four major skills: asking the right questions, listening to the answers, determining whether or not to probe, and using the answers in some application. The most particularly disturbing skill deficiency concerned probing questions. By definition, a customer service representative could not predetermine a probing question. A probing question is always based on the answer that a representative receives from an initial question, or lead. A representative must listen to the answer and then determine whether he or she needs to probe for more information, clarification, or even to show interest.

I conducted a brief informative session for the representatives that introduced them to various questioning techniques that they could use with their customers. Among these techniques were general leads, probes, restatements, or "mirror" questions, pauses, and interpretations. The session concluded with a brief identification exercise and practice in each type of question.

In a subsequent session, we worked with the entire team of customer service representatives in order to give them intensive skill practice and confidence in using fact-finding skills. We asked each representative to complete and return a questionnaire in order for us to construct role plays. The questionnaire asked the representative to provide details for calls from two recent customers, including the items ordered and questions or problems encountered. We then took the questionnaires and embellished them by changing names and including some applications to department policies to see how well each representative identified and dealt with these type of issues. We divided each role play into two versions: one for "customer" and one for "representative," with unique information for each role.

In addition to work on the fact-finding skills, these role plays also provided excellent illustrations of how the customer service representatives could gain an advantage by referring a call to the representative who deals with a particular brand or promotion. One role play was particularly demonstrative: the representative playing herself had to ask more than 15 questions that the customer had already answered on a previous call. Had she referred the caller to the original representative, the call would have been more than 10 minutes shorter and eliminated irritation and aggravation on the part of the customer.

Mandy's follow-up illustrated Situational Leadership principles extremely well. With one representative who seemed to make rapid progress and exhibit the questioning techniques well, she provided support and engaged her in dialogue about her feelings about the new skills. With another direct report who did not catch on as quickly, Mandy used some demonstration techniques and repeated some of the drills that her entire staff had worked with previously.

In some cases, Mandy observed that a customer representative's decision in a role play actually violated the departmental policy. These observations provided her with additional opportunities for presenting learning options and engaging in focused drills.

I asked each of the customer service representatives to send me five email messages, of any length, that he or she had written that week. I copied these and asked Mandy to assess their skill level. Mandy's analysis of four of her direct reports revealed some knowledge, but low confidence in writing memos and recap letters through email. These direct reports were at the D2 level, requiring Mandy to use a coaching style—high direction and high support. One of her direct reports wrote extremely well, causing Mandy to rate her at the D4 level, for which Situational Leadership principles call for Mandy to use a delegating style, with low direction and low support.

I conducted a brief training session on emails with the premise to "write it once" so that the recipient could "read it once." Mandy met individually with the D1 performers and asked them to rewrite their memos in a fashion that met my four criteria:

1. Tell the reader what you want him or her to do early in the memo.
2. Include a descriptive subject line.
3. Carbon copy only the essential people.
4. Tell the reader what is in an attached file and by when he or she should download it.

Over a period that involved several brief meetings and "work-withs," Mandy was able to move most of her staff into the D3 level of development by matching their competence and commitment with the appropriate leadership style. Although none of them had the confidence that he or she was a particularly great writer, they all felt that they had the skill to write memos that would communicate effectively. Rather than continue to focus on skills, Mandy spent her energy in reinforcement and providing confidence and support.

Results

The leadership and quality initiative at Dr Pepper/Seven Up for customer service representatives produced several important outcomes for the unit, the department, and the organization. Due to Mandy's diligence in measuring and tracking results from the training, we identified several critical measurable outcomes.

Error Rates

As the customer service representatives became more familiar with the revised order template form and utilized fact-finding skills appropriately, the department realized significant reductions in errors. Because the representatives now asked the right questions, recorded the right information, and probed for additional information or clarification when necessary, they minimized the frequency of speculation and guesswork.

The impact of getting all the information the first time the customer service representatives had the customer on the telephone provided significant cost savings. Because Mandy had already instituted a system to manage and identify errors, she could easily track the performance of each representative on order errors. If you recall that prior to the onset of the leadership and quality initiative, the error rates for the customer service representatives were as high as 20 percent. Translated, at least one order out of every five for at least one representative included some mistake—wrong items, quantities, billing addresses, purchase order numbers or specifications, among others. In almost every case, these mistakes involved reshipment (usually at priority rates), return freight charges, "fast-time" production charges, or spoiled goods.

Within six weeks of implementing the new system, Mandy's unit reduced the error rates to a high of only 2 percent. The cost savings reduction of 18 percent in error rates was sufficient to pay for one representative's annual salary in just six weeks. In 30 weeks, the reductions produced savings that paid for the entire group's annual salaries.

Time

At the end of the six-week period, I administered a brief questionnaire to the customer service representatives to obtain their own self-assessment of the impact of the leadership and quality initiative. Specifically, my interest was in the impact of time savings they realized from writing and reading memos as a result of the training on emails. I also wanted to determine the percentage of customers that they now had to locate and call back due to a failure to obtain all the necessary information on the first call.

My questionnaire asked the customer representatives to provide estimates as honestly as possible. The results provided evidence of significant cost savings to the unit, the division, and the organization. I asked what percentage of time that they estimated they had cut in writing, reading, and replying to an email memo. The range in percentage of time eliminated on these three questions ranged from 7 to 65 percent. Because Mandy and I knew that prior to the onset of the initiative, the customer service representatives spent approximately 10 minutes per hour of each day involved in reading or writing emails, we could determine the financial impact of these savings. By "writing it once" and "reading it once," the average time saving was 34 percent. Per day, per person, this meant that $16 of a day's work time could be funneled into another area. Per week, this figure was $80. Per month, this figure was $320. Across the group of five representatives, the savings per month were $1,600. Annualized, just through reducing time spent on reading and writing emails, the unit realized an estimated $19,200 in savings.

I also asked the representatives to estimate the percentage of customers that they had reduced the need to call back due to a failure to obtain all the necessary information on the first call. The estimates ranged from 15 to 60 percent. Using the same analysis from the benchmarked time, if a representative spent an average of 15 minutes locating or tracking a customer to speak with him or her a second time, and if he or she spent an average of five minutes gaining the necessary information, this meant that per day, per person, $32 of a day's work time could be spent in some other area of productivity. Per week, this figure was $160. Per month this figure was $640. Across the group of five representatives, the savings per month were $3,200. Annualized, just by asking the right questions and recording the right answers, the unit realized an estimated saving of $38,400.

Customer Satisfaction

Mandy's vision of providing quality services from her unit to bottlers and field salespeople became a reality. The new template for the order form, fact-finding, and writing skills significantly enhanced the reputation of the unit as one that "could get the job done." Mandy sent a memo to all field salespeople announcing the unit's improvements and enhancements and encouraging them to take advantage of the buying power and service that they could find through the corporation.

For a period of approximately six weeks, Mandy sent a one page follow-up questionnaire to each field salesperson or bottler customer who placed an order through the unit. The return rate was 82 percent from internal salespeople, but only 31 percent from bottler customers. The questions called for responses from 1 ("not at all") to 5 ("extremely"). The follow-up yielded an average result of 4.8 on "accuracy in obtaining what was ordered in a timely manner," 4.7 on "satisfaction with the services," 4.5 on "satisfaction with the representative," and a 4.6 on "desire to use these services again." Because we did not have initial surveys to benchmark these results against, I cannot quantify the gain accomplished by the intervention. Intuition tells me that if we had that data, the results would be statistically significant.

Conclusion

This case study represents an application in leadership of the highest order. We would not have realized any of these gains in quality, cost savings, error rates, and customer satisfaction without Mandy's vision and dedication. You can conclude two things from this case. First, leadership requires more than thinking, planning, and delegating. As Mandy demonstrated, leadership takes initiative and hard work. A leader has to "roll up her sleeves," take risks, and do what is right, rather than what is popular. Most managers would never have initiated the kind of development-based intervention described here, choosing instead to complain about, discipline, or dismiss employees. Indeed, several of Mandy's peers remarked that they would never have invested this kind of time for the people in their department. Mandy was a manager but, to be sure, she was also a leader.

Second, leadership is not an end in itself. Effective leadership in an organization results in outcomes important to its success and livelihood. In this case, leadership, not management, was essential in turning around the situation in the department. What is important to note, however, is that a manager should direct his or her efforts in initiating leadership toward tangible and measurable factors that are important to the business. Mandy was not interested in displaying leadership behaviors and qualities so that she could "lead." The best selling point for leadership is that these behaviors result in outcomes that other managers desire to claim for themselves and replicate.

Questions for Discussion

1. Was Mandy correct that this situation called for a leadership intervention, rather than one based on management principles? Defend your position with specifics from the case.
2. Some scholars have argued that leadership is not trainable. Do you believe that Mandy's experiences in this case suggest otherwise? Why or why not?
3. How critical was management's support to the success of this leadership intervention? What difference did it make?
4. What could have helped to make the measurement aspects of this initiative more successful?
5. Suppose that Mandy had taken a "one-best-way" approach in this case and utilized participative-based principles and behaviors. How would the outcomes have changed?

The Author

Karl J. Krayer received his Ph.D. from the University of Oklahoma, specializing in organizational communication. He is currently a consultant for Creative Communication Network, a full-service company offering speeches and presentations, training, and custom consulting and meeting facilitation for individuals, groups, and organizations. Krayer is a nationally renowned speaker, author, and consultant who works with corporations and associations who want to assess and improve competency, teamwork, and communication. He also provides informative, dynamic, and entertaining presentations and workshops for small businesses that want to increase productivity and profitability.

Krayer served on the faculties of Auburn and Texas Christian Universities before serving as training manager for 10 years with Dr Pepper/Seven Up, Inc. He is a past president of Dallas Chapter of the American Society for Training & Development, and was named its "Professional of the Year" in 1990. He is an active member of the National Speakers Association and the DFW Organizational Development Network. You can reach him at 972.601.1537; via fax at 972.414.9961; via mail at Box 38148, Dallas, Texas 75238; via email at karlk224@aol.com; or on the World Wide Web at http://www.creativecommnet.com.

Notes

1. The original work, initiated by Ken Blanchard and Paul Hersey, was entitled Life Cycle Theory. The two founders took their program in separate directions. Blanchard subsequently renamed the program "Situational Leadership II" and modified several components, whereas Hersey marketed his program with the title "The Situational Leader" and retained most of the original elements.

Developing Effective Supervisors

Michigan's Family Independence Agency

Carole S. Aslani and Michael Masternak

Michigan's Family Independence Agency lost many supervisors with an early retirement program in June 1997. The agency needed to quickly implement fast track development of newly appointed supervisors, incorporating competency-based instructional design methods. The human resources director collaborated with other executives to locate and prepare line managers as faculty for the New Supervisor Institute and implemented the "teaching organiza-tion" model to revolutionize the methods of developing agency supervisors.

Background

Michigan's Family Independence Agency (FIA) provides temporary financial assistance to needy individuals and families and protects children and vulnerable adults from abuse and neglect. The FIA employs nearly 13,000 staff located in each of Michigan's 83 counties. The well-being of the most vulnerable of Michigan's citizens counts heavily on the leadership strength of the FIA.

In early 1997, an early retirement program was offered to FIA staff, and by June 1 (the last date to take advantage of the early-out program) more than 1,500 employees had retired from the agency. Over the next several months, most of the mission-critical line staff and first-line supervisors were replaced.

During the same time period, the FIA was revamping the New Supervisor Institute (NSI). The NSI is a competency-based training

This case was prepared to serve as a basis for discussion rather than to illustrate either effective or ineffective administrative and management practices.

program designed to give newly promoted supervisors the skills they needed to provide effective leadership. By the time the first NSI was scheduled, more than 230 new supervisors had been appointed.

An agency reorganization resulted in the placement of the newly created Office of Professional Development (OPD) in the Office of Human Resources (OHR). The OHR director believed that it was critical to be able to offer the NSI to all of the agency's newly appointed supervisors. The institute plan, written by the consultant, provided for up to 80 seats per year, providing 20 seats per quarter. This schedule was appropriate for the quality issues addressed in the plan. Although this schedule would meet the agency's needs for supervisory training given normal turnover, it would not address the cumulative need that had developed since the early retirements. An alternative was needed.

Changing the institute curriculum plan was not an agreeable alternative because we didn't want to compromise quality for speed. The NSI consists of 10 days of classroom training, scheduled over a five-month period, with three consecutive days being scheduled in each of the first three months, followed by a final "graduation day" in the fifth month. The institute plan also included individual training needs assessments (pre- and posttraining self-assessments), interim practical assignments (participants complete these between sessions), and professional reading (participants are given texts).

Supervisors invited to participate in the institute had from zero to 18 months of on-the-job supervisory experience prior to attending. Participants were recruited from county offices statewide, state office sections, and juvenile justice institutions managed by FIA. Each supervisor was responsible for managing one or more agency programs, as well as six to 10 staff members. When asked how much experience they had as workers prior to promotion, the responses ranged from none (they were hired from another government agency) to 30 years. Attendance at the institute was completely voluntary. Each class is limited to 20 participants to assure each participant's questions are answered. All supervisors were new to the tasks of supervising; however, in general, each had technical expertise in their program areas. FIA's focus is primarily social work, assistance payments, and protection of citizens, so each class included participants with master of social work (MSW) degrees, other human services degrees, as well as many with high school diplomas. FIA is currently staffed with 75 percent female employees. NSI participants are 40 percent male and 60 percent female, with representative diversity in all classifications.

This competency-based institute curriculum includes technical topics with faculty composed of subject matter experts (practitioners from the various units of the agency) presenting topics such as selection and hiring, budget, performance management, labor relations, internal controls, affirmative action, automation/systems, and professional development. Other "soft skills" such as mission/vision/goals of FIA, leadership, team building, communication, effective meetings, time management, listening, information management, business ethics, and diversity were to be delivered by a consultant under contract with the agency.

The curriculum design addresses a variety of adult learning principles. Each module involves the learner in one or more activities to assure full participation and engage all the senses in the process of learning. Typical design elements found in the curriculum are games, presentation/discussion, skill practice, peer training, videos, role plays, pretests and posttests, and self-study. We were focused on the supervisor competencies, so we structured activities to promote transfer of learning. Flow of the topics was correlated with the highest rated problem areas identified during the supervisor competency research conducted October to December 1997. We had found performance management and labor relations to be a top priority for supervisors, so we placed it on Days 2 and 3 of the institute, with a follow-up on Day 4.

Support for the curriculum design was immediate from participants because several attendees were dealing with tough employee problems. Supervisors shared the behavior problems of their staff with the office of labor relations trainers and got the policy and procedural support they so desperately needed.

Real employee problem scenarios were gleaned from the experiences of the labor relations files; anonymous names replaced the real names and participants were instructed to use their labor contracts and other employee rule books to find the right way to handle these problem situations.

For example: "You find your employee regularly takes 30-minute breaks in the morning and afternoon and occasionally comes back from lunch 15 minutes late. What action would you take?"

After researching the applicable rules for the situation, each participant reports his or her findings and describes what he or she would do in the situation. Typically supervisors find they are doing some things right and they also find the things they've missed. Participants learn the agency boundary areas and comes away from this training knowing what they need to take action on when they return to their offices.

NSI Curriculum Topics

Day 1 topics covered:

- FIA mission/vision/ philosophy
- Supervisory unit responsibilities/agency structure
- Trends impacting supervisors' roles
- Expectations from above and below
- Diversity at work
- Leadership styles
- Leadership techniques

Day 2 morning topics were as follows:

- Introduction to performance planning
- Techniques of performance planning
- How to address performance gaps
- Performance evaluation/appraisal

Day 2 afternoon and Day 3 discussions and activities covered:

- Leadership: the types of power supervisors use
- Leadership self-assessment
- Understanding the labor contract; utilizing management rights, civil service rules, employee handbook policies, administrative rules
- Reasonable accommodation, Family Medical Leave Act (FMLA), computer/email usage policy, violence response, confidentiality, Freedom of Information Act (FOIA), and the employee assistance program
- Applied problem-solving practice

Day 4 topics:

- Automation applications
- Types/sources of program performance reports
- Utilizing reports
- Writing it Right—policies and methods of responding to employee grievances

Day 5:

- Leading productive meetings
- Meeting functions
- The importance of feedback
- The art of listening
- Time management
- Information management

Day 6:

- Affirmative Action/Equal Employment Opportunity policy and the hiring process
- Employee selection and hiring policy and procedures
- Effective pre-employment interviewing techniques

- New employee orientation: what supervisors need to cover
- Internal controls
    Day 7:
- The team concept
- Evaluating team performance
- Coaching
- Cultivating initiative
- Building enthusiasm
- Quality service in the public sector; a video-based module
    Day 8:
- Introduction to professional development
- Employee professional development: roles of supervisors
- Identifying and utilizing agency development resources
- On-the-job training: how to do it
    Day 9:
- Participant presentations (every supervisor prepares and delivers a 13-minute presentation)
    Day 10:
- Sharing applied practice/exchanging best practices/networking
- Posttraining scoring of Individual Training Needs Assessment (ITNA)/third level evaluations
- Business ethics
- Windows of Change: a video overview
- Graduation ceremony

In addition to the content listed above, the institute design includes 45-minute presentations (usually scheduled at the beginning of the institute day) by various agency administrative, bureau, and office managers. Typical presenters included a group of high-level managers supervisors would not likely meet in the everyday course of their work. Some of these "guest speakers" included the chief deputy director, the manager of child support, the director of the office of re-engineering, the MIS director, the manager of field operations, the director of juvenile justice programs, the director of the office of communications, the director of the office of human resources, and the director of legal affairs. Participation of these "guest speakers" enriches the institute experience. Many participants have said "it broadens my vision of the scope of the agency" or "it puts a face with a name" for many who might not otherwise have a chance to meet these managers.

The consultant and the agency had to be flexible and quickly adopt a new approach to accelerate implementation of NSI. A meeting was scheduled which brought the OPD director, the OHR director, and the consultant together to try to find a way to meet the accelerated training schedule without compromising the quality of the NSI. The consultant had recently read an ASTD *Training & Development* article (July 1998) titled "The Teaching Organization," by Noel Tichy and Eli Cohen, which outlined a model that provided new approaches. The theme of the article is one in which the organization's leaders devote a significant amount of time to teaching their emerging leaders. It was an exciting concept, and after brainstorming practical ideas for implementing it in FIA, the meeting concluded with a commitment for the human resources director to pursue the concept with the top management of the agency.

As a member of the Executive Management Team (EMT), the OHR director had ready access to the top policymakers of the agency. The EMT members include the director, the chief deputy director, and most of their direct reports. At the next scheduled meeting, the OHR director proposed the concept of the "teaching organization" to the EMT members. The concept was greeted with tremendous enthusiasm and support.

It was agreed that the EMT members and their direct reports would nominate individuals within their areas to serve as faculty for the NSI. It was agreed that the individuals nominated would be those holding top leadership positions within the agency but, more important, would be viewed by others to be the leaders among leaders. It was thought to be essential that the adjunct faculty be a diverse group, both organizationally and culturally. They needed to be articulate spokespersons who could share leadership concepts based on their own experiences. It was quickly recognized that the individuals needed for this assignment would be those who had the least amount of time to commit to the project. But it was also agreed that the qualities that got these superstars to where they were in the organization were the same qualities that would excite and motivate the new supervisors. There was a commitment to the importance of the concept of the responsibility of the current leaders to develop the organization's future leaders.

Within a few weeks, a tentative list of faculty nominees had been developed. They were sent a letter explaining the proposed "teaching organization" concept along with some related informational materials. Next they were invited to a half-day meeting so that they would have an opportunity to learn more about the initiative, and determine themselves whether they had the time and the interest to commit to the project. Each invitee was asked to bring his or her planner to the meeting.

The consultant designed a kickoff meeting to build participant spirit as well as commitment to the goal of staffing the institute schedule. She asked the OHR director to give the opening speech. Included in the design were opening testimonials from the OHR director and the participants, a statement of need/purpose, a chronology of the project, an orientation to the institute content and methods of delivery, a request for coverage (stating specific modules we needed coverage for), and a schedule with volunteer forms to complete before departure for lunch.

In his welcoming remarks, the OHR director acknowledged the participants' passion for excellence, their dedication to customer service, and their strong commitment to the agency's mission. Next he challenged them to help teach what they had learned through their experience with the agency. He asked them to help develop the agency's future leaders. The participants were then asked to introduce themselves and to indicate to their colleagues why they had chosen to accept the opportunity to learn more about this new training initiative.

Although their reasons varied somewhat, the overriding theme was an acknowledgment of the debt to someone from prior management ranks who had taken time to mentor or teach them. Helping to develop others would fulfill their desire to repay that debt. A number of them commented on the importance of the role of the first-line supervisor as being the pivotal driving force supporting good customer service.

All but two of the 30 participants agreed to devote the time necessary to fulfill this plan. They signed up to teach modules for which they felt most comfortable delivering the subject. They were given an NSI schedule for the next two years, so they could plan ahead. A schedule of train-the-trainer programs was distributed and participants were encouraged to attend.

Within two weeks of the kickoff meeting, faculty train-the-trainer meetings started. The consultant walked participants through a typical day of training, giving them all the instructional materials, explaining how to present the material (emphasizing the importance of covering the competencies for each institute day), giving some general instruction on adult learning techniques, and describing real experiences with audience reaction to the materials.

As faculty familiarized themselves with the materials they also discussed co-training the modules and posted their desired training dates on the NSI training schedule. Full coverage was achieved on the schedule as faculty eagerly signed up to teach.

To support the faculty and assure that every detail of the participants' NSI experience was a professionally coordinated experience, the agency assigned two professional trainers—human resource developers (HRDs)—to staff the institute schedule and attend to all the faculty support, planning/logistics, communication, guest speaker scheduling, and coordination work for the institute classes. One of two HRDs is in attendance throughout the session on each of the 10 days. They coordinate and provide continuity throughout the institute. They handle every logistical detail so that the faculty, technical staff, and guest speakers are responsible only for delivery of the material and the facilitation of the discussion. These HRDs who serve as NSI coordinators are also prepared to step in and present the NSI modules independently, if faculty are not able to do so. The HRDs often handle most of the group games or exercises, either independently or together with the faculty. The HRDs coach new faculty on methods of presenting the materials and are critical supports for the faculty. They must be able to work with all the faculty needs as a cotrainer, supplying technical support upon demand.

The HRDs are critical supports to the participants of the institute; they are often asked to locate area resources, to solve a participant's problem, or meet a need and provide information on how to get from one area of town to another, how to get a state car serviced, how to locate and meet specific technical experts in state office, and so on, all in an effort to keep participants focused on learning while at the institute.

A good example of the flexibility incorporated into FIA's model of the teaching organization concept can be illustrated by a closer look at Day 1 of NSI. This day begins with an overview of the institute, logistical information, and participant introductions handled through a group exercise. All of this is usually handled by the HRD, although some faculty members have chosen to become actively involved even at this stage. There are three "soft skills" modules to be covered on the first day: the agency's vision and mission, diversity, and leadership.

Some of the faculty have paired to "team teach" these modules with other faculty members, with both individuals being present and interacting throughout the presentation of each of the elements of each of the modules. Another team approach has been for one presenter to handle the morning and another to handle the afternoon of the same day, each adding their comments and support to the others' training. In another instance, the faculty member teamed with the HRD, with the HRD being the primary instructor for two of the modules while the faculty member handled one of the modules.

All of these combinations have proven effective and worked well for the faculty as well as the participants. The one structural requirement that is held firm is the need to effectively cover the supervisor competencies planned for that day. This occasionally requires the HRDs to gently coach the faculty presenter during the break or during a group exercise while the participants are working on an assignment.

The institute plan includes three levels of evaluation, based on Donald Kirkpatrick's (1994) four-level evaluation model. At this time three classes have completed the five-month development cycle and the impact of the institute has been reported by participants through their completion of a third level evaluation form on NSI Day 10.

Participants in these classes have stated the institute is extremely important for them, both professionally and personally. In the next section are some of things graduates have told us (this is a partial listing of the questions asked on the evaluation).

Third Level Evaluation Responses
Number of respondents = 41

What is your overall impression of the institute?

(21) Extremely relevant   (20) Relevant   (0) Not Relevant

Reflecting on the experience of having guest speakers from various administrations, bureaus, and offices; how valuable was this experience for you?

(26) Extremely Valuable   (14) Very Valuable   (1) Valuable

How worthwhile has the institute been for you professionally?

(16) Extremely Worthwhile (17) Very Worthwhile (8) Worthwhile
(0) Marginally Worthwhile   (0) Not Worthwhile

How worthwhile has the institute been for you personally?

(14) Extremely Worthwhile (14) Very Worthwhile (12) Worthwhile
(1) Marginally Worthwhile   (0) Not Worthwhile

How have you improved the performance of your staff since you graduated? Please give specific examples.

- I've encouraged my staff by setting an example. . . . I have made myself available. . . . They know I'm dependable and consistent. . . . I have made sure they know I believe in the mission of the agency.
- They know we are a part of the same team.
- I've helped unorganized staff create order in their office. Reinstated tracking measures of casework performance.
- I am more confident, so my staff is more confident in my ability to lead them.
- Teaching my staff to cope with change.
- Have used OJT to help a low performer improve her stats.

- My county has been trying to impact direction of SOP's. There has been a marked improvement, partly due to performance goal setting.
- I check staff work; then have one-on-one discussion each pay period . . . they know I'm checking and their work is improving.
- My staff meetings are more effective/productive.
- I learned from labor relations trainers how to monitor and correct staff misbehavior, effectively . . . now I'm doing it.
- I'm stronger and more motivated and my staff is more motivated.
- I've counseled on organizational skills, documented performance/quantified outputs and performance is really turning around!
- I responded to a grievance using the materials in our book . . . it worked!
- Providing training.
- One of my staff asked for FMLA and I knew how to respond appropriately, got the forms filled out, and explained options to staff.
- I know how to get the information I need so I can better help staff.
- I coached a staff member who was behind . . . and used the ideas about getting staff to think and come up with their own solutions to problems. I've noticed this staffer has more motivation to improve.

Additionally, follow-up informal phone calls were made by the director of human resources to solicit feedback from both faculty and NSI participants. Although the sample size of phone contacts was not large enough to provide statistically reliable information, this sample echos findings from the formal evaluation process. The NSI teaching and learning experience has been very valuable for both groups as feedback has been extraordinarily positive.

The participants interviewed uniformly stated that the use of managers as NSI faculty proved to be an outstanding experience. A number of them stated that the most important benefit—even more valuable than the material presented—was the message that top management was taking a personal interest in the new supervisor's career. As one of the trainees observed, "It was great to be able to put a face with a name and feel you are actually on a first-name basis. But what I really appreciated was feeling that they were really invested in my success as a new supervisor—in my career." Another stated she sometimes felt "detached from decision makers," and that having an opportunity to spend some time with them in a small group discussion "dispelled the perception of status and rank."

A number of trainees also appreciated having discussions on topics such as leadership, teamwork, vision/mission, and customer service being led by departmental mangers who have "walked the talk." As one of the trainees said, "I have been working on my master's degree in management, and I found much of the content of the NSI to be much more valuable than my college classes because we were learning from managers who have had experience dealing with the same problems in our same environment. I felt the content was much more relevant because the theory was interspersed with a heavy dose of reality. They've had the experiences we're going through."

One supervisor stated she had a terrible negative-attitude problem between her staff and clients. Upon returning to her staff after completing the communication modules at the institute, she told staff if she got any more complaints about rudeness from clients she would invite the client to meet with her and the staff member to discuss the situation. She said she had to do this only twice and the staff behavior changed dramatically; now she gets no complaints from clients.

Others liked having a variety of presenters. When asked if they felt that the faculty were "effective trainers" in terms of their "teaching style," most responded by saying that they liked the variety of presenters and styles. Some stated that they would not like everyone to use the "lecture" format, as some of the faculty did, but that those who used that style were interesting and always open to questions. However, for the most part, the trainees preferred the interactive discussion.

The faculty members interviewed also had very positive experiences with their role in NSI. They all acknowledged that their participation took a significant amount of time and noted that they were spending more time preparing for their presentations than they had expected because they wanted to make the experience as rewarding for the trainees as possible. All stated that they felt it to be a highly worthwhile expenditure of their time, and all plan to continue serving as adjunct faculty.

Some made the observation that the exercise of preparing and delivering the material on a particular topic caused them to refocus on their own management styles and reinforced their commitment to improving their own management skills. One individual stated that she led a discussion on the same topic in her next staff meeting with her own direct reports, because it was a timely issue for them.

Another benefit cited by some of the presenters is that it gave them an opportunity to hear directly from front-line supervisors how things are going at the service delivery level. One manager stated that this "reality check made me rethink how we are communicating some of our policy changes to the field."

Other observations from faculty included:

- "I found out that I had more to offer than I thought."
- "This is not the style of presentation I am accustomed to doing but I found that I felt very comfortable doing it."
- "I had a great time. It was a nice change of pace . . . almost like a day off."
- "It felt good knowing that I was doing my small part to help develop some of our future leaders."
- "It was great to see the enthusiasm of our new supervisors . . . reinvigorated me."

Lessons Learned

Timely organizational change can happen if it is supported from the top of the organization and championed by a dedicated group of administrators who "walk the talk" of the change they support.

Consultants can be most beneficial in their advisory role if they are well read in their field and have tools to offer their clients when a shift of plan presents an opportunity for changing training/leadership models and trying new approaches.

Operational managers with talent and commitment can quickly respond to a call for help and, in the process, find new reasons to like their jobs.

Supervisors benefit from a broad variety of trainer styles. Even more significant is in the managers' new faculty role; by modeling a manner of being a present and approachable support for supervisors, they have shifted paradigms for supervisors and broadened their perceptions of the development roles they can play with their own staff.

There's nothing that spurs success like success. FIA top managers saw the power in the "teaching organization" model to create effective leaders and through their wisdom all NSI partners have experienced success.

At the time of this writing three institute classes have been completed. Six more institute classes are in progress. News of the value of the institute has created a waiting list for NSI. Participants are energized by the role operational mangers are playing in their development, and managers are enjoying being part of the faculty. The consultant has completed the faculty development phase of the project. The HRDs continue to support all elements of the NSI and provide an essential sustaining continuity for all involved with NSI.

This case study demonstrates how committed managers—given the chance—have been able to transform their organization into a "teaching organization" and in the process strengthen everyone involved in the process of developing effective new leaders for the future of FIA. The motto of this agency reads "We strengthen individuals and families through mutual respect and mutual responsibility." At FIA the agency motto is brought to life with the new NSI model for leadership development.

Questions for Discussion

1. Why and how did Michigan's Family Independence Agency implement the "teaching organization" model?
2. What role did the human resources director play in helping the agency to change into a "teaching organization"?
3. Describe some of the win/win impacts of this project.
4. What were the impacts on the participants of the New Supervisor Institute?
5. What needs to be done to maintain the success of this project?

The Authors

Carole S. Aslani is senior consultant with Aslani Associates Consultation and Training of Milford, Michigan. Aslani specializes in organizational performance improvement initiatives and training. She was previously employed by Michigan Family Independence Agency (FIA), where she held various front-line and supervisory positions; she served as a professional human resource developer and supervisor of the Management Skills Section of FIA's Office of Training and Staff Development.

Aslani was selected by FIA to research supervisor competencies and design a curriculum for new supervisors. Previous to founding her consulting practice in 1997, she served as training director of the Michigan Employment Security Agency. She has a master of public administration from Western Michigan University and a bachelor of science education from Michigan State University.

Michael Masternak is the human resources director for Michigan's 13,000-employee Family Independence Agency. As HR director, a position which he has held for the past 12 years, Masternak is responsible for managing all aspects of the human resources function, including labor relations, performance management, recruitment, selection, classification, compensation, benefits administration, training, and professional development. For the 18 years prior to that, he served as the agency's labor relations director.

Masternak has his B.A. in economics from Indiana University, and his M.A. in economics from Michigan State University. While at MSU, he also completed all of the requirements except a dissertation for a Ph.D. in labor and industrial relations. He was an instructor at MSU while working on his Ph.D., and in recent years has served on the faculty of Lansing Community College, where he taught classes in grievance and arbitration, and negotiations and collective bargaining.

References

Kirkpatrick, D. (1994). *Evaluating Training Programs: The Four Levels.* San Francisco: Berrett-Koehler.

Tichy, N.M., and E. Cohen. (1998, July). "The Teaching Organization." Training & Development, 26–33.

Executive Coaching

E.G. Verlander & Associates

Edward G. Verlander

This chapter discusses the concept of executive coaching as a powerful and practical method for developing leaders. First, the business context is discussed as a driver of various leadership development initiatives; then we explore current trends in executive leadership coaching which provide the impetus for three alternative executive coaching methods in current professional practice—shadow, feedback-based, and just-in-time personal coaching. Each is described in detail with specific examples and a set of guidelines needed by the practitioner to ensure that this form of leadership development is successful.

Business Context

For the last two decades or more companies have been dealing with an unprecedented, challenging, uncertain, and very complex business environment. Virtually all companies in all industries have been challenged by industry consolidation, global competition, the rise of nontraditional competitors, the integration of countries into trading blocks, information technology, and the rising pressure to perform from quarter to quarter under the scrutiny of tough analysts in the midst of unprecedented information explosion.

In response to those market pressures, the senior leadership of many companies have launched a rich array of initiatives and programs. Over the last 20 years we have seen centralization, decentralization, matrix structures, outsourcing, de-layering, customer focus programs, total quality management, business process re-engineering, team-based

This case was prepared to serve as a basis for discussion rather than to illustrate either effective or ineffective administrative and management practices.

organizational designs, a range of new ways to think about strategy, and, of course, numerous leadership development initiatives including executive coaching.

What has all this work been trying to accomplish? It could be all boiled down to four basic and simple things. These initiatives have been aimed at making the companies faster, bigger, better, and cheaper: *faster* in terms of helping companies to reduce product development cycle time to bring new products and services to the marketplace quicker than the competition; *bigger* in terms of market share, profits, earnings per share, and return on net assets (not incidentally, bigger in numbers of employees—although, despite the layoffs, it is clear all those who were laid off have found or created new employment); *better* in terms of the quality of the products and services produced and better in terms of value-added services provided to clients; *cheaper* in terms of doing all of the above at lower cost.

To accomplish all of the above, companies have exposed their management to a vast array of organizational change and employee development initiatives. Many have been launched by management consulting firms working in conjunction with internal human resources professionals. Also, the human resources function in most companies has been very busy trying to transform their organizations by creating, designing, developing, and delivering customized versions of the initiatives mentioned above.

Human resources strategies have ranged from empowerment and seven habits to employee stock option programs and leadership development. In fact, for most of the 1990s, leadership development has been a central goal of many companies, in part because a number of well-known academics at leading business schools have focused attention on it, but more important, because the senior management at many companies have realized that the only way that their organizations can deal with the speed, direction, and intensity of the changes affecting their companies is by having a wide and deep force of people who can lead their way out of the highly complex jungle of issues and challenges they now face.

As a result, leadership development has become a major intervention in many companies. It has become: 1) a stimulant for change in many companies that need to be woken up; 2) a source of new talent for rapidly expanding global operations; 3) a tool to implement many of the faster, bigger, better, cheaper initiatives; and 4) a way to sharpen the distinction between internal collaboration and external competitiveness.

Leadership Development Initiatives

What is leadership? How is leadership development implemented in companies and what are the outcomes they want? Researchers from Warren Bennis (1989), John Gardner (1990), and John Kotter (1998, 1990) to Steven Covey (1992), Leonard Sayles (1979), and Tom Peters (1982) have defined leadership in a variety of ways. The old functional definitions of managing (planning, organizing, staffing, and controlling) have been separated from leadership. Kotter, for example, talks about *managing* as controlling complexity through meticulous, detailed planning and execution, and *leadership* as creating, sustaining, and facilitating change. Leadership is about influencing people to accomplish something they did not know they were capable of. It is about visualizing the future and passionately communicating how the organization can and must adapt itself to create that future. It ensures that grand visions are converted into practical goals and plans and that employees are able see how their work fits in and contributes to the big picture. Good leadership skills create a highly committed workforce using innovative performance management and human resource policies. Leadership is building a network of lateral teams across an organization so that a company can share its intellectual capital, resources, and talent—which in turn fosters innovation and creativity. Leadership is about building teamwork and behaving with integrity. And it is about taking people where they have not been before and want to go.

By separating managing from leadership, academics and practitioners of leadership (that is, people who actually lead other people) have been able to research and describe a deeper and richer understanding of leadership. Peter Krass (1998) in his recent book cites many of the key principles that leaders in major corporations have applied to exemplify the role. For example, John Patterson, founder of National Cash Register Company, emphasized the need to create and draw pictures in support of his words (vision) and then to mobilize people with dramatic demonstrations (what we call "walking the talk" today). David Sarnoff of RCA believed in the power of emphasizing future possibilities and progress. Ray Kroc of McDonald's fast-food chain put a premium on self-discipline, a quality available to everyone if he or she chooses it. Robert Haas of Levi Strauss & Co. found that a small number of core values (honesty, promise keeping, fairness, respect for others, compassion, and integrity) provided a way to help company leaders make ethical decisions that balanced those values with the competing needs of multiple stakeholders. Andy Grove of Intel believes it is the ability to make ordinary people do extraordinary things when the odds appear to be against them, by communicating strongly held beliefs with emotion and passion. He says it helps people become believers. Fred Smith of FedEx and Horst Shulze of The Ritz Carlton disseminate leadership by empowering their organization to enable people to lead themselves—enabling people to make quick and important decisions guided with a broad vision, company values, and their own specific business goals.

It is easy to point to high-profile leaders such as Jack Welch, Fred Smith, Lee Iaacoca, Herb Kelleher, and Max DePree (1989). But how did these leaders get that way and what have they done in their organizations to foster the leadership necessary to tackle the challenging external business context? At the personal level, some have done it by instinct, others by logical, practical insight. Some have done it by necessity or have had to face the risk of major business failure. Others have become effective leaders by systematic personal development acquired over many years in a range of increasingly challenging organizational roles. Once in a senior executive leadership role, many have seen the critical need to institutionalize management and leadership development throughout their organizations. In my research I've seen a wide range of such initiatives, including: launching company "universities"; in-tact work group retreats; in-company and university-sponsored seminars and workshops on leadership; attending university summer executive programs; total immersion assessment center programs; outward bound ropes and ladders work; systematic management development programs that carefully track and nurture talent over three to five to 10 years; 360-degree feedback programs; and, more recently, executive coaching.

For more than 20 years, competency-based development has been at the heart of systematic leadership development and is grounded in the idea that if a manager or executive can behave in ways consistent with the competencies, that person will be a better leader. The range of so-called competencies can be enormous—the Center For Creative Leadership, for example, has more than 100 competencies. Nevertheless, proponents of this approach say that their work is based on research that has differentiated effective from ineffective leadership behavior. So, by learning and using the behaviors, together with their generic style and personality, most people will be able to develop stronger leadership capability. The reality is that no single individual can develop all of the competencies, no matter how well defined and aggressively pursued. Indeed, if one looks to the practical world of business and industry and to leaders who lead every day, there are not many examples of the "perfect leader." Even the highly visible, exceptional business leaders have deficiencies and therefore are in need of continuing development. Just as the world's best tennis player or basketball player needs a coach to stay on top, so executives at the top of their game also need a coach.

Executive Coaching Trends

Of all the attempts to develop leaders, I think that executive coaching holds exceptional promise. Coaching has become more important as the pace of change in companies has quickened and the sheer volume of work has increased for all managers. In my consulting, I constantly hear from managers that they feel overworked, burnt out, struggling to handle more things on their "plate" than they can possibly handle. Time is a premium (as well as a major component of strategic business advantage in the "faster, bigger, better, cheaper" world we live in). Because today's executives have unprecedented demands on their time, executive coaching has become an especially attractive form of executive leadership development for three important reasons.

1. Advantages of Coaching

Human resource development (HRD) professionals report a number of advantages to coaching. For example, coaching is seen as a useful way to foster organizational learning and as a faster way to provide individual executives with highly focused and efficient development. At the same time, as an executive skill, coaching (along with mentoring) is now seen in many companies as an important capability at every leadership level. The new mantra is "Every leader a coach." So, executive coaching has become an additional way to help them to understand how to coach others.

2. Coaching Resources

As a managerial capability and training objective, coaching is not new. What is new is that coaching has moved from something talked about in the seminar room to something done in the office. *Importantly, more and more executives are getting personal coaches.* These coaches are usually external consultants hired with specific assignments to work one-on-one with an executive on a set of specific business and often interpersonal issues. I have been working with a vice president at a major utility company for the last nine months to help him address a number of personal leadership problems that his president noted. The president, recognizing the critical role this executive played in the business, used the company's performance management system to focus the executive attention on a number of leadership gaps and problems. Seeking the advice of both the human resources leadership development professionals in his company and his immediate manager, the executive took the initiative to find a personal coach. We have been working together to change his behavior, broaden his thinking, and deepen his understanding of his leadership role in the context of his current business responsibilities. Within two months, his own management team was reporting "seeing more leadership-type behavior than they've seen before." The individualized, personal coaching continues today ensuring follow-through on commitments and reinforcement of the changes we agree he needs to make.

3. Return on Investment Metric

Coaching reflects and supports another recent trend. Even though top management sees competitive advantages to making substantial investment in training and development, they now expect to see a measurable return on that investment. A multimillion dollar investment in a fully fledged corporate university needs to be justified on some measurable basis, just as another business investment is subject to cost-benefit or return on investment (ROI) analysis. Responding to this challenge, many HRD departments are pursuing ways to measure the impact of their work and are using estimation statistics to demonstrate the link between HRD programs and business results (the so-called level 5 analysis). Executive coaching is an excellent way to meet the ROI test because the problems are focused and the results almost immediate.

In sum, coaching is both a noun and a verb in today's office. Leaders are learning to be coaches and more and more leaders are being coached. These two trends intersect as powerful developmental experiences available to HRD professionals to train their leaders. But, turning an executive into a coach is, to say the least, challenging. Coaches are not produced overnight and coaching may or may not come naturally to a person. Thus, I have found that the very process of coaching an executive is itself a way to help them learn how to coach. If done well, as described below, the very experience of being coached becomes a model process that executives can use to guide their own coaching efforts.

A Working Definition of Coaching

Fundamentally, coaching is the facilitation of learning. (Although it is beyond the scope of this work, the reader would be well served to examine the work of David Kolb [1979] and Malcolm Knowles [1978] on this subject to understand the various ways in which we learn.) In general, the goal of this learning is to help executives to: 1) build and enhance self-directedness so they can act with greater autonomy, effectiveness, confidence, and business acumen; 2) learn to trust their own judgment; 3) mobilize personal, continuous improvement with a conviction that change is both possible and desirable; and 4) enable them to create a faster, bigger, better, cheaper organization.

Coaching is a capability with its own set of skills. Skills are needed in diagnosis, advocacy, giving advice, problem exploration, analysis, interpersonal communications, as well as diplomacy, tact, flexibility, and empathy, to name a few. As coaches we also need to be quite conscious of the timing, pacing, and rhythm of the language we use, the logic of our coaching, as well as the tone and manner of our style. These will be discussed below as we consider the three basic approaches to coaching that have emerged in recent years: shadow coaching; feedback-based coaching; and just-in-time personal coaching. I will discuss how each of the three works, the key success factors of each, and results.

Shadow Coaching

One way to coach an executive is through "shadow coaching," which means working alongside an executive as he or she performs regular daily duties. In other words, it means spending a lot of time with an executive on location in the person's office, attending meetings, and participating in social activities.

This intense kind of coaching is useful when the individual in question is seen as having deep-seated, inflexible behavioral patterns and has successfully avoided making the changes necessary to be effective in the new working environment. It is also an effective method when the executive's problem is not clear. The executive's manager may be unclear about what is wrong and the executive senses that something needs to change but cannot articulate it.

HOW IT WORKS. A client of mine, the president of a medium-sized insurance company, had just taken over running the company. Faced with downward pressure on prices, increased competition, and increased client expectations, he determined that the company had to be strongly led and that the company's leadership team needed to make some significant changes in the business. A stronger client focus would mean new sources of revenue; new value-added services in new markets would stabilize earnings; reorganization of management would place talented, aggressive managers in leadership positions; and a revitalized top management team would provide the thought, leadership, and energy to make the hard choices in a very difficult market.

Although the president personally pursued new client prospects and started to make specific and detailed changes internally, he realized that he had to rely heavily on his immediate direct reports. Each individual worked too independently and not as a team and—even worse—although they collectively acknowledged the difficult business conditions, each did not step up (or could not step up) to the *higher level of personal productivity* that the president now expected in his direct reports. He wanted more personal contribution and output, teamwork, tough decisions, a sense of urgency, and radical organizational changes.

With these goals and business problems clear in his mind, the president needed to get the attention of each of his immediate managers, especially one individual who had been especially difficult and recalcitrant about contributing more in his role. In order to convey the seriousness of the need to change and to ensure the executive would "get the message" about his attitude and behavior, I agreed to act as a "shadow coach" to closely observe and guide change. The president and I agreed to the following protocol:

1. The coaching would be for one week. A week was deemed to be sufficient time to observe and assess the executive's strengths and weaknesses and to make specific recommendations.
2. I would provide the executive with confidential feedback and advice during the week, as appropriate.
3. I would write a formal report on my diagnosis and recommendations.
4. The executive in question would review the content with me before any discussions with the president.
5. The executive would agree with me on how my presence would be communicated to his functional organization—that is, the reason for my being there and my role.
6. The president, the executive, and I would meet at the end of the week to discuss the experience, my findings, changes, and next steps.

I focused the "shadow coaching" on five goals: 1) to observe the executive in his everyday, regular work environment—making telephone calls, handling meetings, working with other managers and colleagues, attending various internal and external business meetings, working with staff, and working through his agenda; 2) to analyze and diagnose problems that I observed; 3) to ask questions about the executive's thinking, behavior, style, motivations, frustrations, intentions, and feelings; 4) to offer periodic advice; and 5) to prepare a written report summarizing my findings with specific recommendations for change and improvement.

We felt that a week's worth of time would be enough time for me to get to know the executive's job and for the executive to feel comfortable with my being there (while trying to be as unobtrusive as possible). The executive would not be able to put on false, prepared, or rehearsed behavior to manipulate my observations. I would be able to see a variety of behaviors across a range of work and activity to be able to draw valid conclusions. Finally, a week's worth of work encompassed a wide range of people and situations. This turned out to be true.

Following the on-site week, I called the executive on the average of once a week and then once a month over a three-month period to assess progress, provide reinforcement, offer help and advice, and to provide the executive with the opportunity to talk to a trusted advisor in confidence.

KEY SUCCESS FACTORS. In my experience, shadow personal coaching can be very successful as long as some guidelines are followed:

- **Sponsor Commitment.** Ensure the coaching sponsor (the president of the company in this case) sees this coaching as a priority for the executive and is fully committed to following through on the amount of time committed to the shadow coaching. It will be a major disruption to let other business issues get in the way, to cut it short, break it up into chunks, or simply stop halfway through.
- **Safe Rationale.** The executive may feel embarrassed and awkward about the whole process; so make sure plausible reasons are worked out as to why you are there and what you are doing so the executive can explain it. Put it in broad terms: "... he's here working with me on a number of strategic issues going on in the function and business ..."
- **Unobtrusiveness.** Try to be quiet and unobtrusive, especially when someone else is in the executive's office.
- **Keep Busy.** Always be occupied with something while in the office—taking notes, reading background information, summarizing observations, or analyzing data, or something like that. This reduces the "being stared at" factor.
- **Balanced Analysis.** Prepare a report that points out both the positive leadership behaviors and areas to improve. In either case, be candid and clear, direct and demanding. Shadow coaching is sig-

nificantly weakened if the feedback and advice is "soft peddled" or given as broad observations. The sponsor and the executive in question need concrete ideas about change and improvement.

- **Be Natural.** The coach's presence and behavior will impact the manner of the executive, who may struggle to be natural and normal. So, the coach must be as natural as possible, calm, and sensitive. Take initiatives to put the executive at ease with small talk and humor. Openly acknowledge and try to get him or her to talk about how it *feels* going through the process.
- **Role Model Skills.** During the review meeting at week's end, the president said: "We have the best conversations when you (the consultant) are here." I took this to mean I had done a good job of modeling effective two-way communications, using a lot of interactive listening and making them feel good about how they dealt with issues affecting their relationship—each could engage in some "truth-telling."

RESULTS. Immediate changes were noted. There was a wide range of attitudes from resignation and hostility in the beginning to one of greater candor and acknowledgment about the need to improve at the end. Also, there was an immediate improvement in output because the shadow coaching had focused, in part, on problems of time management, stress levels, productivity, and keeping commitments. Finally, there was an immediate change in the amount and quality of communication between the executive and the new president.

With the passage of time, productivity fell off but did not revert back to the original condition. The quality of the working relationship between the president and the executive and the executive's colleagues improved—not dramatically but to a noticeable degree. An added benefit and additional outcome for the executive was a clearer vision of his role and contribution to the company going forward. Our discussions served to validate a new role he had been considering (and subsequently supported by the president) to play a stronger mentoring and developmental role to middle and new managers, passing on the executive's extensive knowledge of the business and key relationships.

Feedback-Based Coaching

For the last 15 years there has been a growing use of 360-degree feedback coaching. Three-sixty (360) simply means that a process is started that gives the executive input about his or her leadership behavior from the executive's immediate manager, colleagues (peer level), direct reports, and increasingly from other stakeholders such as customers. Thus, the feedback is from all points on the organizational relationship compass.

Three-sixty feedback is an outgrowth of earlier work done with cross-functional and in-tact work team building where all team members would contribute feedback about the contributions and effectiveness of each of the other team members. In many companies it has now become institutionalized as a normal way in which a leader can gain specific knowledge and facts about strengths and areas for improvement.

Concurrently, management development methods, and to some degree organizational development practice, have focused heavily on defining *competencies* for all classes of jobs and job families in organizations. Competency-based training and development has, in some ways, been a linking mechanism whereby career paths, career development, management of high potentials (as company assets), and management development have been linked together with a common set of job-based, hierarchical competencies. Some organizations have built the competencies into their performance management systems. The recent work of Daniel Goleman (1998) has extended the idea of competencies into the area of *emotional intelligence* with five components (that is, competency areas) of emotional intelligence in the work place: self-awareness, self-regulation, motivation, empathy, and social skills. Such components, he argues, are central to leadership success.

Three-sixty feedback can be for any role, job, or job family. In leadership development the competencies are usually the validated behaviors of highly effective leaders. The competencies themselves are the basis upon which employees get feedback, usually in the form of a report that provides graphical and numerical data of how frequently the executive has been observed performing the competencies in a leadership role. In my own work, the behavioral competencies (sometime called *practices*) have been researched, developed, and validated with the client's organization, organized into a logical framework, and then used as the basis for 360-degree feedback and coaching.

HOW IT WORKS. Once a company decides to launch a leadership development process, it can take a variety of forms. In my experience 360 feedback coaching has been part of a senior management, cross-functional training program that addressed many topics, including leadership; it has also been part of a team building process for a single business unit; and it has been a mechanism for helping a single individual to change. It has also been one of a number of programs and initiatives aimed at changing an organization. In this sense, it has been for the leadership of the *entire organization* involved in a change effort.

For example, one recent client in the Philippines decided that the corporate leaders and the top management of each of its business units would participate in a 360 feedback-based leadership development process. A leadership framework was devised, 42 specific leadership behaviors were defined, and dates were organized for leadership workshops where each leader would receive his or her confidential leadership report, be coached, and each business unit would discuss the themes and messages in the business unit's group data.

The process was highly successful and had the following protocols. Preceding the leadership development initiative for the company's five business units, the chairman of the company held a two-day off-site conference for the entire senior management (about 150 managers or so-called "officer corps" of the company). The conference was a forum for managers to talk about the business need for stronger leadership, the new management development system being deployed, and to signal the chairman's endorsement of the investment as a priority for the company.

A package of leadership survey questionnaires was created, printed, and customized for each participant who would attend the leadership workshops; a processing center in the United States was hired to produce the individual and group feedback reports. Each package contained 14 survey questionnaires—one for the workshop participant (a self-questionnaire), one for the participant's immediate manager, six for same-level colleagues, and six for direct reports (that is, subordinates one or two levels down).

An internal procedure was worked out so that the surveys could be completed, sealed, batched, and shipped to the United States for processing. Each survey respondent put the anonymous questionnaire into an envelope, sealed it, and mailed it to a central collection office in the company. (This office was managed by external consultants who batched the envelopes before shipping. When 360 feedback leadership development is done in the United States, survey respondents put the completed questionnaire into a stamped envelope and mail it directly to the processing center.)

Survey questionnaires were shipped for arrival at the processing center approximately three weeks before the scheduled leadership workshops. One week before the workshop, I would receive participants' individual feedback reports and a group report representing data from those actually attending the workshop—in the case of this client, a complete business unit.

I reviewed the group data for themes, patterns in the data, and major messages about the business unit's leadership strengths and weaknesses. This summary data would be distributed and discussed at the workshop and used as a basis for deciding where very specific, additional leadership development work was needed. I also studied each participant feedback report as preparation for the individualized personal coaching sessions.

During the leadership workshop, participants received their data in a way that enabled them to digest the large volume of data and input. The workshops ran for two days including the coaching.

Confidentiality was maintained throughout the entire process. The goal was to ensure that when the workshop participant received his or her leadership feedback report, the participant was the first person (other than me) to see the data. No information was to be given to anyone else, including the person's manager or human resources.

Following the workshop, each participant had a one- to one-and-a-half hour *coaching session* with me. The purpose of the coaching was to help the managers to gain additional insights from the data, validate their current interpretations, understand options and choices about leadership effectiveness, and to apply the messages and ideas from the workshop and feedback to the job. Each walked away with a specific action plan.

Time and time again, feedback-based coaching has proved an important catalyst for action by an individual leader or a whole leadership team. Most executives like data and facts. The competency-based feedback provides data and facts that can be hard to deny. Even though survey data are not 100 percent reliable, it does give the executive a firm basis for returning back to the job armed with insights and new questions about how to be a more effective leader.

Finally, the survey feedback process itself changed people's perceptions and expectations about leadership. Survey respondents who had answered 40 questions about leadership now knew what effective leadership was all about, and could reasonably expect to see changes in their executive's behavior. Feedback coaching was a key element in helping the executive to calibrate a response to those expectations.

KEY SUCCESS FACTORS. In my experience, 360 feedback-based coaching of this kind can be very successful as long as some guidelines are followed:

- **Session Structure.** Think about the coaching session in three parts: opening, middle, and close. Devote the *opening* to gaining more business context and putting the executive at ease; the *middle* to exploring real problems (in the data and/or on the job) that need fixing; the *close* to summarizing actions, next steps, and scheduling follow-up work.

- **Be Well Prepared.** Because the coaching session is organized around the feedback report, the executive expects the consultant to bring expertise and insight. It is important to be well prepared. Study the report ahead of time and work out what you will say about strengths and weaknesses. Therefore, study the gaps in perception between respondents, competencies scored high and low, comparisons with group data, and validations/insights from the written comments.

- **Probe for Answers.** The survey questionnaires usually have a section for written responses from the respondents—what the executive should "stop, start, continue doing." Quite often there are sharp, critical comments that need exploring. Are the comments legitimate? Why? What's causing those remarks? Also, quite often the same comment will crop up several times, such as: "Doesn't listen," "Uses inappropriate language in meetings." A deeper exploration of the psychology driving that behavior is warranted in order to raise the executive's consciousness and to gain commitment to do things differently, to go forward.

- **Balanced Diplomacy.** Candor and directness need to be balanced with tact and sensitivity. This is a judgment call as you quickly size up the person. Is the person receptive and open or defensive and closed? I once told a tall, overweight lawyer that his cigar smoking was a dominant behavior that intimidated some employees, leading them to avoid saying what needed to be said at meetings, and so forth (this was before the widespread ban on smoking in offices). The executive respected my directness, making him conscious of something he simply hadn't thought about before. Not only did he change the smoking habit, he also later recommended me to run a two-day off-site retreat with the company's legal department.

- **Balanced Flexible Style.** Some coaches prefer to ask a lot of questions, some to be highly directive in their coaching. The "Rogerian coaches" ask more questions than make statements or provide advice and believe that questions draw the executive out and will lead to insights and actions. In their view it is important to be nondirective and completely "client centered." Others prefer to be directive, to tell others what the messages are and what to do about them. They believe that with a limited amount of time, executives need quick inputs and straight talk and that their clients will choose whether to follow the advice.

I prefer a balanced approach. Carefully posed questions that probe and draw out underlying motivations and intentions, combined with strongly suggested, specific, concrete, alternative actions, challenges the executive to think out loud, rethink basic assumptions, and to draw conclusions about what is the best course of action.

- **Confidentiality.** Keeping confidences and confidentiality are critical throughout the entire process. I know of no instance where the feedback report or the content of the coaching conversation is available to anyone other than the coach and employee. If you do, please let me know. On the other hand, I always encourage people to share the feedback, although in summary form.
- **Political Insight.** It is a good idea to encourage senior executives to take you into their confidence. This kind of coaching enables you to meet all of the management team and to learn a lot about the political dynamics of the organization. Use this information and insight to help the executive see new ways of understanding people and situations that will in turn lead to more effective leadership behavior.
- **Action Plan.** At the end of the coaching session a follow-up plan is in order, even with the most senior executive. The plan should include: 1) specific behavioral actions and changes based on the feedback and coaching; 2) a plan to meet with the survey respondents to share insights and to engage them in further leadership improvements; and 3) follow-up with the consultant to reinforce, clarify, and encourage change.

RESULTS. Experience shows that feedback-based coaching can be a very useful vehicle to help leaders change and develop. The data are very specific ("I got a 2.3 [using a 1 to 5 scale] on: 'Works to build cross-functional teams'" or "a 1.5 on 'Communicates the vision in a way that excites employees'"), yet, at the same time, by examining the data and scores across 30 to 40 competencies it is possible to see general patterns and habits of behavior which, in turn, can be analyzed and—where appropriate—redirected. For example, one client noted that for the group as a whole, most practices that involved direct face-to-face leadership with its employees such as giving feedback, coaching, resolving conflicts, reviewing performance, and team building, the scores on average were lower as compared to competencies about business knowledge, market trends, and networking outside of the group. The client decided to focus on performance management and interpersonal communications skills as part of its ongoing leadership development efforts. Another client got feedback to stop doing a fake golf swing when talking with other executives and yet another to stop interrupting people and to listen more carefully.

Just-In-Time Personal Coaching

The third and final type of leadership development coaching takes the form of one-on-one, individualized executive coaching or what I like to call "just-in-time" personal coaching. What distinguishes this form of coaching from the others is the focused, single-problem nature of the work, done on a "immediate availability" basis. For example, for a variety of companies in different industries I have been called in to work with individual executives on such things as:

- making an effective presentation to the board of directors
- demonstrating progress on strategic initiatives
- contributing more at executive team meetings
- rethinking the business role of the department and the necessary leadership qualifications to sell that role to the organization
- improving communications skills when thoughts are often muddled and confusing
- developing a stronger leadership team
- improving people-management skills.

Personal coaches have become more widespread over the last five years with many consultants providing services through an emerging service niche called "coaching brokers." All personal coaches work in a similar vein, providing practical help, offering useful advice, and providing an objective outside view that is not colored by a political agenda or narrow interests. These trusted executive coaches have many ongoing long-term relationships with their client companies. Some work with a single individual, some with many individuals in a company. They are successful if they can "parachute in" on a moment's notice, deliver, make an impact, and then engage the executive's share of mind for more coaching.

HOW IT WORKS. Following a performance review with the president of the company, which included the suggestion of getting a personal coach, my client, a vice president of operations, called the manager of leadership development in the company's learning center to inquire about available coaching resources.

After an initial meeting with the leadership development manager to discuss my experience, credibility, procedures, and style, I set up the first meeting with the vice president. The purpose of the first meeting was to review the situation (issues in the performance review), go over several ways to deal with the performance issues, and for the two of us to assess whether we could work together.

Following the initial meeting the vice president told the manager of leadership development he wanted to work with me. We launched a multistep process that required five meetings over three months, followed by a review and a decision about whether to continue. We agreed to initially meet once a week for two weeks so that we could get focused on a priority issue—developing a stronger leadership presence in his very large, geographically dispersed organization and with the president's leadership team.

After the first two meetings we met every two weeks for a month and then once a month. Each session was for a minimum of two hours to discuss progress, actions, issues, and the psychological, political, and organizational barriers to change. Following the three-month review meeting, we decided to open up the development to the vice president's immediate team, which began with a leadership development workshop to give them some of ideas and skills that the vice president and I had covered during the coaching.

KEY SUCCESS FACTORS. Many of the success factors applicable to shadow and feedback-based coaching are useful with just-in-time personal coaching. In addition, the following factors should be kept and mind:

- **Quick Assessments.** Interpersonal skills are always important, but especially so under these conditions where it may be a single coaching event. Careful listening and quick assessment of the needs and problems are crucial for success. Checking and rechecking the problem (using "reframing the problem" techniques) pays great dividends to make sure the coaching is focused on the right issues. There usually isn't much time for a mistake and the executive will size up your competence within a very few minutes.
- **Supporting Diagnostics.** If the coaching is extended over several months, I have found that supplementing my own insights and experience with instrumentation, readings, and diagnostics really helps the executive to gain insights and new perspectives very quickly. One executive, for example, was finally convinced of a point I was trying to make when he completed a leadership diagnostic instrument that pointed out just how little flexibility he had in his thinking and behavior.
- **Background Intelligence Data.** Gain as much background information as you can on the executive before you meet with him or her. This can be gained from internal sources—either from the executive's manager (who may be sponsoring the coaching) or internal pro-

fessional training and leadership development personnel. This information must be immediately validated and confirmed by the information given to you by the executive. This puts a premium on preparation and developing a set of good closed and open-ended questions. I quite like Neil Rackham's (1988) SPIN model for conducting a quick, structured, focused interview at the first meeting, or at the front end of a single coaching event.

RESULTS. Within the first two weeks the vice president reported that his direct reports were saying that he was "acting more like a leader" and that he was "showing more leadership." One immediate concrete leadership change included his making regular visits to his field operations—something he had neglected to do for several years. Other immediate actions occurred. Our conversations brought into focus his need to: 1) establish a personal leadership agenda; 2) to communicate that agenda with his manager and direct reports; 3) to ensure that key elements of his agenda were regularly on the top management team's meeting agenda; and 4) to start making demands of his direct reports that progressed his leadership agenda.

Three months later he agreed to sponsor a management development workshop for his direct reports to help them see how each of them needed to act more as a leader. Today, our coaching continues to unfold on new and emerging leadership issues including cost reduction, process re-engineering, and organization turnover.

Additional Coaching Best Practices and Issues

In addition to the skills, techniques, methods, and interpersonal style issues noted above, there are several other important things to keep in mind when coaching senior executives.

- **The Coaching Dilemma.** Senior executives are used to tough meetings and tangled issues; they expect facts and answers and they want to have their thinking challenged. But they also want respect for their position and authority and therefore expect a certain amount of deference. The effective coach must be able to strike the right balance between those two expectations. Advocacy and directness must be combined with respectful diplomacy.

- **Time.** Senior executives are always under time pressure, so the effective coach must find a way to establish a quick rapport with the executive and to get down to business. In other words, the effective coach must be ready to start the coaching immediately; there may not be much time to think, plan, gather data, or get organized.

- **Client Centered.** Even though consultants and coaches must be concerned about their time, application rates, fees, and their own development, the effective coach always works in the best interest of the client and puts the client ahead of personal concerns. Building long-term relationships with clients is always the goal. A satisfied executive is the best source of new coaching opportunities—with the executive in question or with the executive's organization.
- **Role Modeling.** One of the best ways an executive can learn how to be an effective coach is by being effectively coached. Practice what you preach!
- **Player or Coach.** An executive coach cannot fill the shoes of the leader being coached. So don't try. No coach can play all the positions on the field, nor can the coach be the best player in the world. That's not the job of the coach. The coach sees the field and the players from a unique perspective that the players cannot see. The executive needs that perspective to see blind spots and to lead more effectively. In this sense, the executive neither wants nor expects the coach to be an executive leader.
- **Coaching Reality.** My experience suggests that carefully crafted questions that probe what the executive really thinks and that uncover mistakes, lack of knowledge, or vulnerabilities is always helpful. Facilitating straight talk exposes reality. Those realities can then be turned into practical solutions and, in turn, the coach will earn all the credibility needed to do a good job.

Summary

In summary, executive coaching has become a timely and useful arrow in the quiver of leadership and executive development. Shadow coaching, feedback-based coaching, and just-in-time personal coaching are three ways in which the "corporate coach" can significantly help executives to grow and develop in their leadership roles as they are trying to make their organizations faster, bigger, better, and cheaper.

It is a unique role with requisite skills, ethics, and professional demeanor. As I hope the guidelines and examples outlined here have shown, with the proper application of those skills, ethics, and demeanor, the executive coach can experience a high degree of professional satisfaction while accomplishing significant results with his or her clients.

Questions for Discussion

Although many coaching practitioners have accumulated a large amount of experience, coaching in general, and executive coaching in particular, has been neglected in the literature. In fact, in my travels around the world as I visit bookstores in most capitals, I have found a dearth of books written on the subject of coaching. Although there are more articles written, most of the books are written by American authors writing about experiences in U.S. companies (see Additional Readings on Coaching for a list). This alone suggests that additional research is warranted. Some topics include:

1. How prevalent is executive coaching outside the United States?
2. In what way do non-native American executives working for U.S. companies accept personalized coaching as a legitimate and useful developmental tool?
3. What factors differentiate effective coaching practices from ineffective coaching?
4. What field or fields of psychology provide the dominant underlying constructs and methods in current coaching practice?
5. What role does gender play in the effective practice of executive coaching?

The Author

Edward G. Verlander is president of E.G. Verlander & Associates, an independent management consulting firm located in Oyster Bay, Long Island, New York, specializing in executive coaching, training, conference design and facilitation, and organizational effectiveness consulting for a broad range of clients throughout the world. The author of a number of publications on management development, he earned a B.S. in economics and business, an M.B.A. from the University of Connecticut, and M.A. and doctoral degrees from Columbia University, where he also completed the executive program at the Columbia Business School. He has been an active consultant and coach for more than 20 years. For anyone interested in sharing his or her experiences with executive coaching, Verlander can be reached at 516. 624.2304 or by email: egvassoc1@aol.com.

References

Bennis, W. (1989). *On Becoming a Leader.* Reading, MA: Addison-Wesley.

Covey, S. (1992). *Principle-Centered Leadership.* New York: Simon & Schuster.

DePree, M. (1989). *Leadership Is an Art.* New York: Dell Publishing.

Gardner, J.W. (1990). *On Leadership*. New York: The Free Press.

Goleman, D. (1998). "What Makes a Leader?" *Harvard Business Review*, Nov.-Dec., 92–102.

Knowles, M. (1978). "The Adult Learner, A Neglected Species." Canoga Park, CA: Klevins Pub.

Kolb, D. (1979). *Organizational Psychology*. Englewood Cliffs, NJ: Prentice-Hall.

Kotter, J. (1998). *The Leadership Factor*. New York: The Free Press.

Kotter, J. (1990). "What Leaders Really Do." *Harvard Business Review*, May-June, 1990.

Krass, P., editor. (1998). *The Book of Leadership Wisdom*. New York: John Wiley & Sons.

Peters, T. (1982). *In Search of Excellence*. New York: Harper & Row.

Rackham, N. (1988). *SPIN Selling*. New York: McGraw-Hill.

Sayles, L. (1979). *Leadership*. New York: McGraw-Hill.

Additional Readings on Coaching

Cook, J.M. (1999). *Effective Coaching*. New York: McGraw-Hill.

Fournies, F.F. (1987). *Coaching For Improved Work Performance*. New York: McGraw-Hill.

Kinlaw, D.C. (1989). *Coaching For Commitment*. San Diego: University Associates.

Landsberg, M. (1996). *The Tao of Coaching*, New York: Harper Collins.

Miller, J.B. (1993). *The Corporate Coach*. New York: St. Martin's Press, Harper Collins.

Stone, F.M. (1999). *Coaching, Counseling & Mentoring*. New York: AMACOM.

Additional Readings

Newman, W.H. (1950). *Administrative Action*. New York: Prentice-Hall.

Rogers, C. (1977). Phenomenological Theory of Personality. In W.S. Sahakian (editor), *Psychology of Personality* (3d edition), 231–236. Boston: Houghton Mifflin.

Verlander, E.G. (1990). "The Executive Learner." *Journal of Management Development* (UK: MCB University Press), *9*(4), 4–6.

Verlander, E.G. (1992). "Executive Education for Managing Complex Organizational Change." *Human Resources Planning Journal*, *15*(2), 1–18.

Strategies and Competencies to Enhance Leaders for the New Millennium: A Multicase Study of Three Successful Real Estate Professionals

Affiliated Capital Corporation
Prudential Burnet Realty
Valuation Management Consultants, Inc.

Margot B. Weinstein

Today's real estate organizations worldwide are faced with many new challenges because of recent changes in the business. First, since November 1995, real estate transactions have been listed on the Internet, and technology has become an integral part of most real estate companies. Second, many companies are downsizing, restructuring, globalizing, and forming partnerships with other companies to compete in the industry. Third, changes in the laws on topics such as discrimination, fair housing, and environmental concerns have forced professionals to be knowledgeable about all current laws or face lawsuits or loss of license. Fourth, there has been a tremendous increase in the diversity of real estate professionals as well as their customers. Because of this diversity, it is becoming more challenging to meet the needs of professionals and their customers. Fifth, thousands of real estate professionals practice in many different specialty areas of real estate that need to access information that is not easily ascertainable in formal training and education programs. Because of all the recent changes in the business, leaders must develop new strategies, competencies, and skills in order to lead organizations successfully in this new age. The information gained in this research study uncovered common threads that made up the leadership fabric of three

This case was prepared to serve as a basis for discussion rather than to illustrate either effective or ineffective administrative and management practices.

successful leaders in the real estate business (Weinstein, 1988). This chapter describes the 12 strategies and competencies that these leaders developed to enhance leadership skills at all levels of their organizations.

The definition of leaders and leadership is an elusive concept; although written about often, the concept has been vague and ambiguous. The professionals in this study fit the definition of leaders and leadership by James MacGregor Burns in his 1978 book *Leadership:*

> Leadership is leaders inducing followers to act for certain goals that represent the values and the motivations—the wants and needs, the aspirations and expectations—of both leaders and followers. And the genius of leadership lies in the manner in which leaders see and act on their own and their followers' values and motivations. (p. 3)

This chapter describes the 12 core leadership strategies and competencies employed by three successful real estate professionals who work in three different speciality areas of the field: property management, residential sales, and appraisal. This information adds insight into the strategies possessed by these leaders and how these strategies can be used to enhance organizations in the 21st century.

Methodology

A qualitative or interpretive multicase study was used for the research because an intensive description and analysis of the phenomenon would uncover the interplay of significant factors that are characteristic of the phenomenon (Merriam and Simpson, 1995).

Participants

Exemplar real estate professionals were purposely selected based on Yin's (1994) definition of an exemplar case and the definition of a successful professional listed in the Membership Profile of the National Association of Realtors (NAR; 1996). Each respondent worked in one of the three major areas of real estate: residential sales, property management, and appraisal.

Ruth L. Theobald was vice president and director of property management of Affiliated Capital Corporation in Wisconsin.

Phyllis Kendall Rosen was the managing broker for the Highland Park office of the Prudential Burnet Realty, a residential real estate sales office located in Highland Park, Illinois.

Myron J. Evanich was director of Valuation Management Consultants, Inc., an appraisal company located in Chicago, Illinois.

The first two of the respondents are women, and the third is a man. The ages of the respondents ranged from mid-40s to 60 years old. The respondents had practiced a minimum of 12 years in the business. The respondents had attended college; one had an associate's degree, and one had a Ph.D. All three had real estate licenses as well as several other memberships and designations in real estate. The respondents worked full time in the real estate business. All respondents trained professionals, and two of the respondents were also certified teachers in their field to teach continuing education (CE) in real estate. CE is defined as real estate oriented educational sessions or courses intended to improve the skills of licensees, to keep licensees abreast of changing real estate practices and laws, and to help licensees meet the government imposed educational requirements for license renewal (National Association of Realtors Task Force, 1978). The three respondents regularly took CE courses, and two of the three respondents published in their field.

Procedure

The researcher studied the respondents and their companies for nine months (Weinstein, 1988).

Furthermore, standardization was obtained by taping one formal interview with each respondent, using questions that were designed in advance, and all respondents were asked the questions in exactly the same sequence and manner (Richardson, Dohrenwend, & Klein, 1965).

To examine the data from the formal interviews, tables were designed to display the data, and quotations from respondents and further explanation were presented by the researcher as needed to explain the data. The characteristics that emerged from these in-depth interviews were validated through review of tapes, transcriptions, and field notes of the interviews. The researcher contacted the respondents several times during this study as well as reviewed all published information about their companies and them to obtain accurate information. The respondents also received copies of the final transcribed tapes and edited any personal information that they did not want in the final case study. The information was further validated through documents, journals, literature review, and discussions with other professionals and educators in the field.

After the completion of the data analysis process, another phase of data analysis, a search for themes, was begun. The process used "concept mapping" (Candy, 1990) as a diagnostic tool. A concept map depicts in a diagrammatic form, ideas, examples, relationships, and implications about a particular concept. The center or core idea is placed at the center or top of the page, and radiating from it are a number of spokes or lines leading to other concepts related to, or indicated of, the central idea (Candy, 1990). Concept mapping enabled the researcher to group similar examples of large concepts together, and smaller concepts were set aside until they could be integrated into the larger themes; this process allowed the dominant themes to emerge from the data. The similarity of the process of the information gained in the case studies made possible the rich, descriptive data needed to interpret the phenomenon being investigated as explained by Merriam (1988).

Ruth L. Theobald

The exemplar of a successful, licensed professional from the real estate specialty of property management was Ruth L. Theobald, vice president and director of property management for Affiliated Capital Corporation (ACC). The main office was located in Pewaukee, Wisconsin. She was a well known, successful, and licensed real estate professional and an accredited teacher for real estate CE by the Institute of Real Estate Management (IREM). She specialized in teaching tax-credit housing management. She also lectured and published in many areas in real estate across the country. She is especially successful in developing courses using new technology created for the industry. She embraces women's leadership skills, and she runs ACC utilizing this approach.

Respondent's Biography

Ruth L. Theobald was a 44-year-old woman. Theobald was born in Bloomington, Indiana, and she had one brother and two sisters. She married when she was very young and had two children. At the time of the interview, she was remarried, her daughter had just graduated from the University of Wisconsin at Madison, and her son was going into his second year in college.

In her 20s, she became a divorced mother with two children, no college education, and very limited job experience. In 1981, after she had just lost her minimum-wage job, she entered the Wisconsin Women's Center. Because she needed meaningful employment to support herself and her two children, she joined the displaced homemaker training program titled "Turning Point Program." Through the Women's

Center's efforts, Theobald found work within several weeks in the field of property management, and she has been employed in real estate since that time. She also has attended a community college to gain a better education.

At the time of the interview, Theobald was vice president and director of property management for ACC. Since 1981, she had worked in property management throughout the Midwest, particularly in Wisconsin. She had joined ACC in 1987 and began focusing on tax-credit housing management. She was responsible for creating and implementing ACC's tax-credit compliance program, which had earned the company a distinguished reputation in work with the Section 42 of the tax-credit housing program around the country.

Affiliated Capital Corporation

Affiliated Capital Corporation was a full-service property management company; it provided professional, results-oriented service to its clients and was a member of Accredited Management Organization (AMO). The main office of ACC was located at 21150 West Capitol Drive, Pewaukee, Wisconsin.

The Wisconsin-based firm had properties in Wisconsin, Illinois, and Indiana. ACC opened its doors in 1976 and, at the time of the interview, managed approximately $120 million in real estate assets and had over $100 million of development under way or scheduled to commence in 1997. ACC managed properties for Capital Associates and fee-based clients; its clients included Northwestern Mutual Life Insurance Company, Aurora Health Care, and WISPARK Corporation.

For almost 20 years, ACC had been involved with many forms of government-subsidized housing. In 1987, the company entered the tax-credit housing market. ACC had managed and developed Section 42 properties throughout Wisconsin and was widely recognized for its thorough knowledge of and compliance with the program.

Employees of ACC offered Section 42 knowledge and experience on a consulting basis for training, compliance monitoring, management, and construction. The services provided clients with a vehicle to streamline their operations and put the critical file review and approval process in the hands of dedicated, experienced professionals. They realized that an investor in tax credits understands the risk and responsibility that is placed on the management of the tax-credit program, and they knew that the proper interpretation and implementation of program rules was the bottom line. No matter how good the deal looked on paper, it was meaningless if the program was managed improperly.

Professional Affiliations and Responsibilities

Theobald was a licensed real estate broker and a certified property manager (CPM). Theobald wrote for the *Journal of Property Management*. Her latest article was titled "Managing for Tax-Credit Compliance."

Theobald had designed and taught tax-credit seminars titled "Managing Tax-Credit Rental Housing For Compliance" for ACC for the last three and a half years. The seminars provided information on current U.S. Department of Housing and Urban Development (HUD) qualifying requirements, development issues, terminology, case studies on qualifying households, understanding the 140 percent rule, and tracking minimum set-asides. Theobald taught these seminars using an interactive approach that she had designed. She explored realistic case studies to help students learn the qualifying and management process from start to finish. She used overheads, computer technology, lectures, case studies, and discussion with students, and students worked on laptops, workbooks, and calculators and listened and discussed the subjects with her and other students.

Theobald had been a featured speaker at state and national conferences, including Multi-Housing World conferences and IREM. She also had been featured in a national video, "Compliance: Managing Tax Credits," produced by the Consortium for Housing Assistance Managers in Washington, DC.

Theobald was a member of the IREM, and she was the 1996 president of the Milwaukee chapter. She was a member of the IREM 101 course faculty and received its "Academy of Excellence" award for teaching in 1995. She was also a part-time faculty member at Waukesha County Technical College.

Phyllis Kendall Rosen

The exemplar of a successful, licensed professional from the residential sales area was Phyllis Kendall Rosen, managing director of the Prudential Burnet Realty office in Highland Park, Illinois. She was an outstanding licensed real estate professional and trainer for professionals in her office.

Respondent's Biography

Rosen was raised in Massachusetts. Her mother was English, and her father was born in Boston, Massachusetts. She was the youngest child in the family; she had an older sister, and she had an older brother who died a few years ago at age 65. Her parents pushed her to go to college. Her mother also wanted her to work, and she told her, "Don't think a man will take care of you; better take care of yourself."

She attended Boston University for two years, where she received her associate of arts degree. She moved to the northern suburbs of Chicago in the mid-1960s.

Rosen originally owned three local stores that sold home furnishings. She was a 25-year resident of the North Shore.

Rosen had been active in the North Shore real estate community for many years. She started selling real estate in 1980 and quickly gained a reputation for her outstanding quality and customer service. As a sales associate for Coldwell Banker, she received numerous awards and accolades, including her ranking as top sales and listing producer, and she received the prestigious President's Club Award, which ranked her among the nation's top sales-volume producers. Rosen was the managing broker for the Highland Park area office of the Prudential Burnet Realty.

Prudential Burnet Realty

The Prudential Burnet Realty of the North Shore was part of the Prudential Burnet Realty. The company had more than 27 Chicago offices, more than 1,000 sales associates referring buyers and sellers within the Chicago marketplace, and nearly 35,000 Prudential sales associates in more than 12,000 offices nationwide. The company had one of the largest relocation companies in the United States, which assisted over 100,000 transferees and their families annually, and also employed an international referral service that connected more than 40,000 sales associates in more than 1,600 offices throughout North America, Europe, and Asia. In December 1995, Prudential became part of the Burnet Financial Group, which had more than 65 offices with more than 3,000 sales associates referring clients within the Midwest's largest real estate brokerage. The main offices of the firm were based in Des Plaines, Illinois. The firm offered its clients and customers a complete range of real estate-related solutions all under one roof through a 27-office network and more than 1,100 sales associates serving more than 175 communities in northeastern Illinois.

At the time of the interview, the Prudential Burnet Realty was the number one real estate service firm on the North Shore, according to the *Multiple Listing Service of Northern Illinois for Summer 1997* (Ayers, 1997). For the first half of 1997, the company closed over $317 million in real estate transactions.

Doug Ayers, president of the Prudential Burnet Realty, credited the tenacity of its sales associates along with the Prudential Burnet Realty's one-stop shopping philosophy for its continued success. Ayers (1997) stated:

> We have, without a doubt, the most talented sales associates on the North Shore. Their knowledge of real estate and the North Shore, combined with the broad spectrum of services the firm offers, has made us, and kept us, number one on the North Shore. (p. A12)

Rosen credited her sales staff as the main reason the company was currently number one in selling luxury homes on the North Shore.

Professional Affiliations and Responsibilities

Rosen was actively involved in her profession. She was a certified residential specialist (CRS) and she had a broker's license. She was a member of the North Shore Board of Realtors and had served on the membership, education, hospitality, and grievance committees. At the time of the interview, she was the membership chairman of the Women's Council of Realtors.

Rosen's duties as a branch manager/trainer included:
- hands-on, post-institute training
- periodic goal-setting reviews to "keep realtors on track"
- advice during negotiations and follow-up
- counsel and legal update at company and board meetings and through written correspondence
- coordination of team projects, prospecting, and public relations events
- guidance in areas of problem solving and prevention.

Myron J. Evanich

The exemplar of a successful, licensed professional from the real estate appraisal area was Myron J. Evanich, director of Valuation Management Consultants, Inc., real estate, financial, machinery, and equipment consultants and appraisers located in Chicago, Illinois. Evanich is also an accredited teacher for a real estate appraisal school.

Respondent's Biography

Evanich was born in Pennsylvania in 1940. He was an only child. His father and mother were born in the United States. His father worked as a coal miner in a small town. Both his mother and his father wanted their son to receive a college degree because they did not want him to go into coal mining.

Evanich received his bachelor of arts degree from Wilkes College, Wilkes-Barre, Pennsylvania, in 1963, and a doctor of philosophy degree from the University of Tennessee, Memphis, Tennessee, in 1969.

Evanich worked as a university professor for 29 years. He was an assistant professor at the University of Illinois School of Medicine, Department of Medicine, in Chicago, Illinois, from 1970 to 1977. He then became an associate professor at Tulane University School of Medicine, Department of Physiology, in New Orleans, Louisiana, from 1977 to 1985. During this time, he wrote and published 40 papers. He also lectured to medical, dental, and graduate students at the University of Illinois and at Tulane University School of Medicine between 1970 and 1985.

In 1983, shortly after he was introduced to a real estate appraiser in New Orleans, Evanich left the traditional university setting to enter the field of real estate. He began his real estate career in real estate sales, and, soon after he had entered the field, he began to specialize in real estate appraisal. At the same time, he began to teach courses in real estate appraisal.

Since 1985, Evanich has applied his experience as a former university professor to the real estate profession. Evanich received a real estate broker's license in Metairie, Louisiana, in 1985, and in Chicago, Illinois, in 1987. He became a licensed real estate instructor in Louisiana, and he taught prelicensing and postlicensing courses for salespeople and brokers. He also acted as a school director for the Evanich Educational Institute, a licensed, bonded real estate school in New Orleans, Louisiana, from 1985 to 1987.

Evanich was the president of Evanich and Associates, Inc., in New Orleans, Louisiana, for four and one half years. Evanich then worked as a field appraiser for the Zimmerman Real Estate Group in Chicago, Illinois, for four years. Since 1991, Evanich has headed Valuation Management Consultants, Inc.

Valuation Management Consultants, Inc.

Valuation Management Consultants, Inc. was a real estate, financial, machinery, and equipment consultants and appraisal firm located in Chicago, Illinois. The company conducted appraisal assignments that included commercial, office, industrial, and single family and multifamily residential types of properties, as well as special-use real estate. The properties were located throughout the Midwest region and had appraised values ranging from $500,000 to $50 million. Appraisal assignments included both existing and proposed developments. The services were provided to local and national clients, such as financial institutions, corporations, insurance companies, law firms, and governmental agencies.

Professional Affiliations and Responsibilities

Evanich held an appraisal designation of the Member of Appraisal Institute (MAI) of Chicago, Illinois, and he was a master senior appraiser (MSA) of the National Association of Master Appraisers in San Antonio, Texas. He had received accreditation in the Appraisal Accredited Review (AAR) of the Appraisers Council in San Antonio, Texas. He had also been a national speaker at real estate appraisal conferences.

As the principal of Valuation Management Consultants, Inc., since 1991, Evanich continued to use his expertise in real estate appraisal to conduct all types of appraisals. He conducted several types of appraisal assignments (for example, commercial, office, industrial, single-family and multiple-family residential, special-use properties, and vacant land). He served clients in lending institutions, attorneys, accountants, and private investors for such purposes as first and second mortgages, ad valorem real estate taxation, divorces, successions, and eminent domain proceedings.

Evanich had been a senior faculty member of Lincoln Graduate Center since 1984. He instructed appraisal courses for the Lincoln Graduate Center, San Antonio, Texas, throughout the United States. The courses were approved for state certification of real estate appraisers in Illinois as well as in many other states. He was approved by the Appraisal Institute to teach advanced appraisal courses for candidates and professionals who were advancing to the MAI designation.

Results—the 12 Strategies and Competencies

This section describes the 12 core strategies and competencies developed by these leaders that define their success in the real estate business. These strategies result in the creation of dynamic leaders who enhance leadership skills throughout their organizations.

1. Lifelong Learning

The complexity and diversity of the real estate field have compelled professionals to embrace the concept of lifelong learning. The respondents stated that the opportunity for continual learning was one of the most important reasons they chose and were successful in the real estate business. They used phrases such as "being on the top of the heap," "being innovative," "learning faster than competitors," and "being a quick study," which expressed what made these professionals love the field.

All three professionals loved to learn—that began in their early childhood; they enjoyed school and loved to read. Evanich added that he entered the field of real estate after he had received his Ph.D. and he had been a university professor for 27 years. He said that he liked the fact that real estate was a "more practically oriented career," and he enjoyed the thinking process involved in appraising.

The professionals displayed an intense need to perfect the ability to learn throughout their lives; the process they exercised to learn was a "systems approach." They were able to utilize all the information from their everyday lives in their real estate practice. For example, Theobald stated that by renting properties for her family, she had learned the everyday problems that affect her renters. Rosen expressed that because of aging family members, she had become aware of the needs of elderly people who buy homes.

Respondents explained that from working years in the business, they have become outstanding self-directed learners similar to adults described in the literature (Knowles, 1980; Tough, 1979; Smith, 1982). They know what, when, where, and how to find information. They often reflected on past experiences to understand new information. They also stressed that they learned differently based on their age, sex, and life experiences. These professionals used membership in professional associations to receive literature from experts, attended conventions, and took CE courses through professional associations. In addition, Theobald and Evanich both have taught CE for their professional associations. Theobald read the literature of the IREM; Rosen read the literature published by the Realtors Association; and Evanich read all the information published by the Appraisal Association. They also encouraged their employees to be lifelong learners and to join the real estate associations. In addition, Rosen said that her company provides an excellent library for professionals to receive information about the field.

The professionals expressed that lifelong learning will continue to be a necessity to remain successful because of the constant changes in the business—advances in technology, changes in organizations, diversity issues, and new laws. Theobald stated that Tom Peters (1994), in *The Pursuit of Wow!*, reinforced the need for professionals to continue to learn new information about all the changes that affect their products, their customers, their organizations, and the public.

2. Entrepreneurial Spirit

The professionals in this study embraced qualities of entrepreneurship. They stated that the real estate business capitalizes on principles of entrepreneurship. The professionals debated whether these attributes are inborn or learned, but they all agreed that they possessed the following six entrepreneurial attributes and strategies:
1. creative
2. innovative
3. risk takers
4. interested in concrete knowledge of the result of decision (money as a measure of success)
5. desirous of achievement
6. personally responsible for their learning. (McClelland, 1965)

Throughout the interviews, respondents continually conveyed the importance of being able to use the information in creative and innovative ways to succeed. Their statements affirmed writings by Roberts (1994) that people who are innovative create their future. Roberts stated, "You learn rapidly from experience, and continually improve your ability to take effective action and produce results" (p. 228). He also expressed that innovative people know how to investigate situations by using a variety of strategies to propose innovative solutions.

Theobald asserted that, "It is not only in obtaining the information, but knowing what to do with it in a creative and innovative way . . . that is what makes you successful in this business." Rosen and Evanich added similar statements in their interviews.

Respondents agreed that money as a measure of success was important. Evanich asserted, "I liked real estate because it had prestige and it had money in it."

They also attributed their success in real estate to their ability to maintain personal motivation. Each of the respondents found ways to keep up to date and, at the same time, remain motivated to learn by talking with other professionals and experts, training employees, or teaching courses. Rosen remarked that she often needed "alone time" to re-energize herself and reflect on experiences, and then she regains her personal motivation.

3. Interpersonal Skills

The third leadership strategy these professionals developed to remain competitive in the business was their ability to use effective interpersonal skills. Rosen explained that the real estate business was a "people business" and successful professionals must be able to utilize interpersonal skills to interact with customers, professionals, experts, and the public. Both women attributed the formation of their interpersonal skills to being women in American society. They believed that women, more than men, are encouraged from childhood to learn how to communicate effectively with family members and friends. Young girls are able to express ideas openly, share information, and receive feedback. Rosen emphasized the ability to listen as an important skill professionals need to learn in the business. They also stressed that the ability to deal with nonverbal signs of communication is also a critical skill for leaders to serve diverse workforces, the public, and specific populations. These leaders practice the "open-door" policy. They encourage communication effectively with everyone who is important to their organizations.

4. Value Expertise

The fourth leadership strategy these professionals employed to be successful was their expertise as well as the expertise of others. The respondents had gained knowledge through experience and practice that had enabled them to become experts in their area of the business— similar to the patterns and processes of the expert nurses described by Benner (1984). The real estate professionals explained that they develop a comprehensive knowledge through their everyday practice and experience that enables them to grow from novices to experts. The professionals referred to three stages of expertise: beginning, intermediate, and advanced. They said that the first one to two years in the business, they learned only basic information; the next several years, they learned to understand, interpret, and deduce meaning that they believed beginners in the field could not comprehend. Then, they said, after 10 years in the business they became experts because they had developed an unusual perceptual ability to recognize similarities in clients' conditions even when the presenting of symptoms or situations appeared to be dissimilar or ambiguous; they were able to make sense of ambiguous situations and problems. They expressed that the "real estate business is an art, not a science," and their ability to access reliable information quickly to solve problems, to interpret the information, and to adapt to new learning situations was vital to their success in the business. They asserted that their expertise enabled them to come up with creative new solutions to problems to remain competitive in the business.

The respondents frequently explained that they value expertise, and they constantly seek other experts. They described two types of experts who were very important to their success in the real estate business. The first type included other professionals who were experts in the field of real estate. Evanich stated that he often contacted other professionals in the business. For example, he recently contacted a man who was an expert at appraising nuclear power plants.

The second type of experts that these professionals utilize are those who practice in areas other than real estate. Rosen said that she often talks to lawyers in her business who keep her abreast of important new changes in the laws.

5. Understanding Diversity

The professionals stated that their employees and customers are becoming increasingly diverse. They work with employees and customers of all ages, sexes, ethnicities, disabilities, and differences. These professionals embraced ideas expressed in the words of Work (1996):

> In the final analysis, true leadership brings people of diverse backgrounds and interests together in ways that provide fair and equitable opportunities to contribute their best, achieve personal goals, and realize their full potential. (p. 79)

Therefore, respondents believe that employees must respect everyone's differences and make an effort to continually learn how they can provide the best possible services for their employees and their customers. For example, Rosen explained she has new clients who come from many different cultures who are buying apartments and homes in her area, and she must learn how to find living spaces to meet their specific needs. She stated that the real estate business is a customer-driven business, and she and her employees must be willing to provide customers with the best information and services in their area to be successful. She explained that in order to provide the best customer service, she must learn about their culture, factors such as their communication style, their negotiating style, and their preferences in living spaces. She stressed that there should be more training and education programs to provide employees necessary information to be able to provide excellent customer service.

6. Problem Solvers

The sixth leadership strategy that these professionals applied to stay competitive in their business was their ability to define problems, find solutions, and achieve their goals. The real estate professionals who were interviewed explained that they solve their problems by using their past experiences. Theobald added that she viewed problems by using her personality strengths—such as intuition and introversion—that she learned about herself through taking personality tests such as the Myers-Briggs Type Indicator. Rosen and Evanich expressed that they learned through their daily practice in their careers.

All three professionals use the same "seven-step problem-solving process" and go through the process two or more times using iterations of problem solving. Respondents explained that they used this plan because 1) their problems were very complex, 2) their problems were difficult to solve in the first cycle, and 3) they often took months or years to continue to work on the problems. In this way, they were able to continue to perfect the plan. The seven-step problem-solving model is shown in figure 1.

The seven steps in the "continuous-action problem-solving" model are:

1. Conceptualize plan in his/her head by reflecting on previous similar experiences.
2. Set down the problem on paper in a tentative plan of action.
3. Gather data: talk to professionals, read, and so forth.
4. Analyze alternative approaches.
5. Develop more complete plan by redesigning plan to reflect new insight.
6. Act on plan.
7. Evaluate results based on consequences of outcomes of action.

The professional continues through the process to reflect and refine the plan as new information on the problem is gathered. Professionals may continue to go through the entire process several times, or they may use only one or two steps to update the plan. However, the interviewed professionals used reflection continually throughout the problem-solving process. They stated that their problems in-

Figure 1. Seven-step problem-solving model.

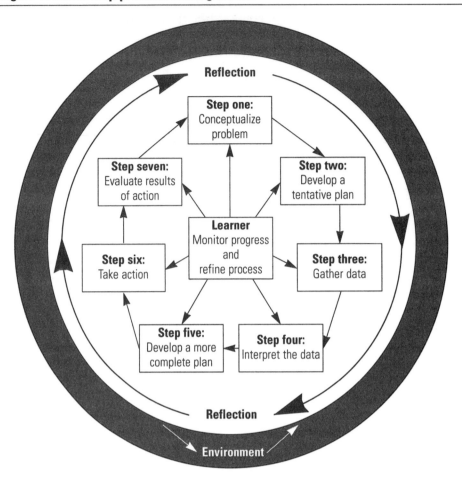

The professionals solve their problems by following the seven-step process listed in the boxes within the circle. The arrows surrounding the boxes in the white circle represent that professionals monitor and refine the process by continual reflection. The arrows pointing to and from the gray circle indicate a feedback loop in which professionals continually interact with everything in the environment.

volved cycles of problem solving because they usually could not solve their problems in one or two cycles.

Theobald, for example, stated that when she acquired a property, she went through the seven-step process. However, she stated that as long as she managed the property, she needed to constantly reflect and improve the plan when it is necessary in order to keep abreast of all the changes in the business, and that they usually update their management plans at least twice each year to reflect such factors as market trends, number of apartments available in area, and the number of vacancies on the property. Evanich explained the process in relationship to appraising real estate buildings, and Rosen talked about how she repeatedly goes through a cycle of problem solving when a house does not sell in the first 30 days. Rosen explained that residential homes frequently do not sell in 30 days, and luxury homes may take more than two years. The "continuous model of problem solving" is repeated until the goal is reached by the professional (figure 2).

The diagram contains five circles and each circle represents a problem-solving cycle that contains the seven steps. The process consists of iterations or cycles of continual learning. The plan becomes increasingly refined with every iteration, and the learning continues cycle after cycle—similar to ideas explained in literature by Argyris and Schön (1974, 1978) and Redding and Catalanello (1994). During the process of problem-solving, these professionals work with employees individually, as well as in groups to resolve problems. They demonstrated the ability to trust their employees and delegate jobs and responsibility effectively to solve their organizations' problems.

7. The Strategy of Networking

The professionals believed that networking was an important strategy for their professional survival. Networking was more than just a job-hunting tool; it was a way to gather useful information, build a pool of professional contacts, and position themselves for new opportunities in the long term. The respondents explained that they were constantly networking to find experts who could provide them with the

Figure 2. Iterations of continuous cycles of seven-step problem-solving model.

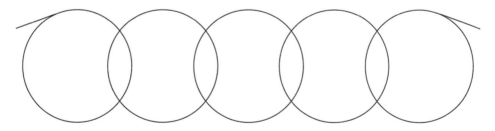

Because their problems are complex and difficult to solve in one cycle, professionals usually repeat the process of reflecting and refining the plan as new information on the problem is gathered. Professionals may continue to go through the entire process several times, or they may use only one or two steps to update the plan.

answers to problems. Theobald and Rosen expressed that women are often better than men at networking because they develop this ability from childhood, and they are able to make relationships through friendships—at PTA meetings, family activities, and community functions, to name a few. All three professionals remarked that they work at enhancing their ability to network to find experts throughout their careers with employees, other professionals, at functions held by professional associations, and through teaching and training. They believed in the words expressed by Eitington (1996), author of *The Winning Trainer*, who clarified how professionals in business utilize this strategy:

> The adage, "It's not what you know, but who you know." That purpose is indeed a significant one. Probably more valuable are (a) the outside contacts that can help to keep us alive and growing, (b) the new ideas which external associates can provide us so that we can do our jobs better, (c) the capability of our network to function as a worthwhile part of our overall support system, and (d) in some cases, the professional camaraderie it can bring. (p. 462)

The respondents also remarked that they believed that in the future, the Internet and email will provide them with another valuable way to network.

8. Embrace Collaboration

The eighth leadership strategy acquired by these professionals for success was their ability to collaborate effectively in groups or teams. Respondents develop their ability to learn in groups in a variety of situations (for instance, with employees, in courses, in lectures, at conventions, in teaching or training sessions, and the like). Respondents stated that leaders must have the skills necessary to work in groups effectively because of factors stated by Stouch (1993).

> Work today has become more collaborative. People meet to solve problems. To work in groups, we must be able to learn in groups. Such collaborative learning requires communication skills, observation and reflection skills, and planning and consensus skills. (p. 66)

Theobald and Rosen used the term "brainstorming session" to explain how they learned through talking to other professionals in groups to solve their problems.

9. The Strategy of Using Technology.

The ninth leadership strategy necessary for professionals was technology. Respondents explained that technology has not played a significant role in their learning strategy in the past. However, with the development of newer technologies and the fact that real estate transactions are now on the Internet since November 1995, they all agreed that new technologies will be a very important strategy to aid them to remain successful in the business in the 21st century. Recently, authors in the literature of real estate have stressed that technology will play an important role in the future success of real estate professionals: to access information, to teach, to train employees, to keep records, and to evaluate (Shield, 1996; Wadsworth, 1997).

Theobald developed her ability to use technology through teaching; Rosen learned through other employees; Evanich stated that he learned through practicing on the computer. Evanich said that he is a "hands-on" learner, and he had just built a new computer before the taped interview.

Respondents stated that they currently used technology for many purposes (for instance, problem solving, simulations, computer-managed instruction, information management, word processing, training, teaching, email, advertising, and computer literacy), and they perceived an even greater use of technology in the future. Rosen's office now has an Internet site, and professionals as well as customers use it to find homes. Rosen believed that "if one is not able to use technology, one should get out of the business." She added that younger agents used technology much more than older professionals, and she believed that this trend would continue. She also stated that it is important for training and education programs to be designed to teach professionals how to use technology in their business.

Respondents also cautioned that there may be many liabilities, frauds, and insurance problems in using technology, and they plan to continue to monitor these aspects of technology. For example, Rosen explained that they often advertise a home by showing a video of it on television; however, there will be security issues that arise from this practice.

10. Value the Mentoring Relationship

The tenth leadership strategy was the importance of the mentoring relationship. They described mentors who had been essential in enabling them to become successful professionals. The respondents stated that teachers were mentors in their early schooling. According to Knowles (1980), the behavior of the teacher is an important influence on the learner. Cohen (1995) stated,

> The mentor-mentee relationship, whether it occurs in education, business, or government, is a learning activity essentially created for the benefit of the mentee and offers a guiding but not controlling influence on the mentee's choices and goals. The mentor and mentee assume a transactional process of learning, which involves active involvement with a mentee as a collaborative partner in the learning. (pp. 14-15)

Daloz (1986) proposed that the mentee is an adult learner who has consciously undertaken a developmental journey that engages three key functions of the mentor: support, challenge, and vision. Daloz further referred to the experience of learning within the mentoring relationship as a complex process that promotes learning in the mentees as well as the mentors, and they are therefore interpreters of the environment. Evanich explained that a friend who had a real estate license was instrumental in helping him choose the field. Later, he met professionals in the appraisal business who encouraged him to pursue a license and business in real estate appraisal. Theobald was mentored by women in the beginning of her career, and she now mentors other women to continue the cycle of success. Rosen sat near one of the top producers in the field when she began her career in residential sales, and she believes that woman contributed to her success.

11. Leaders as Trainers and Teachers

The eleventh leadership strategy that respondents claimed was essential to their success was to continue to train and teach in the business. The adages "good leaders are good teachers" and "you don't know what you know until you teach it" applied to these professionals. All three respondents train employees, and Theobald and Evanich both are certified instructors in the field. They discussed how they learned how to teach through the process of training employees and teaching courses, and through constantly taking training and educational programs throughout their careers. They also gained valuable information through assessment forms and feedback from their employees and students. They affirmed that in a training or teaching session, adults must be involved, receive content that relates to their specific work setting and expertise, and have an atmosphere or setting that is comfortable. Theobald uses overheads, computer technology, lectures, and case studies. She has learned through years of teaching how to involve students through dialogues, questions, and group discussions, and she continues to learn in the field by teaching, using laptop computers, and humor to interact with adults.

12. Embrace Women's Leadership Styles

The final and the most important leadership strategy that these professionals utilized to lead their employees and their organizations was to embrace qualities associated with women's leadership styles. Both Theobald and Rosen noted that women and men learn differently in the real estate business, and they discussed how they employed women's leadership skills to lead their organizations. They believed their success at leading in business was their ability to use the qualities they had grown up with: nurturing, enjoying family relationships and friendships, playing in cooperative team sports, being responsive to community members and issues, and having mothers as role models.

Theobald and Rosen went on to explain that women were more interested than men in relationships, and that these relationships with family members, their spouses, friends, colleagues, students, clients, and their business partners or bosses were important resources that they utilized to gain support, information, understanding, and nurturing. Baskett, Marsick, and Cervero (1992) stated:

> It is clearly fallacious to assume that professional learning occurs in isolation. Colleagues, clients, family and friends, as well as many others influence the way in which professionals learn and change. Women often learn by interacting with one another and by connecting the themes in their lives with social forces—based on race, gender, and class—that constrain as well as trigger learning. (p. 111)

Women's literature has supported that women learn differently, which affects the qualities they utilize as leaders (Baskett et al., 1992; Helgesen,1990; Gilligan, 1982). Theobald and Rosen continued to explain that they were more interested than men in listening to stories about customers' and employees' lives and that they tried to use the information in their business. Theobald added that her leadership style is based on being a woman. She said that when she began in the business, she tried to lead as a man would, but she learned that she was more effective using her abilities as a woman. As a woman, she has been both a nurturer and family-oriented, and

she is more interested than most men in trying to manage properties with this in mind. She believed that relying on her woman's abilities allowed her to learn to be an excellent boss and property manager.
Although Evanich debated the issue, he said that women's knowledge
on certain subjects affected how and what information they learned.
His stories further confirmed how he learned differently based on
his gender.

Rosen and Theobald thought that there should be more training and education programs for women because almost half of the
real estate professionals were women. They felt that such courses would
be very effective in empowering women to lead in ways that are natural to them.

In addition, the respondents agreed that organizations must believe in the abilities of their employees and allow them to continue
to learn and to make decisions. Respondents presented a clear picture of how organizations should be designed to embrace qualities
and skills discussed in this chapter.

Organizational Design

The professionals explained that organizations need to improve
their services as 1) the competition for both professionals and funds
continues to increase, 2) the changes in the business persist, 3) the
increase in diversity of professionals and customers continues, 4) technology plays a larger role in the business and training of professionals,
and 5) the public continues to pass laws to force professionals to practice ethically and competently.

In order for organizations to respond to the needs of professionals,
their customers, and the public, they must design a learning organization that combines the ideas and strategies of a Total Quality Management (TQM) Learning Organization described by Deming (1986)
with that of a model of the "open organizational learning system" discussed by Senge (1990). Organizations should provide a renewed focus on quality in training, education, and customer satisfaction. As
explained by Deming (1986), major tenets of TQM to which organizations must subscribe in order to satisfy customers include:
1. being committed to a common, organizational vision, set of values, attitudes, and principles
2. understanding the need to constantly review procedures to improve services to customers
3. believing that the work of each of its members is vital to customer
satisfaction
4. valuing the input of customers.

In addition to factors of a TQM organization, organizations that provide training and education to professionals must also operate as "learning organizations" to keep up with changes in the business and the environment. Senge (1990) best described the importance of utilizing a systems approach of learning organizations:

> Systems thinking makes understandable the subtlest aspect of the learning organization—the new way individuals perceive themselves and their world. At the heart of a learning organization is a shift of mind—from seeing ourselves as separate from the world to connected to the world. (pp. 12-13)

Senge (1990) further described three elements that are important in these learning organizations: a) visions, values, and integrity; b) dialogue; and c) systems thinking. Senge added that the successful organization of the future must inspire a commitment and capacity for people to learn at all levels. "Learning organizations are possible because, deep down, we are all learners" (p. 4).

The respondents in this study stated that they also wanted:
- organizations that encourage open communication at all levels
- organizations that establish an environment that values and empowers individuals to be responsible, productive, and creative
- organizations that have a shared goal/mission that everyone in the organization knows, agrees on, and is committed to accomplishing
- organizations that value the diversity of people as an asset, that encourage opinions, ideas, and experiences of others, and have the ability to be sensitive to others
- organizations that constantly evaluate their practices by employees, trainers, professionals, as well as the public
- organizations that can make immediate changes as necessary to satisfy the needs of professionals
- organizations that require better assessment techniques and evaluations regarding all issues that are important to employees, customers, and the public.

Limitations

Because the study was limited to three case studies, the study cannot attempt to predict successful leadership styles of all real estate professionals. Although the case studies lead to deeper insights, findings from case studies cannot be generalized in the same way as the findings from random samples. For this reason, this study should be the first step to further research on the subject.

Conclusions

The research study presented the core strategies and competencies developed and employed by three successful leaders in the real estate profession. The chapter tried to establish the connection between the strategies and competencies utilized by successful leaders in the real estate business and the type of organization and training programs that would be enhanced by these skills. As we enter the millennium, visionary leadership is needed to succeed in competitive and changing workplaces. Women's leadership styles may play a larger role in the skills leaders need to develop to succeed in the business. It is clear that leaders in the real estate business must be more responsive to the needs of employees, customers, and the public. Licensed real estate professionals must respond to society's new expectations for competence and accountability by following the code of ethics in the preamble of NAR (1995):

> Under all is the land. Upon its wise utilization and widely allocated ownership depend the survival and growth of free institutions and of our civilization. Realtors® should recognize that the interests of the nation and its citizens require the highest and best use of the land and the widest distribution of land ownership. Such interests impose obligations beyond those of ordinary commerce. They impose grave social responsibly and a patriotic duty to which Realtors® should dedicate themselves. (p. 8)

Questions for Discussion

1. What are the main problems facing the real estate business?
2. Do you think other types of organizations are facing the same problems as the real estate business?
3. What were the 12 strategies and competencies embraced by these leaders?
4. How did the leaders develop the 12 core strategies?
5. Do you think these leadership strategies and competencies will work in other businesses? If so, which ones and why?
6. What additional leadership strategies could be used by leaders in the future?
7. How could you implement these leadership strategies into training programs in your organization?
8. Could you use the seven-step problem-solving design in your organization?
9. How do you think their ideas for organizational change would work in other businesses and industries?

The Author

Margot B. Weinstein has been vice president of Kingston Group, Inc., a commercial real estate company located in Northbrook, Illinois since 1978. She has been a licensed real estate professional in the business since 1972. Over the years she has held various leadership positions as a manager, teacher, trainer, human resource developer, and counselor. Throughout her career, she has continued to pursue both formal and informal education. From National-Louis University in Evanston, Illinois, she received a baccalaureate degree in 1992, a master's degree in adult education in 1994, a second master's degree in psychology in 1997, and she received a doctoral degree in education from Northern Illinois University in May of 1998. She is a member of the Kappa Delta Pi International Honor Society in Education. She is an adjunct professor for returning adults in the bachelor's degree for School of New Learning at DePaul University, and she conducts private career counseling for adults. She wrote a chapter titled "Continuing professional education in the real estate" in *Continuing professional education in transition: Visions for the professionals and new strategies for lifelong learning*, edited by William H. Young and published in 1998 by Krieger Publishing. She also published and presented at conferences, conventions, community groups, organizations, and schools throughout United States for the last 25 years.

References

Argyris, C., and D. Schön. (1974). *Theory in Practices: Increasing Professional Effectiveness*. San Francisco: Jossey-Bass.

Argyris, C., and D. Schön. (1978). *Organizational Learning*. Reading, MA: Addison-Wesley.

Ayers, D. (1997, August 28). "Realtors: Service Rates Prudential Offices on Top." *Highland Park News*, p. 4.

Baskett, H.K.M., V.M. Marsick, and R.M. Cervero. (1992). Putting Theory to Practice and Practice to Theory. In H.K.M. Baskett and V.J. Marsick (editors), *Professionals' Ways of Knowing: New Findings on How to Improve Professional Education*, 109–188. San Francisco: Jossey-Bass.

Benner, P. (1984). *From Novice to Expert: Excellence and Power in Clinical Nursing Practice*. Menlo Park, CA: Addison-Wesley.

Burns, J.M. (1978). *Leadership*. New York: Harper & Row.

Candy, P.C. (1990). How People Learn to Learn. In Smith & Associates (editors), *Learning to Learn Across the Life Span*. San Francisco: Jossey-Bass.

Cohen, N.H. (1995). *Mentoring Adult Learners: A Guide for Educators and Trainers*. Malabar, FL: Kreiger.

Daloz, L.A. (1986). *Effective Teaching and Mentoring: The Transformational Power of Adult Learning Experiences.* San Francisco: Jossey-Bass.

Deming, W.E. (1986). *Out of the Crisis.* Cambridge, MA: MIT Center for Advanced Engineering Study.

Eitington, J.E. (1996). *The Winning Trainer.* Houston: Gulf Publishing.

Gilligan, C. (1982). *In a Different Voice: Psychological Theory and Women's Development.* Cambridge, MA: Harvard University Press.

Helgesen, S. (1990). *The Female Advantage: Women's Ways of Leadership.* New York: Currency.

Knowles, M.S. (1980). *The Modern Practice of Adult Education: From Pedagogy to Androgogy* (2d edition). New York: Cambridge Books.

McClelland, D.C. (1965). "Need Achievement and Entrepreneurship: A Longitudinal Study." *Journal of Personality and Social Psychology, 1* (1), 389–92.

Merriam, S.B. (1988). *Case Study Research in Education: A Qualitative Approach.* San Francisco: Jossey-Bass.

Merriam, S.B., and Simpson, E. (1995). *A Guide to Research for Educators and Trainers of Adults* (2d edition). Malabar, FL: Krieger.

National Association of Realtors. (1978). *Manual of NAR Task Force.* Washington, DC: Author.

National Association of Realtors. (1995). *Code of Ethics.* Washington, DC: Author.

National Association of Realtors. (1996). *Membership Profile.* Washington, DC: Author.

Peters, T. (1994). *The Pursuit of Wow!* New York: Vintage Books.

Redding, J.C., and R.F. Catalanello. (1994). *Strategic Readiness: The Making of the Learning Organization.* San Francisco: Jossey-Bass.

Richardson, S.A., B.S. Dohrenwend, and D. Klein. (1965). *Interviewing: Its Forms and Functions.* New York: Basic Books, Inc.

Roberts, C. (1994). What You Can Expect from the Practice of Personal Mastery. In P.M. Senge, A. Kleiner, C. Roberts, R.B. Ross, and B.J. Smith (editors), *The Fifth Discipline Fieldbook: Strategies and Tools for Building a Learning Organization,* 198–200. New York: Currency.

Senge, P.M. (1990). *The Fifth Discipline: The Art and Practice of the Learning Organization.* New York: Dell.

Shield, C. (1996). "The Face of Leadership: Meet the 1996 Officers of the Illinois Association of Realtors." *Realtors Magazine,* 8–9.

Smith, R.M. (1982). *Learning How to Learn: Applied Theory for Adults.* New York: Cambridge.

Stouch, C.A. (1993). What Instructors Need to Know about Learning How to Learn. In D.D. Flannery (editor), *Applying Cognitive Learning Theory to Adult Learning,* 59–67. San Francisco: Jossey-Bass.

Tough, A.M. (1979). *The Adult's Learning Projects* (2d edition). Toronto, Ontario: Ontario Institute for Studies in Education.

Wadsworth, K.H. (1997). "Found Time: Do You Really Have Time to Be Reading This?" *Journal of Property Management,* Nov/Dec, 20–25.

Weinstein, M.B. (1998). *Learning to Learn: Strategies of Successful Real Estate Professionals: Implications for Continuing Professional Education.* Unpublished doctoral dissertation, Northern Illinois University, DeKalb.

Work, J.W. (1996). Leading a Diverse Workforce. In F. Hesselbein, M. Goldsmith, R. Beckhard (editors), *The Leader of the Future,* 71–79. New York: Peter F. Drucker Foundation.

Yin, R.K. (1994). *Case Study Research: Design and Methods* (2d edition). Newbury, CA: Sage

Training Tomorrow's Leaders Using Yesterday's Techniques

Sandia National Laboratories

Linda K. Stromei

This case study examined mentoring as a training method for middle managers. The participants were mentors and protégés in a formal mentoring program at Sandia National Laboratories. The study looked at transfer of leadership skills using pretest and posttest instruments and an instrument designed to assess the satisfaction of the protégé. The data were analyzed using t tests, multiple regressions, ANOVAS, correlations, and descriptive statistics. The case concluded with the development of a model for a formal mentoring program, Arranged Mentoring for Instructional Guidance and Organizational Support (AMIGOS™), which incorporated the results of the analyses. This study provided statistical evidence that mentoring is an effective method of training for transfer of leadership skills.

Background

"During the past year Linda has used the Sandia mentoring program as a subject for her research in the area of mentoring. Her research concluded with positive results not only for Sandia but also for the research community as a whole. The key finding from Linda's research is that we now have objective, documented evidence that Sandia's Corporate Mentoring program enhances the transfer of skills/knowledge between mentor and protégé." So wrote Charline S. Wells, program manager of the Mentoring Leadership Program at Sandia National Laboratories. What were the events that led up to this glow-

This case was prepared to serve as a basis for discussion rather than to illustrate either effective or ineffective administrative and management practices.

ing pronouncement of a consultant's research into and evaluation of a formal mentoring program?

Organizational Profile and Rationale for Leadership Program

Sandia National Laboratories (Sandia) is a large research and development national laboratory with its main facility located in Albuquerque, New Mexico. Sandia Corporation, a Lockheed Martin Company, operates it for the United States Department of Energy (DOE). Sandia provides scientific and engineering solutions to meet national needs in nuclear weapons and related defense systems.

Sandia employs about 8,100 employees, of which about 900 are managers, directors, or vice presidents. Approximately 60 percent of Sandia's employees are in technical and scientific positions, with a large percentage of this group holding doctorate and master's degrees. A provision of their most recent contract with DOE mandated the implementation of a mentoring program for managers within two years. As the output of Sandia was changing to meet new challenges in science and technology, while at the same time continuing in their traditional efforts in national security, a mentoring program for leaders was sought to "foster agility in the workforce and to provide a mechanism for developing people to be better able to respond to changing requirements and complex customer needs" (Stromei, 1998, p. 56). Sandia currently has a large retirement eligible population in its ranks and a mentoring program could utilize the expertise of these employees prior to their retirement.

Sandia National Laboratories implemented its mentoring program to fulfill several organizational objectives. One of the primary objectives was to enhance employee contribution through increased knowledge of Sandia National Laboratory culture, strategy, and programmatic direction. A major concern was to provide an additional mechanism for the transfer of leadership skills and knowledge at risk due to retirements, and as an additional mechanism for developing future leaders.

Description of Program

The mentoring program at Sandia tried to imitate mentoring in its "natural" setting, and imposed little structure on the participants. Although the program planners initially favored the loose structure, they found themselves rethinking that issue. The program was set up so the participants all volunteered for the one-year program. Participation was solicited for both mentors and protégés from all of the 900 managers and senior level technical staff who manage projects at Sandia. Because the program was aimed at increasing the number of women and minorities in leadership roles, those groups in particular were targeted for participation. In the end, however, it was strictly a volunteer program, in terms of participation and commitment.

The volunteer participants were paired together by the program coordinator, or in some cases paired themselves if they had someone in mind. The pairings then met together for a kick-off luncheon, after which time they would meet three to four times throughout the year as a group in a luncheon format, with a speaker/trainer who talked about various areas of interest. Attendance at these luncheons was strictly voluntary.

There was no structure in the program as to how often the pairs would meet throughout the year. The pairings were provided packets with information that contained suggestions for meetings and possible activities that could enhance the mentoring relationship. The amount of contact between the mentor and protégé and the type of projects the protégé completed was left up to the individual pairings to arrange and coordinate. Also included in the packet was an agreement that the mentor and protégé were to complete outlining their expectations for the program. This was to be signed by both the mentor and protégé.

The program coordinator periodically sent an email to all of the participants asking for feedback. She was available for questions and concerns throughout the program. She reported receiving only a small number of calls and only a very few end-of-the-year evaluation forms. However, at the end-of-the-year luncheon, all those who attended reported they were pleased with the mentoring leadership program.

Charline Seyfer Wells is the program manager for leadership training at Sandia, which includes the mentoring leadership program. The mentoring program was a very important initiative in the leadership training division of Sandia. The president of Sandia participated as a mentor in the pilot program, and in the present program both the vice president of human resources and the human resources director were volunteer mentors. Other vice presidents and directors at Sandia also volunteered as mentors.

Charline felt that the mentoring pilot program had been successful. She had volunteered as a mentor herself to demonstrate her commitment to the project and had been on hand at the final luncheon to witness the positive feedback. However, she needed something more tangible than reports that everyone enjoyed himself or herself. She wanted tangible evidence that the protégés had really learned something from their mentors. She wanted proof of the actual leadership skills transfer. She needed an in-depth evaluation of this program.

Sandia was like most large organizations in the United States who spend a disproportionate amount of their training budget on the training of their managers. Because companies invest large amounts of money on training their managers, it is important for them to evaluate the success of this training to justify the expenditure.

Charline knew Linda as a consultant who had both a strong interest in and had conducted research of formal mentoring programs. She related to Linda that it was her understanding that, to date, most of the research done on the benefits of mentoring had been inconclusive, subjective, and based on "smile sheets." With this in mind, Linda agreed to conduct an objective evaluation of Charline's program.

At the time that Linda became involved, the second group of mentors and protégés had been paired for about three months. This group contained 62 pairs, with same and mixed gender pairings. The mentors were all upper level managers or senior level technical staff who manage projects; directors; or vice presidents of the organization. The protégés were middle level managers and senior technical staff; some did not currently manage people, but managed projects and at some time might be called upon to manage subordinates.

Formulating the Evaluation Plan

As Linda planned her evaluation, she looked at the format of the current mentoring leadership program. It was easy to see why Sandia started a mentoring program for their managers. The literature abounds with instances of the duality of mentoring and leadership; mentors are leaders, and leaders are mentors. Mentoring as a method of training has been successful in achieving a desired organizational culture. Through mentoring, the organizational culture is passed from one manager to another in a cyclical fashion. Mentoring has its roots in the apprenticeships of the medieval trade guilds and is a phenomenon that has appeared in almost every large corporation to some extent.

Yet Linda was aware that few mentoring programs have actually succeeded and that often the "forced pairing" of a formal mentoring program violates the true spirit of mentoring. Linda wondered if the "forced pairing" of a formal mentoring program was something like the "forced marriages" of yesteryear, legitimate on paper yet lacking the passion required to make them truly successful. She also wondered if this "passion" could be duplicated or if it existed only in those natural pairings.

As Linda searched for benchmarks, she discovered there had been scarce research conducted on any *one* particular mentoring program in either a business or governmental setting, with most research concentrating on mentoring programs in educational settings. Most of the surveys previously conducted were sent to unrelated people in different organizations asking if they had received any mentoring in their career. Linda found that most of the evaluations focused on satisfaction and perceived career advancement, and none had really looked at the skills transfer to the protégés.

Seeking to provide her client, Charline, with the objective tangible evidence of skills transfer that she desired, while at the same time curious to see if the "passion" and satisfaction of the naturally occurring mentoring relationship could be found in a "forced pairing," Linda proposed the following questions:

1. Are the managerial and leadership skills of the protégés improved as a result of the mentoring relationship?

2. What factors of the mentoring program will increase the satisfaction of the participants and have a positive effect on the protégés?

The first obstacle facing Linda was how to collect the data necessary to answer these questions. The second obstacle was how, in a purely voluntary program, would she get the mentors and protégés, who were already stressed for time, to commit to completing numerous data collection instruments? Linda decided to study the format of the current program and design her evaluation around the activities of that program. Figure 1 illustrates the format of the mentoring program and how the evaluation fit in with it. The data collection design turned out to be the easy part. The data collection itself proved to be the most challenging part.

Choosing the Tools

Because Sandia was interested in measuring the transfer of leadership skills, Linda decided to use Blanchard's Leader Behavior Analysis (LBAII) instrument. The LBAII instruments were designed to provide information about the respondent's leadership style and to determine their effectiveness and flexibility with certain managerial functions. Linda used the LBAII-A at the beginning of the program to establish a baseline of the participants' skills, and then used the LBAII-B at the end of the program to measure the change in leadership skills. The LBAII-*Other* was completed by the mentors as a way to corroborate the self-report scores. All three versions of the LABII consist of 20 management scenarios, and the respondent is asked to choose from one of four choices given. The LBAII instruments were

Figure 1. Sandia mentoring program and research study.

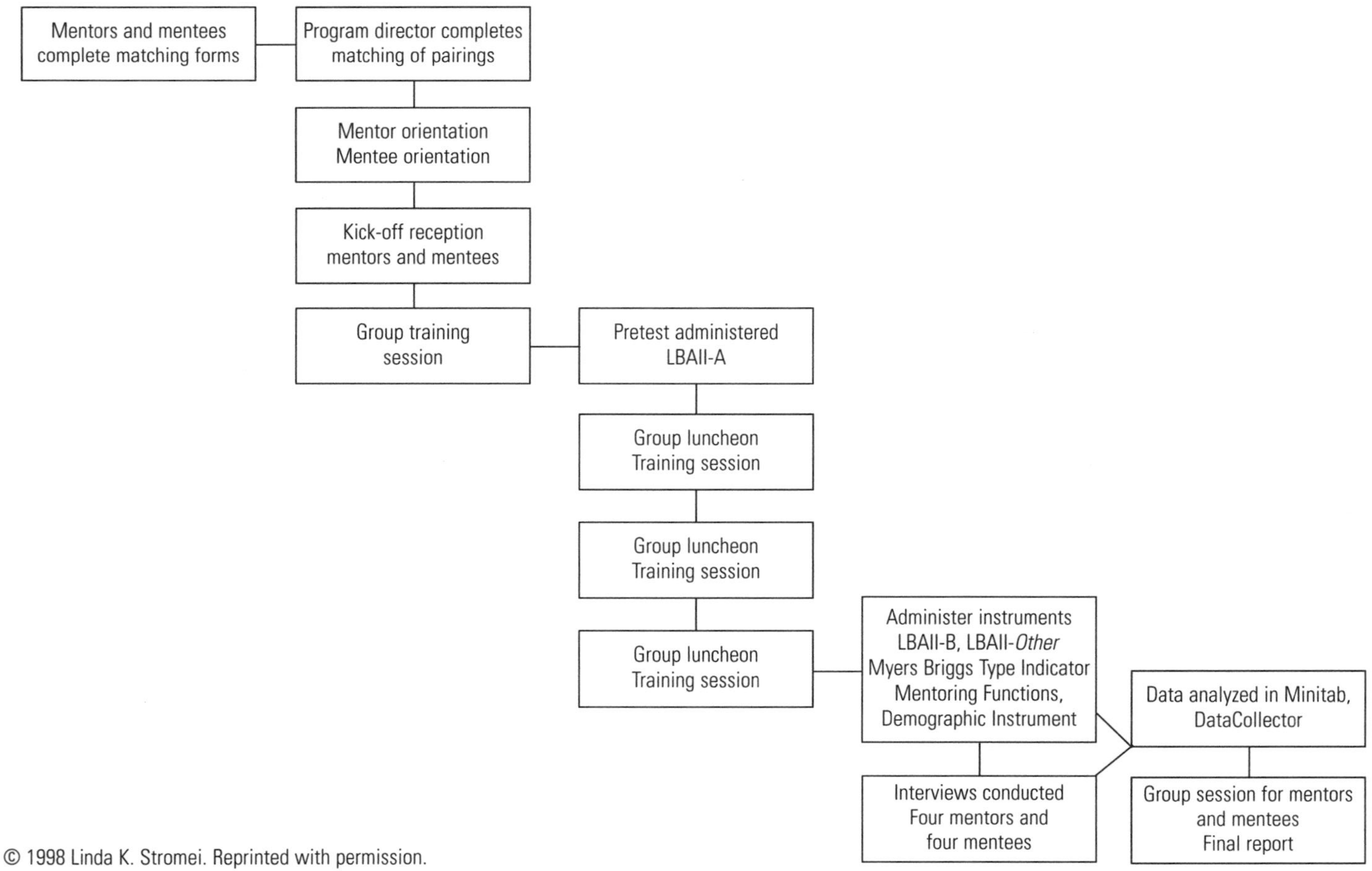

© 1998 Linda K. Stromei. Reprinted with permission.

chosen because they measure two facets of leadership and their designers have established both their construct validity and reliability.

To examine the correlation between personality type and both satisfaction and effectiveness, the Myers-Briggs Type Indicator was administered to both the mentor and the protégé. Because previous studies looked at the satisfaction level of participants of a mentoring relationship, Linda thought it would be helpful to compare satisfaction with the other variables. As she searched for an instrument to measure satisfaction, she found only the "happy sheets" that merely asked if the parties were satisfied. So Linda designed an instrument she called the *Mentoring Functions Scale,* which was designed to measure the protégés' attitudes about predictors of success and how these factors actually contributed to their success. Demographics were also collected to aid in comparisons. After collecting and analyzing the data, Linda decided to conduct interviews to clarify some areas. Interviews were then conducted with four randomly chosen pairs.

Implementation of the Evaluation

This proved to be the most challenging part for Linda for several reasons. Linda attempted to hold sessions immediately following the group luncheons where participants were encouraged to stay for a few minutes and complete the instruments. This was only marginally successful. Because Sandia is a national laboratory, most of its facilities require either a security clearance or an escort to enter, making access to the participants more difficult. It was arranged for Linda to hold several sessions in a conference room outside of the secure area where participants could come and complete the instruments.

Time was a crucial factor for the first set of instruments (the pretest) because they were used to establish the baseline skills. Therefore it was important for all of the protégés to complete these in basically the same time frame. The 62 pairs represented a wide age group, with both same and mixed gender pairings. Table 1 illustrates the breakdown of the pairings of the 62 participants.

Table 1. Sandia mentoring program original participants.

Number of pairs	Mentor age range	Protégé age range	Same gender pairs male/male	Same gender pairs female/female	Mixed gender pairs male/female
62	31-59	26-57	22	18	22

Despite her best efforts, Linda was only successful in getting 42 of the 62 pairs to complete the instruments. Table 2 illustrates the breakdown of the 42 pairs who actually completed all of the instruments and were included in the final evaluation.

Support of Key Stakeholders

For any leadership program to succeed, it needs the support of upper management. The mentoring program at Sandia appears to have the full support of its management. As mentioned earlier, the president of Sandia participated as a mentor in the pilot program, and the program that was evaluated boasted several vice presidents and directors as mentors, including both the vice president of human resources and the director of human resources.

Answers to the Questions

As Linda analyzed the data she had collected, she began to put together the pieces that would answer the questions she had proposed to answer for her client. The answers she found to each of the questions follow.

To the first question, "Are the managerial and leadership skills of the protégés improved as a result of the mentoring relationship?" the answer was yes, absolutely. Using the data collected on the LBAII-A (pretest), Linda established a baseline score for the protégés on the scales of Leader Effectiveness and Leader Flexibility. It was important to know where each of the protégés was in terms of these skills when he or she started the program in order to determine an increase at the end of the program. Scores on the effectiveness scale can range from 20 to 80, and the mean score for the protégés on the pretest was 50. This indicated that the protégés as a group already possessed above average leader effectiveness skills. However, the mean score on the LBAII-B (posttest), administered at the end of the mentoring program, was 56.4, an increase of 13 percent, which indicated that the

Table 2. Sandia mentoring program final evaluation participants.

Number of pairs	Mentor age range	Protégé age range	Same gender pairs male/male	Same gender pairs female/female	Mixed gender pairs male/female
42	31-59	26-57	11	13	18

protégés did learn more about leadership effectiveness as a result of being in the program. These data were analyzed using a paired *t* test. Table 3 shows these results.

Traditionally, results of a mentoring program are sometimes not evident in the first year because it often takes longer for the protégé to learn the nuances of the organization's culture. Therefore, this significance on the difference between the pretest and posttest scores on leadership skills taken before the end of the one-year program was positive and highly encouraging.

To further corroborate the significance of the pretest and posttest of Leader Effectiveness, the LBAII-*Other* was given to the mentors. This parallel allowed for meaningful comparisons between the respondent's (protégé's) self-perception and those who "experience" the manager's style. There was no significant difference in the means (56.4—protégé self-report; 55—mentor report on protégé) on the effectiveness scale. It appeared that the protégé's perception of his or her leadership effectiveness and the mentor's perception of the protégé's effectiveness was almost identical. These data were analyzed using a paired t test, which looks at the differences in the individual's scores. Table 4 shows these results.

The effectiveness score is thought to be the most important score derived from the LBAII instrument. It is a numerical representation

Table 3. *t* test LBAII-B (posttest) scores and LBAII-A (pretest) scores, effectiveness.

t test: Paired Two Sample for Means	Posttest Effectiveness	Pretest Effectiveness
Mean	56.35714286	50
Variance	65.21080139	29.12195122
Observations	42	42
Pearson correlation	−0.035820044	
Hypothesized mean difference	0	
Df	41	
T Stat	4.173353888	
P(T<=*t*) one-tail	7.61064E-05	
T Critical one-tail	1.682878974	
P(T<=*t*) two-tail	0.0001152213	
T Critical two-tail	2.01954208	

Table 4. *t* test LBAII-B and LBAII-*Other* scores, effectiveness.

t test: Paired Two Sample for Means	Posttest Effectiveness	Other Effectiveness
Mean	56.35714286	55.04761905
Variance	65.21080139	90.53426249
Observations	42	42
Pearson correlation	0.180074301	
Hypothesized mean difference	0	
Df	41	
T Stat	0.749911387	
P(T<=*t*) one-tail	0.228794947	
T Critical one-tail	1.682878974	
P(T<=*t*) two-tail	0.457589895	
T Critical two-tail	2.01954208	

of the respondent's appropriate use of the chosen style in light of the situation described. On the LBAII-A, the effectiveness score is an indicator of the respondent's diagnostic skill in choosing the appropriate style advocated by the model. On the LBAII-*Other,* the score represents the perceived behavior of the manager by the mentor. The fact that these two are so closely aligned lends credibility to the relationship of the pairing, and to the validity of the scores.

The second scale on the LBAII instrument measured the protégé's Leadership Flexibility score, a numerical indicator of how often the respondent used a different management style in each of the 20 situations in the LBAII. The more evenly the four choices appeared, the more flexibility is shown in the score. Scores can range from 0-30.

The protégés' mean score on the LBAII-A (pretest) for the flexibility scale was 17, indicating again that many of the protégés reported they already used above average flexibility in their leadership style. The mean score on the posttest, taken at the end of the program, was 20.8, an increase of over 22 percent. Table 5 shows the results of the paired *t* test.

The second question was, "What factors of the mentoring program will increase the satisfaction of the participants and have a positive effect on the protégés?"

This question looked at what factors had a positive effect on the protégés and those that increased the protégés' satisfaction with the

Table 5. *t* test LBAII-B (posttest) and LBAII-A (pretest) scores, flexibility.

t test: Paired Two Sample for Means	Posttest Flexibility	Pretest Flexibility
Mean	20.80952381	17.0952381
Variance	20.49941928	21.356562214
Observations	42	42
Pearson correlation	0.306296542	
Hypothesized mean difference	0	
Df	41	
T Stat	4.466981496	
P(T<=*t*) one-tail	3.05559E-05	
T Critical one-tail	1.682878974	
P(T<=*t*) two-tail	6.11118E-05	
T Critical two-tail	2.01954208	

program. To gather data to evaluate this question, Linda used a mentoring functions questionnaire which asked the protégés to rate various aspects of the program and to give information regarding their relationship with their mentor. The demographics instrument asked them the number of times they met, where they met, number of phone calls, and other methods of communication.

Correlations were used to determine whether there was a relationship between various aspects of the program, its benefit to the protégés, and their overall satisfaction. Linda found that there were several aspects of the program that were beneficial to the protégés. These were the number of times they met, the quality of projects they worked on together, the extent to which the mentor was available to the protégé, and the commonality of their values.

A regression analysis in which all the factors were examined together indicated that the most important factor was the quality of projects or assignments on which they worked. Table 6 shows these results. This finding was further substantiated by the interviews conducted with four of the pairs. In an interview conducted with one of the protégés who doubled her score from the pretest to the posttest, she related how her mentor worked with her on various projects and problems she encountered. Although the mentor did not provide specific answers, he gave guidance and was available to assist and work with the protégé on the problem while the protégé found her own answers.

Table 6. Best subsets regression of four variables and satisfaction.

Response is Satisfaction

Vars	R-Sq	R-Sq (adj)	C-p	S	1	2	3	4
1	47.5	46.2	12.2	0.42037		X		
1	17.0	14.9	41.4	0.52839				X
2	56.2	53.9	5.9	0.38897		X		X
2	53.5	51.1	8.5	0.40066	X	X		
3	61.2	58.1	3.1	0.37067	X	X		X
3	57.3	53.9	6.9	0.38897		X	X	X
4	61.3	57.1	5.0	0.37512	X	X	X	X

The four variables are: number of meetings (1), quality of projects (2), commonality of values (3), and availability of mentor to protégé (4).

Creation of a Model

As a final synthesis of the data analysis, Linda incorporated those determinants identified in the evaluation and put together a model for a formal mentoring program. It incorporated those activities that proved to be beneficial to improving the skills transfer, satisfaction, and psychosocial benefits, based on the reported preferences of the participants of this study.

The proposed model is entitled AMIGOS, which is an acronym for Arranged Mentoring for Instructional Guidance and Organizational Support. The model is proposed for a formal mentoring program in an organization. The AMIGOS model is based on a dual benefit for the mentor and protégé. The model shows the mentor and the protégé together in the center, interacting with the four centers of the model. Figure 2 is a graphic representation of the model, and Figure 3 is a flow chart for implementation of the model.

The model has four centers: the IDEA center, which is an acronym for Individual Diagnosis, Evaluation, and Assessment; the TIPS center, Training Instruction Practical Tips; the COPE center, Center for Organizational Problem Enlightenment; and the FUN center, Friendship, Understanding, and Nurturing.

The first step of the model is the IDEA center. Because the protégés of this study reported a preference for a mentor who shared their same values, beliefs, and work ethic, someone whose work behavior they could model and whose personality "clicked" with theirs,

Figure 2. Formal mentoring program model.

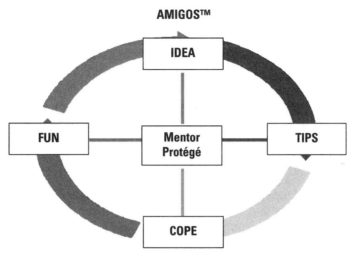

the pairing was identified as the most important part of the model. A profile of the mentor and protégé should be prepared to assist with matching, using various assessment instruments. The IDEA center of the model is one of the most critical and must be completed before the participants can move to the next stage.

It is important to note at this point that for the proposed model to work in an organization, it requires full organizational support from the top level on down. Sufficient resources and personnel must be allocated for it to be successful. The training proposed in the mentoring program must be integrated into and become a part of the overall organizational objectives and mission.

Once the diagnostic/assessment phase is completed, the preliminary matched pairs move forward to the next step of the model. The pairs meet in a retreat or other social setting, which will take place in the FUN center of the model. The mentor and protégé move in and out of the various centers of the model, sometimes in tandem and sometimes separately.

Next the participants move to the COPE center. A problem-based activity should pair the mentor and protégé together. These activities could be modeled around the action learning sets, where participants bring real problems from their workplace, and the teams brainstorm and identify potential solutions, which have been described

Figure 3. Flow chart: Implementation of the AMIGOS™ model of a formal mentoring program.

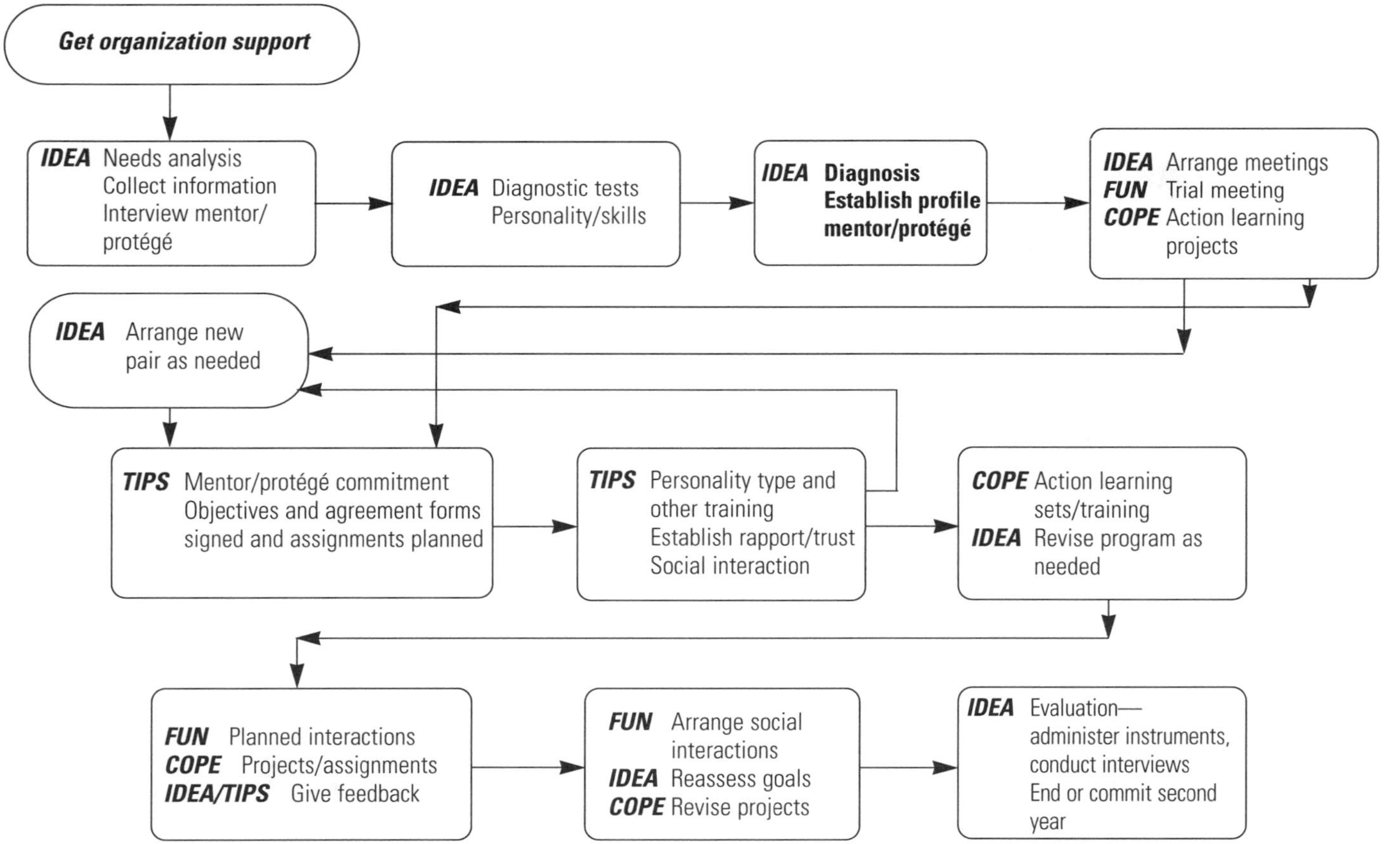

Get organization support

IDEA Needs analysis
Collect information
Interview mentor/protégé

IDEA Diagnostic tests
Personality/skills

IDEA **Diagnosis**
Establish profile
mentor/protégé

IDEA Arrange meetings
FUN Trial meeting
COPE Action learning projects

IDEA Arrange new pair as needed

TIPS Mentor/protégé commitment
Objectives and agreement forms signed and assignments planned

TIPS Personality type and other training
Establish rapport/trust
Social interaction

COPE Action learning sets/training
IDEA Revise program as needed

IDEA Evaluation—administer instruments, conduct interviews
End or commit second year

FUN Planned interactions
COPE Projects/assignments
IDEA/TIPS Give feedback

FUN Arrange social interactions
IDEA Reassess goals
COPE Revise projects

© 1998 Linda K. Stromei. Reprinted with permission.

previously. These sets could put together two or three mentors and protégés and give each of them the opportunity to observe their partner in a problem-solving activity related to their work. The TIPS center is where they will receive hands-on training for the various skills they will need and they will be provided with resource materials.

The model includes incentives for both the mentor and protégé, and methods of interaction between the mentor, protégé, and their home departments. The initial length of this model for a formal mentoring program is one year, but it is recommended to renew it for another year.

Presentation of the Results and Suggested Improvements

At the conclusion of her evaluation, Linda met with her client, Charline, along with the vice president of human resources and the human resources director. Although they were pleased with most of the aspects of the evaluation, they were interested in ways to improve their current program. One area in particular that was of concern to them was the lack of structure in the current program, and they were interested in finding ways to increase the structure yet still remain a voluntary program. Another area of concern was the lack of participation of all of the mentoring pairs in the evaluation, especially when their participation could impact the future direction of this important program. Linda pointed out areas of her model that would help them with these and other areas for improvement.

Areas of Implementation

Charline felt the key finding from Linda's evaluation was that Sandia now had objective, documented evidence that the mentoring leadership program enhanced the transfer of skills/knowledge between the mentor and protégé. In addition Sandia was pleased with Linda's model and used the information from her evaluation as well as the model as a foundation for their new internal knowledge management program for interns. As the evaluation report was distributed, other departments within Sandia used the data and the model to enhance the work of their career development mentoring teams.

This case is a good example of continuous quality improvement in progress. Linda continues to meet with Charline and explore ways to further refine the mentoring leadership program. Charline continues to meet with other managers at Sandia and explore ways to expand this current mentoring program to other divisions and to include other skills in addition to managerial/leadership skills.

Charline Wells and Sandia National Laboratories are to be congratulated on their efforts to evaluate their leadership training programs and to constantly look for ways to improve them.

Teaching Note

This chapter, "Training Tomorrow's Leaders Using Yesterday's Techniques," should stimulate an interesting discussion about mentoring programs and their use as a training method, particularly for specific skills. There has been a resurgence of interest in mentoring in organizations today, particularly for accelerating the transfer of leadership skills. Because many of today's organizations have flatter hierarchies, there is a shortage at the middle management level to replace the upper management nearing retirement age. Organizations are waking up to this fact and are seeking ways to maintain their knowledge base and prepare new leaders to be ready to step in.

This case could best be discussed with a facilitator managing the discussion. All participants should have read and be familiar with the case. The facilitator would then guide the discussion and have participants identify the key players, what they were doing, why they were doing it, sequence the actions according to time frame, and identify the perceived goal(s) or objective(s) of the participants.

Once these key points are identified, the facilitator could divide the participants into small groups to discuss the suggested discussion questions. This could be done one of two ways, depending on the time available. Each group could answer all of the discussion questions, and the facilitator could debrief all of the groups' answers, or, if time is limited, the facilitator could assign each group specific questions to answer and then report back those answers to the main group.

The facilitator would record all answers on a flip chart as the groups report, then summarize answers for each question and ask follow-up questions to stimulate more discussion.

There are many compelling issues in this case study, with space permitting only limited discussion of some. Some issues that could be expanded could be the challenge of how to motivate the participants and the role that each stakeholder plays. The issue of security and lack of access to the participants necessary due to the type of organization presents other issues, such as: would an internal consultant have been more effective due to his or her increased access? Or was the external consultant more effective because she had no alliances within the organization and could promise the participants anonymity with their answers? Would the participants have been re-luctant to share candidly with an internal employee conducting this same type of evaluation?

Another issue that could be discussed would be the sensitivity of some participants to attend training sessions, especially in soft skills areas such as those surrounding mentoring. Many have the perception that they are too "touchy-feely" and they do not see the purpose. Ask how participants have overcome these personality and ego issues with their own training experiences.

This case could be used in a variety of venues. It could certainly be used for training consultants who work with organizations to evaluate training. It could be used in classes for HRD, organizational behavior, adult learning, and evaluation. Simulations and role-plays could easily be constructed using the detailed information provided, and participants could augment the given material with ideas of their own. A long-term project could be to encourage participants to design their own model for a year-long training program for leaders, perhaps including the mentoring component.

It is hoped that this case study could stimulate the participants' desire to identify some of the methods used so that they could incorporate them into their next project.

Definitions of Terminology Used in this Study

The following definitions are given as to their relation and meaning in this study. These definitions are made up of a composite of this researcher's readings and work with mentoring programs, unless otherwise noted.

- **Mentoring**—A complex, interactive process occurring between individuals of differing levels of experience and expertise who have been deliberately paired for the agreed-upon goal of having the lesser skilled person grow and develop specific competencies, which incorporates interpersonal or psychosocial development, career and/or educational development, and socialization functions into the relationship. This one-to-one relationship is developmental and proceeds through stages which help to determine the outcomes of the process.

- **Mentor**—A person at a higher level of responsibility in the organization, who agrees to act as a wise or trusted counselor, leader, and role model to a person who seeks to grow and develop professionally.

- **Protégé**—From the French verb, protégér, to protect, it has come to mean the recipient of the mentor interest, the one whose protection and development is the primary interest of the mentor.
- **Formal Mentoring Program**—A specifically designed process or program created to set up the deliberate pairings of individuals of differing skill levels to guide the development of those individuals in the enhancement of skills, to provide assistance in the structure of the training, and to evaluate the results for the benefits of the participants and the organization.
- **Informal Mentoring**—The natural pairing of individuals who come together, not in an official program, for the purpose of enhancing their career and psychosocial development.
- **Pairing**—The matching or placing together of the participants in a mentoring relationship, the mentor and the protégé. For the purpose of this study, this was done by the program director of the mentoring program.
- **Psychosocial Functions**—Those aspects of the relationship that primarily enhance sense of competence, clarity of identity, and effectiveness in the managerial role.
- **Career Benefits/Functions**—Those aspects of the relationship that primarily enhance career advancement.

Questions for Discussion

1. Was the method of evaluation Linda chose appropriate for this program? What other evaluation models could have been used?
2. What could Linda have done to encourage more participation in the evaluation?
3. How well do you think a voluntary mentoring program will develop leadership skills? What would be important components in such a model to ensure leadership development?
4. In this case Linda used an instrument to evaluate the gain in leadership knowledge. What are some other ways to evaluate a protégé's leadership knowledge?
5. Is a mentoring program helpful in career development of employees, and particularly for women and minorities?
6. Based on this case study, how could you modify your existing leadership program to provide more tangible evidence of leadership skills transfer?
7. How much time does a successful leadership program need to run? Is a year long enough for a program such as the one described?

The Author

Linda K. Stromei is owner of LINCO, a consulting firm whose clients include public and private sector organizations. Stromei consults in all areas of human resource development and instructional design and training, and specializes in establishing formal mentoring programs. She teaches part-time at the University of New Mexico (UNM) and Southern Illinois University at KAFB, where she has taught courses in human resources, instructional design and training, adult learning, and learner assessment/evaluation. Her current research interests include evaluation of formal mentoring programs and in particular leadership skills transfer and soft skills training for technical employees, as well as the influence of personality types on working relationships.

Stromei holds a Ph.D. in organizational learning and instructional technologies from the University of New Mexico and a master's degree in public administration from UNM—both with honors. Her research and the AMIGOS model for a formal mentoring program were awarded the 1998 International Society for Performance Improvement International Award of Excellence for Outstanding Research Product, and an Outstanding Research Product Award from the International Mentoring Association for her research of formal mentoring programs.

She has been a national conference presenter for ASTD, International Society for Performance Improvement (ISPI), the International Mentoring Association, the Center for Application of Psychological Type and has been on the board of the local chapters of ASTD and ISPI in the Albuquerque area. She is also on the local board of the Society for Human Resource Management (SHRM), is in charge of professional development for the SHRM State Council for New Mexico, and is on the national SHRM College Relations Board. Linda is chapter advisor for the UNM Student Chapter of SHRM.

Reference

Stromei, L.K. (1998). *An Evaluation of the Effectiveness of a Formal Mentoring Program for Managers, and the Determinants of Protégé Satisfaction.* Unpublished doctoral dissertation, University of New Mexico, Albuquerque.

Transformational Coaching: A New Paradigm for Executive Development

Haywood Insurance

Raymond P. Harrison

Traditional approaches to the coaching and development of executives have relied heavily on interventions and counseling over extended periods of time. Although these may be effective in some cases, there remains a type of individual who often seems impervious to these more traditional types of approaches. This article examines a radically different approach that borrows heavily from research in cognitive and social psychology of the last several decades.

Transformational coaching presumes that people can change dramatically and quickly, given the right set of experiences at a critical point in the executive life cycle. It eschews techniques based largely on argumentation or persuasion in favor of a behavioral approach. However, unlike other types of behavioral approaches that rely on simulations or games, this approach attempts to recreate actual events that have occurred in the executive's life. The individual is given a minimal amount of counseling but a maximum amount of practicing new ways of responding, so that new behaviors can be fully mastered and locked into a behavioral repertoire. Changes at the cognitive level are eventually expected, but they will follow behavioral change.

Organizations today are characterized by rapidly shifting, unpredictable, ambiguous demands placed on executives. Executive development programs in previous decades could use five-year, ten-year, or even longer-term horizons to map out the knowledge, skills, or abilities their future leaders would need. The world is much less predictable now. Although it is still useful to groom executives for gen-

This case was prepared to serve as a basis for discussion rather than to illustrate either effective or ineffective administrative and management practices.

eral competencies or characteristics, there is often a disconnect between the abstraction of a competency and its execution as an actual behavior. In addition, organizations need to have methodologies that allow executives to change rapidly and dramatically enough so that it is immediately apparent to others.

Simulations, tests, assessment centers, and the like are all useful developmental tools. But often the most useful kind of development comes from direct, real-world experience. Unfortunately we do not generally get the chance to relive our experiences. Usually, if we are lucky, we get to apply the learning to the next similar situation we encounter and hope for the best. But there are methodologies available that, in essence, allow us to relive the same experience over and over again until we get it right. And in getting it right, really mastering the challenge, rapid and dramatic executive growth can occur. This article will describe a set of techniques centered around this notion and review the underlying principles on which it is based.

Haywood Insurance

Haywood Insurance is a property and casualty insurer with assets of approximately $22.4 billion. The company is nearly 40 years old. It has been a solid financial performer in its industry up until three years ago when it suffered heavy losses due to a year of particularly frequent natural disasters. Since then, the organization has come under heavy scrutiny and sometimes criticism from Wall Street for its failure to adequately assess its risk exposure.

The organization has a history of sending people to various management development programs off site. Until about five years ago, however, these activities tended to be ad hoc and disconnected from any kind of coordinated, integrated, organization-wide effort at executive development. In response to increasing pressure to retain and develop existing talent, a position of director of executive development was created and filled by Jack Prescott, a long-term human resources manager with the company, but not an expert in executive development.

Mary Lamarro is the organization's vice president of human resources. Mary, along with Jack, has been a driving force in creating a Corporate Values initiative which was linked to a 360-degree assessment process, the first the company had ever done. She reports to Richard Crowes who is president and chief operating officer of the company.

These three executives all have a vested interest in developing and retaining top talent for the company. An immediate concern for them is George McGowan, the controller for the company. George is about to be thrust into a new role in the organization for which he is not ready. He started with Haywood as an actuary right out of college and came up through the ranks to his current level. At a superficial glance his career trajectory seems to be a highly successful one, but closer scrutiny reveals that his success was largely a result of superior technical skills, not executive ability. In fact his technical excellence forced the organization to gloss over some of his more glaring deficits until now. Now the moment of truth has arrived when Jack, Mary, and Richard must confront the problem and quickly:

> We've really managed to box ourselves into a corner. Harry's decision last week to leave the company means we've got to fill the SVP spot at least two years before I anticipated. As far as I'm concerned George McGowan is the only person that has the executive potential to do the job, but I'm well aware of his reputation. He's had such strained relations with the other VPs that if we promote him, we'll have a major revolution among the troops. On the other hand, if we bring someone in from the outside, I'm sure that George will go ballistic and resign. And he's really the only one in that group who's known and respected by Wall Street right now. If he leaves, we'll have another major problem on our hands.

Richard Crowes was clearly exasperated with the situation. He sat with Mary Lamarro. "Mary, why didn't we deal with this problem long ago?"

Mary Lamarro responded somewhat defensively, "We have tried to deal with it. I specifically wanted Jack in this meeting to go over some of the things we've tried."

Jack Prescott began, "As you'll recall we first became aware that we had a problem with George about five years ago when we came up with our new values statement and began a regular 360-degree executive assessment process. He got murdered in the evaluations particularly by his peers and every year since then the ratings have remained essentially unchanged. I've worked with George off and on since then and, at my suggestion, the organization has sent him to a number of outside programs to supplement my coaching. He's had university-based programs, experiential learning at several outside institutes, and leadership training. I've also continued to spend a lot of time coaching him one-on-one, but to no avail. George and I have spent countless hours talking about his abrasive, abusive, competitive style. I know you've spent some time with him on this issue too. He doesn't disagree with what we point out to him, but it never seems to impact his behavior. He's one of these people who seem absolutely impervious to any outside influence.

"His basic assumption seems to be that people are either at your throat or at your feet. He gets a lot done but at a terrible cost to morale and teamwork. He believes as long as he gets the job done, he will be rewarded and, by the way, so far it's been true. He's been promoted twice in the last five years and Mary tells me he's well compensated for his level.

"I can't honestly recommend an executive development initiative at this point. His relations are so damaged they may be irreparable no matter what he does and I don't know what else we can do to get him to change, especially given the fact that we need to do something quickly."

The scene just described is probably reenacted with slight variation several hundred times a day across corporate America. Organizations are filled with high level, high potential, proven performers who are at best plateaued in their careers and at worst in danger of imminent derailment. Flaws that may seem trivial become major obstacles later in a career. Organizations are often conflicted in terms of what they really want from an executive. In George's case, he may have been talked to about his behavior, but he was still regularly promoted and handsomely compensated. Small wonder he didn't take it seriously.

Also, it must be said that the ground has shifted under the feet of executives today. It is still necessary to produce results, but those results may have to be obtained in a particular way. A small sampling of the challenges and constraints with which executives must now contend include:
• dealing with continuous, complex, massive change
• increased attention to corporate values and guidelines for behavior
• regular use of 360-degree assessments which may not only include superiors, peers and subordinates, but customers, business partners, or others
• flattened, re-engineered, restructured organizations with fewer people to do the work and increased emphasis on getting things done through people who may not report to you directly

- wider spans of control and supervision of people whose work may be unfamiliar to you, requiring more delegation, trust, openness, communication, and allowance for autonomy
- more focus on teamwork and project-based management, with increased emphasis on collaborative, cooperative, consultative skills from managers
- fast-paced, impatient, unforgiving organizational environments that can't allow executives the luxury of making small, incremental improvements in their competence to handle these situations.

This list is representative, certainly not exhaustive, but underlying each challenge is the theme that, just as organizations are going through abrupt and dramatic change, their executives are also being called upon to transform themselves quickly and dramatically.

Given the challenge facing executives today, it is remarkable that so many of them are able to respond to the traditional forms of executive development. However, there remains a core group of executives in almost any organization who have been sent to all the traditional executive development programs, who have been mentored, who have been coached and yet they remain largely unchanged.

Fortunately, behavioral and organizational research has progressed over the last 20 years to a point where alternate types of interventions are available that hold the promise not only for dramatic, transformational change, but change that can occur in remarkably short periods of time.

The "Victim Of Your Success" Paradox

Ironically, some of the most seasoned and successful executives are the ones who will have the most difficulty making the change. First of all, their very success in their career acts as a major reinforcer to keep doing what has worked so well in the past. Second, most senior executives have distinct, strong personalities and reputations to match. This very strength may make it more difficult for them to change their behavior or attitudes. Third, even when they do, organizations have a way of perceptually pigeonholing executives. Once a perception is created of being abrasive, abusive, autocratic, political, deceptive, power hungry, and so forth, small, incremental improvements are not likely to be noticed. That which is not noticed is not likely to be reinforced. Behavior which is not reinforced is likely to be extinguished in favor of old patterns that were previously successful. The circle of the self-fulfilling prophecy becomes complete when the behavior reverts and reconfirms everyone's assumption that a tiger cannot change his or her stripes.

All of this conspires to create a particular kind of executive profile that is intractable and impervious to traditional coaching interventions. Instead, the new realities of the workplace mandate an intense, concentrated process, which can produce rapid, dramatic new executive behaviors that will be perceived and reinforced immediately by the organization. But a huge body of research on personal change from a variety of disciplines has shed light on how to create this kind of executive metamorphosis. Because of the magnitude and rapidity of the change produced, the term "transformational coaching" best describes the process.

Principles of Transformational Change

Following are eight identified principles for the challenge of transformation.

1. Capitalize on "Teaching Moments"

In the life of all executives there are moments when you have their attention about management style issues. In the earlier case illustration, George McGowan is about to enter such a moment. Either he is going to get the job—which will pose a new set of challenges— or he won't and that will be a teaching moment as well.

In their book, *The Lessons of Experience,* Morgan McCall, Michael Lombardo and Ann Morrison highlight the importance of timing in executive development. Times of triumph, disappointment, personal crises, leaps in level of responsibility, demotions, and so forth are periods that executives often cite retrospectively as being key in their later development. These periods of heightened emotionality and vigilance are also opportunities for learning because as executives flounder to regain balance, they will also be most receptive to new ideas and suggestions from others. Organizations and their coaches are wise if they strategically identify these periods in advance and plan for them.

2. Organizations Arrive at Impressions About People as a Result of "Critical Events"

Many executives have reputations that precede them, but these reputations were originally founded on specific events that were observed by others. The key question is, "how do we know what we *think* we know about the executive?" It may be based on one-on-one interactions or observations made during meetings. In most organizations, people can cite specific *critical* events that led to the creation of perceptions about the executive or that serve to maintain those perceptions.

Undoubtedly executives possess individual stimulus characteristics as well that contribute to these perceptions. A tall, heavy-set, male executive might more readily create an impression of being intimidating than a petite, soft-spoken, female executive who might enact the same behavior and be judged as unassertive. But stimulus characteristics aside, in each case, people have come to their conclusions about the executive as a result of specific interactions with him or her or observations of the executive interacting with others.

3. Memory for Critical Events is Notoriously Faulty

A fundamental technique of most executive coaching interventions is that you talk to the executive about problematic things that have happened in the past, what might have been done differently, and what needs to happen differently in the future. Depending on the orientation of the coach, a number of other interventions may also be employed, but the basic problem with this approach is that people either:

- lie
- selectively remember
- distort the recollection
- unconsciously create events that never happened.

Mark Twain used to say that he wasn't so astonished by the number of things he could remember as the number of things he could remember that weren't so. Since the late 1950s psychologists have been regularly able to demonstrate Twain's observation.

Elizabeth Loftus is a distinguished researcher in the field of memory. In addition to her scholarly research, she also regularly testifies in court as an expert witness in the areas of eyewitness accuracy and false memory. *Witness for the Defense* (Loftus and Ketcham, 1991) is a riveting account of just how fallible memory can be, particularly when observers may have preconceived notions or are in heightened states of emotion. What is particularly striking is how absolutely certain witnesses can be, even in the face of proven contradictory facts.

Memory can become tainted at several points. The physical appearance of the participants, distractions, emotions, or preconceived notions can all contribute to distortions in what is initially perceived. These are called attentional processes. Later long-term memory processes can create further biases, distortions, or outright invention of things that never happened.

The practical implication is that it isn't sufficient just to get critical events about an executive's behavior; but it is necessary to get descriptions of the event from multiple sources. We call this the *Rashomon technique,* in tribute to the ancient Japanese story of the same name about a robbery and rape told from multiple perspectives. Even then there is no assurance that the event represents objective reality. But identifying a specific critical event and hearing it described from the multiple perspectives of participants as well as observers gives us an organizational perception which has a certain reality all its own. Ultimately, the executive has to deal with these collective perceptions.

4. Practice to Mastery

Learning researchers have been aware of this phenomenon for several decades. Practice to mastery refers to learning an activity not just to the point of competence, but to the point where the behavior can be produced easily or automatically. It is one thing to learn how to consciously drive a car with a stick shift. It is quite another to shift gears so easily that the process essentially becomes automatic and unconscious. If one learns to drive a stick shift on only one occasion and then doesn't practice it again for 10 years, it is likely that most of the previous learning will have been lost, a process learning theorists call *regression*.

When an activity is practiced and learned to the point of mastery, it is also more likely that *transfer of training* will occur. If one fully masters a four-speed transmission, he or she can usually master a five-speed easily. Likewise, if one has to learn to drive some other form of machinery such as a truck, tractor, or boat that requires shifting gears, the learning will generally occur more quickly and easily.

One of the important implications of these findings for executive development is that activities must be over-learned and practiced to the point where the executive can reproduce them easily. Once learned, they must be practiced immediately in the workplace and not just whenever the opportunity arises. In the absence of such practice, regression will likely occur.

Practice to mastery is also crucial because it facilitates transfer of training to related situations that can't be anticipated by the executives or their coaches. For example, if one fully masters the techniques of giving employees accurate, specific, and constructive performance feedback, it will be much easier to use many of the same techniques to a subordinate who comes seeking career guidance.

5. Behavior Drives Attitudes

It might seem from the foregoing discussion that this is a strict behaviorist approach. But almost no serious researcher today disputes the importance of mental functioning in behavior change. Changes in ideas, assumptions, and attitudes as well as emotions and motivation are critical if lasting change is to occur. Otherwise the participant is just "going through the motions."

But how to change attitudes? Surprisingly, direct methods of verbal persuasion have often been shown to be worse than useless. Studies in smoking cessation, for instance, have shown that when subjects are given didactic presentations about the evils of nicotine they are even less likely to stop than groups receiving no treatment at all. Psychologists now understand that what happens as a person is being harangued to behave in a particular way is that they react to the threat of diminished personal choice with silent counter arguments. This process, coined *psychological reactance* by the social psychologist Jack Brehm, results in participants coming out of the experience even more entrenched in their positions than before.

Real-life examples of psychological reactance abound. Several years ago the town of Kenneshaw, Georgia, enacted a law requiring every adult resident to own a gun and ammunition, under penalty of six months in jail and a $200 fine. Gun sales shot up almost immediately. Unfortunately, almost all of the purchases were made by out-of-town residents!

Similarly, Dade County, Florida, imposed an antiphosphate ordinance prohibiting the use or even possession of laundry products containing phosphates. Residents began almost immediately to form "soap caravans" with neighbors to smuggle in phosphate detergents. Even more interesting was the fact that in independent consumer surveys, residents became absolutely convinced that phosphate detergents were better than nonphosphate detergents. Apparently once phosphates became forbidden fruit, they became more attractive.

So how do you change attitudes, or can you? An overwhelming amount of literature and the practical experience of many consultants is that attitude change will follow behavior change. In the example of smoking cessation research given above, it was discovered that interventions like asking subjects to role-play picking up a cigarette and putting it away or role-playing the refusal of an offer of a cigarette resulted in a greater likelihood of subjects giving up smoking. This basic finding has been replicated many times across many kinds of situations.

Why this occurs is not completely understood. We know that the actions of people are not necessarily linked to espoused attitudes and values. We all know people who say one thing and behave very differently. But the reverse doesn't seem to be true. Once a behavior is exhibited, the individual is more likely to gravitate to ideas and attitudes consistent with the exhibited behavior. Apparently behaviors are a more potent source of attitude change than attitude is a driver of behavioral change.

This observation about human behavior dates back at least to the time of Machiavelli, but it first began to be studied systematically by researchers after the Korean War. The noted organizational psychologist Edgar Schein headed a team of investigators who debriefed returning American POWs in North Korea. Schein noted that POWs returning from Chinese prison camps in North Korea were treated significantly differently from those who had been held by the North Koreans. The North Koreans gained compliance from their prisoners by savagery and harsh punishments. The Chinese favored what they called a "lenient policy" which in reality was an intense and sophisticated psychological assault on their captives.

The Chinese approach was simple as well as insidious: first get the POWs who had been trained to offer only name, rank, and serial number, to make small, inconsequential concessions. As an example, prisoners were asked to make statements like, "The United States is not perfect." Once this was accomplished, related, more substantive requests followed. A prisoner who admitted the United States was not perfect might then be asked to indicate a few ways this was so. At each step there was relatively little direct coercion to perform, but rewards were given for compliance. He might then be asked to make a list of such items and then sign it. Eventually he would find himself to be a "collaborator"; having given aid and comfort to the enemy. Once the prisoner had engaged in the collaborator behavior, his self-image eventually changed to be consistent with the deed.

In this way the Chinese officials in North Korea were able to get nearly all U.S. POWs to collaborate at one time or another. The magnitude and duration of the change was evidenced by the fact that after the close of the hostilities a significant number of POWs preferred to stay in North Korea as citizens of the communist regime. Many of the prisoners stayed for decades afterward and, in fact, it is estimated that there are still several former POWs living in North Korea today.

The relevancy of this research is clear: logical methods of persuasion such as information giving, argumentation, logical analysis, and disputation have little lasting effect on attitude change. Changes in ideas, attitudes, and values will result in long-lasting behavioral change, but this is likely to be preceded first by actual changes in behavior. If the individual is resistant to the change in behavior, then small, nonthreatening, incremental behavioral changes should be undertaken under noncoercive conditions.

6. Stakeholder Analysis and Action Planning

But in planning what behaviors need to be produced in the workplace, events cannot be left to chance. Each executive faces her or his own set of unique challenges on the job. But each executive also works in a larger environment of superiors, peers, subordinates, customers, and other business colleagues who may have the same, similar, overlapping, or competing challenges and goals. Analyzing who your key stakeholders are and developing productive relationships with them is essential for success in today's organizations.

In most cases tasks should be analyzed first and then, working backwards, the executive needs to determine what alliances are necessary to accomplish the tasks. Normally one's boss and perhaps other superiors will be part of the equation. But some issues have to be dealt with largely through peers, whereas others may need to be tackled through subordinates.

Once this key constituency has been determined, specific initiatives need to be taken with each stakeholder. Gene Boccialetti (1995) has developed a simple yet effective conceptual scheme for analyzing and planning stakeholder initiatives. His system revolves around analysis of three key dimensions: *distance, deference,* and *divergence.* Distance refers to the amount of intimacy and informality in a relationship. Executives who are high on the distance factor favor relationships at work characterized by formality, little self-disclosure, and a no-nonsense task orientation. Deference refers to the degree that an individual feels comfortable in voicing or receiving opinions from others. Executives high in deference tend to be good soldiers who want structure and will follow orders. In their relations with peers they are not likely to volunteer ideas in the their peers' areas of responsibility about how work could be done more effectively. Divergence refers to the degree that one sees his or her goals in competition or opposition with others in the organization. Executives who are high on this factor are likely to view their relationships with colleagues as competitive and adversarial.

In our earlier case example of George McGowan, we know that he has a problem with his peer relationships. It may be that he is too distant in his relations with them. If this is the case, then specific actions such as inviting them to lunch or arranging informal meetings might be suggested. If deference is the problem, then the executive needs to work at listening to the opinions of others as well as volunteering opinions in a nonaggressive manner. If the problem lies in the domain of divergence, then discussions around basic business strategy and goals need to occur and these differences need to be resolved.

In the real world, it is more typical to find a mix of these problems, but triangulating each of these domains in a stakeholder analysis will yield specific tactics for creating, building, or repairing the critical relationships needed for success.

7. Measure What You Want to Change

Feedback about one's performance is critical to any kind of ongoing learning. Feedback not only serves to tell us how well we are performing, but it also keeps us focused and motivated for continued improvement.

We know in the case of George McGowan that he had undergone some form of 360-degree assessment and that his ratings have not improved with peers over the past several years. Often the problem with many 360-degree instruments is that they assess too wide a range of generic management variables. Real gains or losses in progress may be washed out in the averages on many different factors.

In George's case some form of ongoing assessment like this will be critical, but if a 360-degree process is used, it probably should be on a more restricted set of variables related to specific problem behaviors. It may also be the case that a full 360 degrees (superiors, peers, and subordinates) is unnecessary because the problem seems to reside only with peers.

An essential aspect of feedback is that if it is to be helpful, it must be fairly immediate, allowing for quick course corrections. The value of doing an assessment with a more limited population of raters and a more restricted set of factors is that it may make it easier to assess George more frequently and assess him on a more specific and relevant set of factors.

Whatever methodology is used, selection of the specific behaviors needed for change is essential. George needs to identify specific critical events with peers that have contributed to their negative perceptions of him. He and his coach need to then devise other, new behaviors that will begin to challenge those perceptions. Timely and accurate feedback will be needed to discern whether he is making progress on these dimensions.

8. Reward What Has Been Changed

Individual change occurs most effectively when it is supported by systemic sources of support and reinforcement. The only meaningful assessment George has had so far has been via his compensation. We know he has been "handsomely rewarded," so he has been heavily reinforced for the behaviors that are now getting him in trouble.

Organizational psychologists know that in any organization, who gets promoted and how people are compensated are powerful messages about what's really important. The dilemma for Richard Crowes, the COO, is that if he promotes George, he is once again reinforcing problematic behavior and sending a signal about executive success to the rest of the organization. If George is refused the promotion, Crowes risks losing a valuable employee.

A partial resolution of this dilemma is to outline for George very specifically the things he must change in his management behavior in order to be eligible for future promotions. This will be a tough conversation for the COO to have, but it must be done. However, once the new behavioral goals are outlined, it is important to outline a plan for attaining those goals. Nothing is more demoralizing than to be made aware of a problem and then be given no escape route to deal with it. The COO will be creating a "teaching moment" and it is up to the organization as well as George to capitalize on it.

Mapping Out a Plan of Transformational Change for George McGowan

From all of the foregoing principles of change it is possible to outline a preliminary sequence of events that must occur if George has any chance of transforming himself in the eyes of his colleagues:
1. George should not be given the promotion at this time and the difficulties he has had with his peers should be given to him as the prime reason.
2. The COO should emphasize his continued confidence in George and discuss with him a preliminary plan for solving the problem with his peers.
3. Coaching services should be immediately engaged for George, initially focusing on the "critical events" that have contributed to the perceptions his colleagues have of him.
4. Critical event interviews using the Rashomon technique should be undertaken with each of George's peers in order to get the fullest, most comprehensive picture possible of what actually happened during these critical moments.

5. From these interviews a specific list needs to be developed for the purpose of identifying, then practicing new behaviors that will challenge earlier perceptions of George.

6. These new behaviors need to be practiced to mastery to allow for easy reproduction of the behaviors in the actual work setting as well as transfer of training to other situations. It is not necessary and perhaps undesirable to discuss at length the rightness, wrongness, theoretical, or philosophical underpinnings of these actions. What is important is that George be willing and able to produce them at will.

7. If resistance is encountered in practicing any of the behaviors, George should be given smaller, more incremental steps that he will not resist.

8. A "stakeholder analysis" should be conducted for each of George's peers and specific actions should be planned for each of them. Upon return, George should begin using the newly acquired skills immediately.

9. Upon return to the work setting, regular and frequent assessments of his progress should be made and this feedback given to him as quickly as possible.

10. When progress can be documented, George should be rewarded. Rewards can take many forms and verbal recognition by the COO or others can be one of them.

11. Whoever serves as George's coach should continue to probe for changes in George's assumptions and attitudes about how to work with people.

12. Others in the organization such as the COO, the vice president of human resources, and others should take every opportunity to comment publicly about the changes George makes, so that the changes are recognized by the larger organization.

If these things are implemented immediately in the case of George McGowan, he has a very good chance of making a dramatic and rapid change in his executive behavior. More important, a powerful message will have been sent to the entire organization about what is really required for executive success.

The Sequencing of Steps in the Coaching Process for George

If George agrees to one more attempt at executive development, the following are the things that must happen.

1. Develop a List of "Critical Events" for Re-enactment

An example of a critical event would be a specific incident where George blew up at someone. Rather than have an abstract discussion about it, the executive coach should recreate the event with George by way of role-playing it just as it happened. Although the primary purpose of coaching at this point is not to elicit thoughts or feelings, getting him "into the moment" may spontaneously allow him to re-call the triggering states which contributed to his explosion.

This kind of coaching is labor intensive and may not be one-on-one, but two- or even three-on-one. But ultimately it will have greater impact. It is also is helpful to videotape the process and let the individual see how he or she appears to others during such an event.

2. Re-enact the Event Again, This Time Using Role-Reversal

It is often helpful to have the individual experience what it is like to be on the receiving end of such behavior. It also sets the stage for being more receptive to other ways of handling a situation.

3. Model, Don't Attempt to Explain New, More Effective Ways of Interaction

Lengthy discussions about why one should be more participative, listen more, delegate more, and so on are likely to be useless and may even add to psychological reactance.

4. Have the Individual Practice What He or She Has Just Seen

This may take many attempts, not just to get the performance to an acceptable level, but to get it to the level of mastery. It can be a tedious process, but mastery is necessary to avoid a later return to unacceptable levels of performance. It is at this stage that one often finds individuals spontaneously offering, "I guess I can see how this might have been a better way to handle it."

5. Use the Newly Acquired Behavioral Repertoire to Begin Challenging Underlying Assumptions or Attitudes

This is much easier to do once behaviors have changed. Attitudes follow behavior more easily than the reverse.

6. After Retrospectively Reviewing Things That Have Happened, Begin Prospectively Rehearsing Things That Must Happen

A big mistake that many executive development programs make is that after the coaching, the coach sends the person off and hopes for the best. It is far better to plan with the individual the things that he or she must do upon the return to the work setting. Specif-ically, things should be planned that will start to build or repair strained relationships or things that will immediately and dramatically chal-lenge people's preconceived perceptions about the individual.

This aspect of rapid and dramatic change is a frequently over-looked topic in the executive development literature. Without these two ingredients, any changes that do occur are likely to be incremental. Incremental changes are not likely to be noticed by others and the individual is not likely to get much, if any, reinforcement. Without reinforcement, the stage is set for rapid regression to former behaviors. It is somewhat analogous to the principle in physics of escape velocity. If a rocket doesn't achieve quick and certain acceleration in its first few moments after launch, it will inexorably be pulled back to earth by gravity.

In George's case, for instance, it seems likely that he needs to plan to have specific and conciliatory discussions with his peers. What he says, when he says it, and how he says it need to be carefully planned and practiced to mastery. If this seems phony, perhaps it is but again that attitude will follow behavior. If he acts long enough, often enough in a conciliatory way, eventually he will begin to feel and think differently about his relations with his peers. This will be especially true if he gets any reinforcement from them or the organization for his efforts.

7. Measure What Changes May Take Place

Follow-up measurement can take many forms, such as more in-terviews, or another 360-degree type survey. Measurement will have the dual impact of charting what progress has been made, if any, as well as increasing the likelihood that changes will be made in the first place. If George knows that he will be evaluated at some point later on, he is more likely to work diligently to improve his ratings.

8. When Change Occurs, Reward George

After a decent interval has passed, the reward of a promotion or other benefit will be appropriate. Along the way verbal praise or other types of recognition can have a powerful effect to maintain changes in executive behavior.

Summary

There is certainly a place for executive development programs that can proceed for months or even years. But it is equally true, that in the rapid, continuously changing environments of today's orga-nizations, an alternative paradigm is needed to address the need for rapid and dramatic change. The conceptual underpinnings for such an approach have been around for many years, but are rarely used, perhaps because of ignorance by many executive development specialists or perhaps because of a deeply held suspicion that people can't really change, especially quickly. A wealth of scientific and anecdotal evidence does not support this pessimistic view. The techniques described here work.

Questions for Discussion

1. George McGowan has apparently been a problem manager in the organization for some time. In what ways has the organization tried to help him and in what ways might it have conspired to maintain those problem behaviors?
2. The article places a great deal of emphasis on the concept of "teaching moments." What events in George McGowan's career might now be acting to create such a moment?
3. What aspects of transformational coaching seem radically different than other kinds of coaching or counseling, or is it truly different at all?
4. A key assumption of the transformational approach is that behavior drives attitudes. What experiences have you had that would confirm or disconfirm that notion?
5. If George responds to the transformational coaching approach, how might it be seen or measured within the organization? What specific kinds of behaviors or other measurable criteria should be examined?

The Author

Raymond P. Harrison has nearly 20 years of experience as an organizational consultant, author, and industrial/organizational psychologist. He currently serves as Manchester's national practice leader for Executive Development Services, the group within the company devoted to delivering executive coaching, leadership development, career development, and newly appointed leader coaching, as well as other executive development services. During his career at Manchester, he has also been regional director of Manchester Consulting and general manager of Manchester's Philadelphia, Princeton, and Washington, D.C. offices.

Harrison began his career as a counselor in 1972, working with dislocated workers under a grant from the National Institutes of Mental Health. His work in the mental health field culminated in his being named director of Psychiatric In-Patient Services at Nanticoke State General Hospital. In this role, he focused heavily on the vocational needs of patients returning to the community. After several years, he returned to academia and published numerous articles on issues related to counseling. As a result of his work, Harrison has lectured throughout the United States and Europe and several of his articles have been translated into Spanish, German, and Portuguese. Prior to joining Manchester, he served as senior vice president and general manager for Drake Beam Morin, winning its Professional Excellence Award three consecutive years.

For 10 years Harrison was also associated with the University of Pennsylvania Medical School, where his responsibilities included positions as assistant professor of psychiatry and clinical director of the Center for Cognitive Therapy. In these roles, he provided coaching and counseling services to students and faculty of the Medical School, Law School, and the Wharton School of Business. From 1989 to 1992, he served on the board of directors for the Association of Outplacement Consulting Firms (AOCF), co-chairing its Standards Committee, the group responsible for developing and maintaining standards of professional and ethical practices for the entire outplacement industry. More recently, he has been a board member of the Association of Mental Health (AAMH), and the chair of that organization's Strategic Planning Committee. Harrison received his Ph.D. from Pennsylvania State University where he also taught in the Division of Counseling and Educational Psychology. His postdoctoral education has included advanced study at the Wharton School of Business and at Drexel University.

His professional affiliations include the Consulting, Industrial/Organizational and Counseling Divisions of the American Psychological Association and the Pennsylvania Psychological Association of which he is a past president of the Industrial/Organizational Division.

Since joining Manchester Consulting, Harrison has championed a number of new directions for the company. He was creator of Manchester's first organizational recovery program and the principal author of Manchester's Survey of Separation Policies and Practices, derived from a study of more than 500 organizations located throughout the Northeast United States. In recent years, he developed Manchester's first executive coaching manual, its first New Leader Assimilation program and authored the Manchester Survey of Executive Behaviors, an assessment device designed to measure progress derived from executive development interventions. Most recently, he has been principal architect of Manchester's Transformational Coaching program, a radically different approach to coaching which produces rapid and dramatic behavioral change.

References

Boccialetti, G. (1995). *It Takes Two.* San Francisco: Jossey-Bass.

Loftus, E. and K. Ketcham. (1991).*Witness for the Defense.* New York: St. Martins Press.

McCall, M., M. Lombardo, and A. Morrison. (1989). *The Lessons of Experience: How Successful Executives Develop on the Job.* Lexington, MA: Lexington Press.

Additional Readings

Cialdini, R. (1993). *Influence.* New York: HarperCollins.

Heatherton, T.F. and J.L. Weinberger (editors). (1996). *Can Personality Change?* Washington, DC: American Psychological Association.

Schacter, D. (1996). *Searching for Memory.* New York: Basic Books.

Implementing Quality in Higher Education: A Must for Leaders in the New Millennium

Ohio State University

Lee Jones

Higher education is experiencing a metamorphosis of sorts. Many external and internal stakeholders are challenging the fundamental assumptions upon which universities have traditionally operated. This has caused the university to review its mission and examine the type of leader it wishes to lead the academy into the next century. This chapter highlights the success of Ohio State University's attempt to implement quality improvement initiatives throughout the Division of Business and Administration. Finally, the chapter offers recommendations and poses challenging questions for those who seek to explore proactive leadership initiatives to ensure quality in higher education.

The Challenge of Quality in Higher Education

There is growing unrest about the quality of higher education from local, state, and federal levels of government. The poorly prepared college graduates, uninformed professionals, outdated instructional methods, dysfunctional workflow processes, leader unwillingness, and inability to change are just a few of the challenges that higher education is experiencing. Other challenges include a major dispute over the mission of the university, meeting the needs of a more diverse student population, the mistrust that many external constituencies have of the university, and fiscal exigency (Cornesky, McCool, Byrnes, and Weber, 1992). There is a major erosion of confidence in the lead-

This case was prepared to serve as a basis for discussion rather than to illustrate either effective or ineffective administrative and management practices.

ership and the quality of higher education in this country. Respect for colleges and universities is in grave danger.

Universities are generally seen as large enterprises that have assets in excess of a billion dollars. The faculty and administrative staffs of America's universities are the largest group of intellectuals in any formal educational setting. Although universities spend millions of dollars for faculty and administrative salaries, universities are still an enigma and a paradox (Anderson, 1993). Many within the university do not know where the university is headed. The problems within universities are not necessarily with faculty/staff salaries, rather with the university's unwillingness to respond to the needs of society and leaders who are unable to respond to change.

In the past decade, higher education seemingly settled into a conglomerate of intellectual islands where the educational and social needs of a variety of students were met. During the beginning of the decade of the 1980s, higher education enjoyed what many in the academy called "fiscal flexibility" (Rhodes, 1992). The academy had the twin luxuries of sincere collegiality and expanding budgets that resulted in a leisurely workplace and an increase in academic and administrative departmental spending. Universities had no real or pressing issues that threatened their future. In fact, many of the faculty and administrators saw the university as a safe haven where accountability for the academic and administrative performance was not an issue. The university functioned practically without worry of major external influences.

Like many other profit and nonprofit organizations, higher education has been plagued with consistent criticism about the lack of administrative and academic leadership to manage these organizations, given the major transformation that is occurring. Problems with administrative leadership range from their inability to actually manage the changing organizational dynamics to operating a dysfunctional system that is based on fear. The lack of vision, insight, and administrative skill contributes to the lack of formal and informal management training.

During the rapid growth of higher education in the 1960s and 1970s, unskilled or inefficient managers set the stage for long-term problems associated with strategic planning and development, fiscal management, and organizational development (Cornesky, 1992). Administrators without leadership qualities or visionary ability generally yield to their fear of the unknown when confronted with change.

These and other problems with higher education's leadership affects how employees view the organization and the level of trust they have in their leaders' ability to manage them. No longer can universities ignore the public's criticism of its leadership as a mere expression of "intellectual shallowness" (Keith and Girling, 1991). Economic forces, among other drastic societal changes, have forced the university to explain itself, defend its central character, and demonstrate that its services are worth the cost. The tensions and conflicts that beset the university are just a mere reflection of the problems that all governmental, profit, and nonprofit business organizations are facing.

The journey of self-reflection that leads to a quality-driven organization is a struggle for higher education because of its long history and traditions. In an attempt to ensure that higher education's customers are satisfied, and to take the pressure off the academy from its external stakeholders, many institutions have begun to implement quality initiatives. If leaders within higher education follow the points of the quality gurus, like W. Edwards Deming, Philip Crosby, Joseph Juran, and Imani, they will have:

• constructive competition
• shared values and unity of purpose
• collaboration on broad issues
• simulations and synergistic planning
• emphasis on responsibility to contribute
• decentralized partnerships built upon situational management
• team accountability
• constancy of purpose
• win-win resolution to conflicts via conflict management
• probably most important, a superior professorate, student body, and administration.

In summary, the organizational culture will be transformed and frontline employees will become a part of implementation of organizational goals.

There are many reasons that make it difficult to incorporate continuous quality improvement (CQI) principles into the university. Today's state universities find themselves competing with other state agencies and business sectors for limited tax dollars. In response to the consistent dissatisfaction with higher education's graduates, many corporations offer their own specialized training programs. There is also competition between and among departments on campus. To survive, universities must rethink their critical processes and how they can more effectively provide services that meet the needs of their students.

Deming (1989) offered the following management recommendations that need attention when implementing the continuous quality improvement process:

1. develop top leadership commitment
2. recognize quality improvement as a system
3. define it so that others will recognize it
4. analyze change behavior that leads to service
5. measure the quality of the system
6. develop improvements in the quality of the system
7. define who the customers are
8. measure the gains of quality and link them to customer satisfaction
9. develop plans to ensure constant results
10. attempt to replicate the improvements in other areas of the organization.

The university's passionate convictions and traditional ways of doing business and its tightly held assumptions about quality make it difficult to incorporate a shift in the way it does business.

There are at least four major assumptions that are the basis for why universities and public colleges must change and consider implementing continuous quality improvement initiatives (Lewis and Smith, 1994):

1. It builds on the traditions of concern for quality that has characterized higher education in the United States and throughout the world.
2. It recognizes the need for the continuous development of the people who are a part of the higher education system, whether faculty, staff, or students.
3. It involves principles applicable to institutional administration and classroom teaching, thus bridging the gap between traditionally separate parts of the system.
4. It helps us to meet the challenges of the 21st century.

The perception that many external constituencies have of universities is that universities have focused much of their energies on meeting the needs of a few self-centered faculty and have lost control of and knowledge about who its real customers are. The university's quest for faculty personal achievement has lost perspective on the changing student demographics and why these students are demanding more from universities. CQI's goal within the university is not to change the mission of higher education; rather, it is to ask fundamental questions: What is the role of the university? Who are the university's customers? How does the role of the university lend itself to the changes that are taking place externally? How must we change to align ourselves with society's needs? These and other questions challenge universities to review their role and mission. These questions force the university to rethink how they operate and how their contributions impact positively on the students.

Lewis (1993) cautioned the university on making the assumption that CQI can resolve all the issues surrounding the functions of a university. However, if universities approach the CQI process as a way of reviewing the critical processes and examine ways that will connect all of its "loose" parts to better serve the students—and ultimately make a measurable impact on society—then they will initiate a quality program that will be successful.

A review of the quality literature indicates that there has been little written about applying CQI to higher education (Holt, 1993). There is even a smaller body of literature about implementing CQI within higher education and the perception that employees have about its principles. Much of the quality literature focuses on business and industry.

It is apparent that quality initiatives are applicable to higher education (Abernethy and Serfass, 1992; Danne, 1993; Teeter and Lozier, 1993). The significance and benefits of investigating employees' perceptions of managers' commitment to implementing CQI is of major relevance. Almost all the literature on quality (Juran, 1988; Crosby, 1989; Deming, 1986; Collard, 1993) purports that if CQI stands a chance of surviving in any organizational setting, there must be strong leadership commitment from the top.

Universities that have adopted the principles of CQI are faced with the inevitable challenge of making significant organizational cultural changes. The American Society for Quality recently published a list of more than 100 colleges and universities that have begun to implement CQI within their organizations (Hittman, 1993). Unfortunately, most of the universities that have begun to implement CQI have focused their CQI techniques on employees' participation in decision making. This approach is typically implemented without the benefit of assessing the need to change the culture of the organization so that it can take full advantage of the experiences and skills of its human resources. Barriers to the successful implementation of CQI within the university fall in two categories:

1. Universities see themselves as participatory. Because they are structured both in a hierarchical and matrix form, they assume that faculty and staff input is present and effective.
2. Tradition and standard organizational culture determine the receptiveness to and application of CQI.

The Role of Leaders While Implementing CQI in Higher Education

Higher education seems to be the last bastion of resistance in implementing CQI (Sink, 1992). There are those who would rather cling to the "good old days," those who are early adopters but are not quite sure what they are adopting, and those who are skeptics or at least cautious observers of the situation. One reason there seems to be such resistance to implementing CQI in higher education is that the current structure in education seems to embody much of what CQI warns against.

CQI calls for teamwork. In universities, teamwork does not exist. Professors are autonomous and administrative offices create silos to protect their turf. CQI calls for a flat organization. In universities there are layers upon layers of bureaucracy that prohibit their effectiveness. Because of their size and ties to the community, local colleges are at the forefront of implementing CQI initiatives. This section deals with the role of leadership in implementing CQI.

The role of the university leaders while implementing CQI, during a time of transformation and fiscal constraints, is a difficult one. In the face of redefining the institution's mission, the criticism has continued to mount for higher education. For example, Kirk (1987) purports that higher education has lost all sense of purpose. He suggests that higher education is nothing more than an industry that hires thousands of people and supplies "research" to satisfy the egos of the faculty.

He characterizes higher education's curriculum as a "cafeteria style" setup whereby students come to the campus and pick and choose courses with little direction. He further suggests that the size of many large universities is "inappropriate" and is designed for constant failure of students. Although these claims may be an unfair examination of what the university is about, the cries of criticism from many of its internal and external stakeholders is worth examining.

The leader's role in facilitating change in a university setting is a difficult one during these times. It brings about many questions as universities look at how they can position themselves for the 21st century. Higher education will need to discuss ways to redirect its energies while examining the fundamental mission of the university. The mission statement for the university can at least give purpose for and direction to what the university is and what it "ought to be" (Bogue and Saunders, 1992). Writing a mission statement requires a careful review of the university's unique dimensions that set the institution apart from other institutions.

The university leader's role is also to look carefully at how the institution can invest its human and fiscal resources. Finally, the mission statement must reflect the increasing changes that are occurring outside the university; the cultural diversity of society in and outside of the university; changes in the state and federal economy; the expansive growth in knowledge technology and communications; and so forth.

In writing such a mission statement, many questions should emerge. What unique contributions should the university make to society? How does what the university teaches relate to what is happening in the broader society? Which programs should be given priority in the areas of research, teaching, and community outreach? Should the university's aim be focused on community outreach? The answers to these questions will cause many heated debates by faculty and staff and several long discussions on compiling supporting data that will justify counterclaims with regard to the mission of the university. A university's purpose should be neither career development nor character building. Rather, its mission lies in training the mind to critically analyze and debate "truth, realities, and assumptions." Denny (1982), however, sees the mission of the university as "the opportunity of each person to develop his/her intellectual, moral, aesthetic, and spiritual capacities."

With whatever purpose higher education chooses to identify, it cannot view itself as all-encompassing. The leader will have to be a facilitator in dealing with the multiple points of views that will emerge as a result of rethinking the academy's mission.

Today's effective leaders within higher education must have an understanding of the organization's goals and norms. The leader must be able to succinctly communicate those goals and norms and convince the organization members that their individual and group actions are consistent with the broader organizational goals (Argyis, 1974).

The effective leader must also be able to diagnose a situation and develop strategies for improvement. To do this well, the leader must have the ability to perceive and apply a multitude of different perspectives or frames as described by Argyis and others. Imagination, openness, and listening skills seem obvious prerequisites for this type of process (Schein, 1980). There is considerable evidence that formal training in these areas as well as in radical reframing can greatly improve a leader's ability in this area.

The leader must be flexible in personal behavior. This requires the ability to be either authoritative or cooperative, antagonistic or conciliatory, as dictated by the diagnosis of the specific situation at hand. This flexibility is akin to change and is often difficult to initiate within organizations (Bowers, 1985).

To create change, a leader must exhibit the above qualities to maximize effectiveness. Those common characteristics include the unique power distribution between students, alumni, faculty, and staff (between academic departments).

As nearly every experienced leader in higher education will attest, it is always a mistake to neglect the political model when implementing change. Universities, with their dependence on external funding and their physical and philosophical barriers among groups of faculty/staff and students, tend to be highly political in their behaviors. Clark Kerr (1998) suggests that a United Nations type of decision-making model is appropriate to this environment. Obviously, considerations from other models are also essential, but the political model should always be included.

Goals for both the organization and any particular subgroup should always be developed with as much input and involvement from as many members of the organization as possible. This will increase ownership and support. The primary goal should always be on education. As mentioned earlier, these goals must be congruent with each other and easily understood by all members of the university community (Austin, 1985).

Incentives and reward systems should be designed to encourage each individual to assist the organization to achieve the goal. Just as people are different, they are motivated differently. The leaders should identify with and motivate each individual and build him or her into a diverse reward system for the organization (Galbraith, 1987).

In short, colleges and universities should strive to develop organizations that are flexible and responsive to change from within and without, that value input from all members and strive to solicit that input, and that are openly inclusive of diverse perceptions of the organization and its impact.

Within the context of higher education, implementing quality initiatives is becoming the paradigm of choice. At Ohio State University (OSU), under the courageous leadership of Vice President Janet Pichette, the university attempted to implement quality training for

1,200 employees in the Division of Business and Administration (B&A). The goals of this massive training model were 1) to shift the chain of command to one of chain of confidence through offering a training program for all front-line, middle managers, and top-level employees of the division; and 2) to investigate the factors related to how front-line employees within the division perceive their managers' commitment to implementing major concepts of quality on the job.

I will summarize how these two goals were achieved, and recommend how organizations might deduce from this successful quality implementation initiative.

Training Model

The population of this extensive training program consisted of the employees and middle managers within the Office of Business and Administration at OSU, which is a complex organization that employs 1,300-plus front-line employees, secretaries, shift supervisors, middle managers, department directors, assistant vice presidents, and a vice president. The mission of B&A is:

> All individuals of B&A are committed to providing services, facilities, and technology to preserve and enrich a quality learning environment that advances education, scholarship, and public service.

The office is made up of the following university departments and areas: Property Management, Trademark and Licensing, Air Transportation, University Bookstore, Food Supply, Mail Services, Printing, Purchasing, Receiving, Reprographics, Stores, Traffic and Parking, Transportation, Travel Services, University Repair, Physical Facilities, Human Resource Management, Utilities, Building Services, Maintenance, Environmental Health and Safety, Engineering, Buildings and Grounds, University Architect, Wexner Security, University Police, and Telecommunications.

Business and Administration provided five days of classroom instruction to more than 1,200 employees over a two-year period. The purpose of this training was to provide all the employees with the tools necessary to implement continuous quality improvement throughout the organization. The continuous quality improvement training also addressed organizational cultural issues and their importance to quality initiatives. The training reviewed the basic principles of quality management, the university and the B&A mission statements, and the six essential elements of continuous quality improvement (commitment, communication, education, fact-based decision making, proactive approach, and continuous improvement).

The significance of this training was that all top-level and middle managers were engaged in the training with the front-line employees. Employees from all levels were trained to teach the five-day class sessions. The vice presidents and other senior leaders throughout the organization were heavily involved in the development and actual teaching.

Additionally, the division invested in a CQI library for its employees. More than 500 books and quality manuals were purchased. The library was made available 24 hours a day for employees, as there were several employees who worked shifts outside the regular work day. The books provided an opportunity for employees within the division who desired a more in-depth understanding of quality and its applications. To further assist employees with implementing quality within their work environments, "quality forums" were offered. The forums were designed to update the employees on the new developments of the division's quality initiatives.

Front-Line Employees' Perception of Implementing CQI

The study's purpose was to investigate the factors related to how front-line employees within the Office of Business and Administration at Ohio State University perceive their managers' commitment toward implementing CQI on the job. Of specific interest, the study explored the relationship between middle managers' perceived knowledge and skills of and commitment toward CQI and front-line employees' perception of their managers' commitment toward implementing CQI on the job.

Research Design

The research design selected for this study was a combination of descriptive and correlational survey designs (Campbell and Stanley, 1966). The purpose of descriptive research is to accurately describe the characteristics of subjects and to report the way things are. Descriptive research is also concerned with the assessments of attitudes, opinions, demographic information, conditions, and procedures. Objective one was achieved by using the descriptive methodology. Correlational research, on the other hand, investigates possible relationships among variables without trying to influence those variables. The major purpose of correlational research is to study the relationship between two or more variables without any attempt to influence or manipulate them. Objectives two to four were achieved using the correla-tional methodology. Pearson Product Moment Correlation Coefficients were used to determine the magnitude of the relationships between the dependent variable and the independent variables.

Survey questionnaires are typical ways of gathering data for this type of research. Survey research allows the researcher to frame questions in a way to collect information and describe some characteristics from a large population. The independent variables are 1) middle managers' perceived knowledge, 2) front-line employees' perception of their own knowledge and skills of CQI, and 3) middle managers' commitment to implementing CQI on the job.

The extraneous variables are 1) front-line employees' attitude toward their managers and their job, and 2) front-line employees' and middle mangers' length of time on the job. The main dependent variable was the front-line employees' perceptions of middle managers' commitment toward implementing CQI on the job.

Population

To achieve this assessment, the on-the-job (OTJ) and middle managers' instruments were developed. Part one of the instrument consisted of three five-point Likert scale questions designed to collect information on front-line employees and middle managers' perception of their knowledge and skills of CQI. Part two of the instrument has five questions based on five-point semantic differential scales used to measure employees' attitudes toward their jobs and their manager. Part three of the instrument was designed to measure employees' overall perception of their management commitment as well as report the number of years employees have been on the job. Both instruments were similar except the middle-management instrument contained an additional 21 open-ended questions. The open-ended questions allowed the middle managers to respond in detail about their perceptions and knowledge of CQI.

The OTJ instrument was administered to all the front-line employees and was designed to measure the employees' perceived knowledge and skills of CQI. The instrument also provides data on employees' attitudes toward their departments, the division, and their managers. Additionally, the instrument gathers information about employees' familiarity of CQI and other demographic information (for instance, number of years on the job). The survey is presented as figure 1.

Figure 1. On-the-job CQI survey.

**The Ohio State University
Division of Business and Administration
On-the-Job CQI Survey**

Please complete this survey whether or not you have participated in any CQI training. Your opinion is very important. Please be frank in your responses. No information you share will be linked with your name in any way. THANKS!

1. Which ONE of the following sentences best describes what you know about CQI? (Circle the letter of the sentence.)

   a. I really do not have any idea what CQI is.
   b. I have somewhat of an idea of what CQI is.
   c. I have a general understanding of CQI.
   d. I have a good understanding of CQI.
   e. I have an excellent understanding of CQI.

2. Rate the following situations which you may be CURRENTLY experiencing in your job. (Circle one number for each situation.)

	Not a Problem		Somewhat of a Problem		A Real Problem
a. co-workers argue/many conflicts	1	2	3	4	5
b. boss's words and actions don't match	1	2	3	4	5
c. decision-making slow	1	2	3	4	5
d. most employees not involved in decision making	1	2	3	4	5
e. not much communication up and down the line	1	2	3	4	5
f. solving problems is confusing; sometimes full of conflict	1	2	3	4	5
g. important information is not always shared with everyone	1	2	3	4	5

3. Indicate your agreement or disagreement with each of the following statements. (Circle one number for each.)

	Strongly Disagree	Disagree	Neutral	Agree	Strongly Agree
a. Employees in my department could improve a lot in working together.	1	2	3	4	5
b. Customer service is the major focus in my department.	1	2	3	4	5
c. The quality of the outputs in my department can vary quite a bit.	1	2	3	4	5
d. Quality is very important in my department.	1	2	3	4	5
e. My department shares in decision-making activities.	1	2	3	4	5
f. Employees in my department don't seem to care very much lately.	1	2	3	4	5
g. Even if employees wanted to follow CQI principles, my boss wouldn't be encouraging.	1	2	3	4	5
h. Employees in my department work together to solve problems.	1	2	3	4	5
i. In my department, we do not use a good process to solve problems.	1	2	3	4	5
j. Things appear to be changing for the better in my department.	1	2	3	4	5
k. The leadership in my department is committed to quality.	1	2	3	4	5
l. My department has the attitude that it can always improve customer service.	1	2	3	4	5
m. In my department, customer satisfaction is not that important.	1	2	3	4	5
n. In my department, "the left hand never knows what the right hand is doing."	1	2	3	4	5
o. Communication is a problem in my department.	1	2	3	4	5

continued on page 162

Figure 1. On-the-job CQI survey (continued).

4. Mark your feelings about your job by circling a number between each of the pairs of words.

MY JOB

BAD	1	2	3	4	5	GOOD
UNFAIR	1	2	3	4	5	FAIR
WORST	1	2	3	4	5	BEST
BORING	1	2	3	4	5	FUN
HATE	1	2	3	4	5	LOVE
UNIMPORTANT	1	2	3	4	5	IMPORTANT

5. Mark your feelings about your department by circling a number between each of the pairs of words.

MY DEPARTMENT

BAD	1	2	3	4	5	GOOD
UNFAIR	1	2	3	4	5	FAIR
APART	1	2	3	4	5	TOGETHER
BORING	1	2	3	4	5	FUN
HATE	1	2	3	4	5	LOVE
UNIMPORTANT	1	2	3	4	5	IMPORTANT

6. Mark your feelings about your boss by circling a number between each of the pairs of words.

MY BOSS

BAD	1	2	3	4	5	GOOD
UNFAIR	1	2	3	4	5	FAIR
INCOMPLETE	1	2	3	4	5	COMPLETE
UNABLE	1	2	3	4	5	ABLE
HATE	1	2	3	4	5	LOVE
UNIMPORTANT	1	2	3	4	5	IMPORTANT

7. Mark your feelings about your co-workers by circling a number between each of the pairs of words.

MY CO-WORKERS

BAD	1	2	3	4	5	GOOD
STRANGE	1	2	3	4	5	FAMILIAR
SAD	1	2	3	4	5	HAPPY
BORING	1	2	3	4	5	FUN
HATE	1	2	3	4	5	LOVE
UNABLE	1	2	3	4	5	ABLE

8. Mark your feelings about the Division of Business and Administration by circling a number for each of the pairs of words.

THE DIVISION OF BUSINESS AND ADMINISTRATION

BAD	1	2	3	4	5	GOOD
UNFAIR	1	2	3	4	5	FAIR
UNORGANIZED	1	2	3	4	5	ORGANIZED
WORST	1	2	3	4	5	BEST
UNIMPORTANT	1	2	3	4	5	IMPORTANT

9. When they happen, how often are you INVITED to participate in the following activities in your department?

	Never	Rarely	Sometimes	Often	Almost Always
a. Reading written communications from department leadership	1	2	3	4	5
b. Writing communications for others within the department to read	1	2	3	4	5

continued on page 164

Figure 1. On-the-job CQI survey (continued).

c.	Being on a work team	1	2	3	4	5
d.	During decision-making, being consulted by leadership as to your opinion	1	2	3	4	5
e.	Participating as an "equal" in decision making	1	2	3	4	5
f.	Participating in a group problem-solving process	1	2	3	4	5
g.	Attending an on-the-job training session	1	2	3	4	5
h.	Other _____	1	2	3	4	5
i.	Other _____	1	2	3	4	5

Thinking about your job in general terms, how would you compare your situation today with the past? N/A = Does not apply to me; I haven't been here that long.

	Yes, Much Worse	Yes, Worse	Things are the Same	Yes, Better	Yes, Much Better	N/A
10. Are "things" different in your JOB today than they were....						
a. several years ago?	1	2	3	4	5	N/A
b. last year?	1	2	3	4	5	N/A
11. Are "things" different in your DEPARTMENT today than they were...						
a. several years ago?	1	2	3	4	5	N/A
b. last year?	1	2	3	4	5	N/A
12. Are "things" different in the DIVISION of BUSINESS & ADMINISTRATION today than they were...						
a. several years ago?	1	2	3	4	5	N/A
b. last year?	1	2	3	4	5	N/A

	Yes, Much Worse	Yes, Worse	Things are the Same	Yes, Better	Yes, Much Better	N/A

13. Are "things" different at OSU today than they were...

	Yes, Much Worse	Yes, Worse	Things are the Same	Yes, Better	Yes, Much Better	N/A
a. several years ago?	1	2	3	4	5	N/A
b. last year?	1	2	3	4	5	N/A

14. Now, think about your department over the last year. Mark your agreement or disagreement with the following statements.

	Strongly Disagree	Disagree	Neutral	Agree	Strongly Agree
a. Communication within my department has seemed to improve.	1	2	3	4	5
b. Employees appear to be arguing more among themselves.	1	2	3	4	5
c. Work is going much smoother.	1	2	3	4	5
d. Deadlines are being met most of the time.	1	2	3	4	5
e. Quality of service seems to be sliding downhill.	1	2	3	4	5
f. People in general appear to be happier in their jobs.	1	2	3	4	5
g. Problems are not getting solved.	1	2	3	4	5
h. Employees are consulted more than they used to be about decisions being made.	1	2	3	4	5
i. Bosses are less friendly than before.	1	2	3	4	5
j. There seems to be more confusion than usual.	1	2	3	4	5
k. Conflicts are solved more easily than they used to be.	1	2	3	4	5

continued on page 166

Figure 1. On-the-job CQI survey (continued).

Thinking about your own work situation and your answers to this survey, what kinds of "help" could the leadership of Business and Administration offer to employees like yourself? (Circle ALL that apply to you.)

15. I WOULD LIKE TRAINING OR INFORMATION ABOUT...

    a. conflict management

    b. work skills

    c. communication

    d. balancing work and family

    e. quality control

    f. other _____

16. I WOULD LIKE BETTER FACILITIES FOR...

    a. working

    b. taking breaks

    c. recreation

    d. friendly conversations

    e. personal needs

    f. other _____

17. I WOULD LIKE BETTER RESOURCES FOR...

    a. my work

    b. my physical workplace

    c. break areas

    d. other _____

18. OTHER IDEAS?

a. _____

b. _____

c. _____

d. _____

e. _____

19. Please share the following information about yourself.

a. What is your job classification (front line, supervisor, etc.)? _____

b. What is your department? _____

c. How many years have you been in this job? _____ years

d. How many years, total, have you been with OSU? _____ years

20. About how many of your co-workers in your department have already completed the five-day CQI training? (Circle your best guess.)

Less Than 25%   25%   50%   75%   Almost All   100%

21. Has your direct supervisor completed the five-day CQI training? (Circle your answer.)

YES   NO   I DON'T KNOW

22. What level of commitment do you think your supervisor has toward implementing CQI? (Circle one number.)

NONE   SOME   MUCH
  1   2   3   4   5

23. Have you completed the five-day CQI training yet? (Circle your answer.)

YES   NO   I AM CURRENTLY IN THE TRAINING

continued on page 168

Figure 1. On-the-job CQI survey (continued).

If YES, please answer the following:

23a. About how long ago did you complete the five-day training? _____ months

23b. What 1-2 things (if any) are you personally doing differently on the job, as a result of your CQI training?

_____

_____

24. What level of commitment would you say you have to implementing CQI? (Circle one number.)

NONE		SOME		MUCH
1	2	3	4	5

25. What other ideas or comments would you like to share about…

CQI?

YOUR JOB?

YOUR DEPARTMENT?

ANYTHING ELSE?

THANKS FOR COMPLETING THIS SURVEY!

Content validity was determined by soliciting the support of the stakeholder panel. The stakeholder group is a panel of informed customers consisting of managers, front-line employees, and internal and external customers of B&A. The stakeholder group's major functions were to identify evaluation questions, assess and draft instruments that would answer the questions, make decisions about data collection techniques, review the pilot study data, and recommend changes on instruments. The stakeholder team helped to develop the instrument. Step one consisted of generating all possible questions that the stakeholder team might want to ask on the instrument. A total of 94 different questions led to the next step. A synthesis of the trends helped guide the development of the final instrument. Finally, the research team developed proposed operational definitions for all the variables. The final instrument was much more comprehensive than needed for this study.

The content of the final instrument was assessed by a panel of experts and a field test. The panel consisted of experts in CQI and measurement. The panel was given a month to determine the completeness of the content and the appropriateness of the language used. The field test included a similar review by persons representing the proposed populations for the study. There were six individuals who reviewed the instrumentation for face validity and content validity. Results of the panel and field test were used to modify the instrumentation.

Pilot Study Summary

A pilot test was conducted to determine the reliability of the OTJ instrument. The reliability of summated scales was determined using Cronbach's Alpha procedure. The instruments were administered to an existing class of employees who were entering their first day of a five-day CQI training class (N = 70). The class completed the instrument as a part of their CQI training. The instruments were examined to ensure that they were accurately completed. Instruments that were less than half complete were not used. Fewer than 10 of the instruments returned were not usable. Data were entered and analyzed using SPSS PC for Windows.

As a result of the pilot analysis, no questions were removed or reworded. The instrument was deemed valid and reliable and ready for use with the study. The data were analyzed as one specific group (class).

Data Collection

Data were collected over a six-month period. The instruments were administered on site by the researchers who attended a special middle managers' meeting for each department within B&A. The special meeting with the managers was divided into three parts. First, the managers were given a brief lecture on the purpose of the study. The managers were then given an opportunity to ask questions. Second, the middle managers were give 45 minutes to complete the instruments. The evaluation team was present during the entire time. After the instruments were completed, the managers were given a ten-minute break. Third, the managers were asked to identify one person in each of their areas who was viewed as "trustworthy" by their peers, to disseminate the OTJ instruments. To ensure the possibility for a high response rate from front-line employees, the instruments were given to a peer within this group (not the supervisor) to monitor the completion. The designated person(s) within these departments was asked to collect the instruments from each person in his or her area or department. The names and phone numbers of each person responsible for disseminating the OTJ instruments were given to the evaluation team for follow-up. The employees were given a total of two weeks to complete the instruments.

The instruments were collected on site once they were completed. The belief is that employees did perceive the process to be confidential and responded to the questions to the best of their abilities, leaving little concern that the data were skewed by the data collection process. Ongoing follow-up for those who did not complete the instrument was achieved by communicating with the designated persons from each department. A follow-up memo was sent by the research team to all managers, reminding them of the deadline date to return instruments. Given the confidentiality of the instruments collected, there was not an identification code on the instruments; thus, no follow-up with nonrespondents was conducted. The total number of instruments received from middle managers was 86. The total number of front-line employee instruments returned was 732.

At least 50 percent of the instruments needed to be completed to be included in the assessment. The final number of 818 middle managers and front-line employees was used for the data analysis. Choosing this form of data collection achieved two goals: 1) allowed for the highest possible return rates from those participating in the study, and 2) made the completion of the instrument easy and comfortable for both front-line and management.

Data Analysis

Appropriate statistics were used to analyze, organize, and summarize the data for each of the objectives. First, preliminary descriptive statistics were run to verify the integrity of the data. All data that were not usable were coded as missing data. The variables that were reverse coded were recoded for consistency in scoring. Variables consisting of more than one item were combined to create a summated variable. Middle managers' means by department were determined and placed with the appropriate front-line employees' file.

For objective one, descriptive statistics were used to organize the data. Frequency distributions, cumulative distributions, means, standard deviations, percentages, and cumulative percentages were used to describe the independent variables.

Front-Line Employees' Perceptions of Managers' Commitment To Implementing CQI on the Job

Overall, employees viewed their managers as having moderate to high commitment in implementing CQI on the job. Only 61 employees felt that their managers would not be supportive if they wanted to follow CQI principles. More than 270 employees felt that management was committed to quality, whereas only 50 said that their managers were not committed to quality. Surprisingly, many employees felt that managers were moderately interested in implementing CQI on the job. This disparity suggests that managers may be knowledgeable of CQI, but are unsure of how to implement its principles. This may also suggest that managers may need ongoing training to assist them in understanding the importance of their role when implementing CQI.

Managers must understand the critical role they play in the workplace. The literature review suggests the traditional role of managers, which focuses on planning, controlling, staffing, and directing their employees. Modern day organizational development theorists (Seymour, 1989; Deming, 1986; Juran, 1988; Crosby, 1989) recommend focusing managerial energy on the four Cs: coaching, consulting, cheerleading, and coordinating. These competencies will help managers to learn the following new skills:

- use management by walking around in order to build relationships and stay in touch without being a spy
- transfer complex knowledge
- redesign organizational systems to align with the values of team work and quality
- build strong and lasting alliances with others

- catalyze action without taking responsibility for the work
- build shared vision
- manage interconnectedness with a self-directed environment.

There are at least four major obstacles that prevent managers from implementing CQI on the job: priority, resistance, skill, and arrogance (Brown, 1992). In the day-to-day functions of managers, quality has yet to become a priority. Many have not assimilated into practicing CQI because the principles are simply not a priority for them. CQI cannot and will not be achieved in any organization without a drastic change in management philosophy. Managers must adopt a new philosophy in how they view the customers and how they examine employee involvement in transforming the organization. Second, many managers are resistant to changing their way of managing. To assist managers in getting over the obstacle of resistance, Brown, Hitchcock, and Willard (1993) offer many suggestions in their book, *Why TQM Fails:*

1. Establish an employment policy emphasizing that everyone's role will change but that no one will lose his or her job due to this change.
2. Sell the need more than the solution. Make sure that everyone understands the pressures of the underlying change.
3. Take managers on site visits to other organizations that are further along in the transformation process. There they will learn from disinterested peers that, although the change was difficult, the new role is far more rewarding.
4. Help everyone define a new, inspiring role for him- or herself. Employees should be involved in the redesign of their own jobs.
5. Provide additional training so that they can be taught the skills they will need when they will most need them and have time to practice and get feedback on the job.
6. Implement meetings where employees can learn from each other. These meetings may come in the form of informal focus groups.
7. Use active, creative training techniques that draw managers in despite their resistance.

Third, few managers have the necessary skills to implement quality on the job. Much of the training managers are provided does not relate the CQI to their roles as managers. Finally, managers' arrogance is reported to play a critical role in their willingness to implement CQI. Managers routinely underestimate the amount of changing they themselves must do. Organizations must set into motion escalating opportunities for managers to get feedback on their performance.

Recommendations for Practice

1. If CQI is to have a positive impact, front-line employees must feel that their managers are committed to fully implementing CQI on the job. Business and Administration must begin to measure management commitment in more practical ways. Managers' commitment must be measured not only by the amount of money saved, but by the amount of quality time spent with front-line employees. Managers must spend time with customers and constantly probe how customers are feeling about services received from their departments.

2. Front-line employees must feel that their managers are invested in their roles. Managers must re-evaluate how they spend their time. Managers should spend more time evaluating the effectiveness of the CQI initiatives. Front-line employees will begin to feel more content about their managers' commitment if they actually witness the sincerity of their managers' efforts.

3. Managers need to make a concerted effort to include front-line employees in decision making within their departments. One way this can be accomplished is to develop a communication system that would first ensure that information about decisions is disseminated widely throughout the organization. Second, managers could review the impact that these decisions will have on individuals within the organization.

Given the current flux and transformation that higher education is experiencing, it is imperative that every facet of the organization be involved in meeting the challenge. The leaders within higher education will play a critical role in ensuring that they are committed to transforming the university while implementing CQI. Additionally, employees will need to play a critical role in the transformation process. This means that managers will have to change the way they manage to ensure that an organizational climate is developed that will include the knowledge and skills of all employees.

Questions for Discussion

1. What are the skills needed for those who are currently training to take on key leadership roles for the new millennium?

2. How might universities begin to implement leadership training programs to better prepare leaders to take on the challenges of higher education?

3. How might leaders and employees of the academy work together to ensure there is a shared quality improvement model in place for the organization?

4. What behaviors should leaders demonstrate to ensure that employees understand their level of commitment toward quality improvement within and throughout the organization?

The Author

Lee Jones serves as the associate dean for Academic Affairs and associate professor in the Department of Educational Leadership at the Florida State University. Prior to his current role, he served as director for the Division of Multicultural Affairs and assistant professor of Educational Leadership at Washington State University. He also served as assistant to the vice president for business and administration for continuous quality improvement at Ohio State University. A prolific speaker, Jones has been invited to speak around the country on leadership development. He is the host and producer of the Your Voice television talk show, which airs in Florida and reaches more than 4 million viewers. Jones has received more than 150 awards for his leadership in several academic, social, civic, and community affiliations. His motto is the Bottom Line is Results, Anything Else is Rhetoric.

References

Abernethy, P.E. and R.W. Serfass. (1992). "One District's Quality Improvement Story," *Educational Leadership, 50*(3), 14–17.

Anderson, M. (1993). "Impostors in the Temple." *The Review of Education,* 15(3-4), 317–321.

Argyris, C. (1974). *Theory in Practice: Increasing Professional Effectiveness.* San Francisco: Jossey-Bass.

Austin, J.S. (1985). "Comparative Career Accomplishments of Two Decades of Women and Men Doctoral Graduates in Education." *Research in Higher Education, 22*(3), 219–249.

Bogue, G., and R. Saunders. (1992). *The Evidence of Quality.* San Francisco: Jossey-Bass.

Bowers, C.A. (1985). "Culture Against Itself: Nihilism as An Element in Recent Educational Thought." *American Journal of Education, 93*(4), 465–490.

Brown, H. (1992). "Staff Development in Higher Education—Towards the Learning Organization?" *Higher Education Quarterly,* 46, 174–190.

Brown, M.G., D.E. Hitchcock, and M.L. Willard. (1994). *Why TQM Fails.* Burr Ridge, IL: Irwin Professional Publishing.

Campbell, D.T., and J.C. Stanley. (1966). *Experimental and Quasi-Experimental Design.* Boston: Houghton Mifflin.

Collard, E.F.N. (1993). "The Impact of Deming Quality Management on Interdepartmental Cooperation." *Human Resource Development Quarterly, 4*(1), 71–79.

Cornesky, R.A. (1992). *Using Deming to Improve Quality in Colleges and Universities.* Madison, WI: Magna Publications, Inc.

Cornesky, R., S. McCool, L. Byrnes, and R. Weber. (1991). *Implementing Total Quality Management in Higher Education.* Madison, WI: Magna Publications Inc.

Crosby, P.B. (1989). *Let's Talk About Quality: 96 Questions You Always Wanted to Ask Phil Crosby.* New York: McGraw-Hill.

Danne, D.J. (1993). *Total Quality Management in Industry and its Implications for Secondary Education (Education Restructuring).* Doctoral dissertation, Pepperdine University, 1992. Dissertation Abstracts International, 54/02A. University Microfilms, No.9316428.

Deming, W. (1989). "Out of the Crisis." *The American School Board Journal, 176,* 28+.

Deming, W.E. (1986). *Out of Crisis.* Cambridge, MA: The Massachusetts Institute of Technology, Center for Advanced Engineering Study.

Denny, A. (1982). *An Oration Delivered at Worcester.* Worcester, MA.

Galbraith, M.W. (1987). "Readership Survey Evokes Association Response. (American Association for Adult and Continuing Education)." *Lifelong Learning, 10,* 10–14.

Hittman, J.A. (1993). "TQM and CQI in Postsecondary Education." *Quality Progress, 26*(10), 77–80.

Holt, M. (1993). "Deming on Education." Phi Delta Kappan, 75(4), 329–330.

Juran, J.M. (1988). *Juran Planning for Quality.* New York: The Free Press.

Keith, S. and R.H. Girling. (1991). "Education, Management, and Participation." *Educational Evaluation & Policy Analysis, 13,* 203–205.

Kerr, C. (1998). "Clark Kerr's Perspective on Leadership Challenges." *Change, 30,* 10–11.

Kirk, P. (1987). "Young Exam for Old Heads." *The Times Higher Education Supplement, 778,* 17.

Lewis, J., Jr. (1993). *Leadership Styles.* Arlington, VA: American Association of School Administrators.

Lewis, R.G., and D.H. Smith. (1994). *Total Quality in Higher Education.* Delray Beach, FL: St. Lucie Press.

Rhodes, L.K. (1992). "Readers and Writers with a Difference." *The Reading Teacher, 46,* 163–164.

Schein, B.E. (1980). *Following the Way: The Setting of John's Gospel.* Minneapolis, MN: Augsburg Publishing House.

Seymour, D. (1989). *Causing Quality in Higher Education.* New York: McGraw-Hill.

Sink, C.V. (1992). "Education for Employment." *National Business Education Yearbook,* 1992, 159–166.

Teeter, D.J., and J.P. Lozier (editors). (1993). "Pursuit of Quality in Higher Education: Case Studies in Total Quality Management." *New Directions For Institutional Research, 15*(2).

A Leadership Education
and Dialogue Model:
Creating a Learning Organization for
Continuous Leadership Development

University of North Carolina Health Care

Donna L. Kaye

As the title suggests, this case describes the conditions leading up to, and the implementation of, a new model for continuous leadership development. Past experience with a 360-degree developmental feedback pilot, and guiding principles established by an internal learning organization, had identified the need for a new leadership development model that allowed for partnership and accountability between new leaders and their managers and staff. By treating the expectations of staff as valid data to be acted upon in the external environment, we learned that leaders are better able to live competencies such as creating a customer service environment and fostering teamwork. We also learned about the importance of creating vehicles and processes that inculcate the concept of leader as teacher and employee as customer. For example, the competency of "foster teamwork" is lived by requiring participating leaders to meet with their managers and staff before a class intervention to obtain perceptions of team and operational performance. After class, leaders are also expected to meet with staff to share back the analyzed data and partner with them to put an action plan into practice. Often these action plans include working with teams to clarify goals or involve them in implementing new initiatives. The case highlights two specific programs in which this education and dialogue model have been implemented.

If you have had any encounter with the medical system, you know that health care has been in the midst of major changes. As a consumer we feel the impact when we have to choose among health main-

This case was prepared to serve as a basis for discussion rather than to illustrate either effective or ineffective administrative and management practices.

tenance organization (HMO) plans, when our hospital stays are much shorter, and when procedures that would normally take place in a hospital are now done at outpatient facilities. For the health-care industry as a whole, and for University of North Carolina (UNC) Health Care in particular, the following transition is occurring (table 1).

Organizational Profile

At UNC Health Care, these transitions manifest themselves in several ways, ranging from UNC Hospitals' formal merger with UNC School of Medicine physician group in October 1998 to become UNC Health Care to the expansion of satellite clinics, the increase in joint ventures with other health care institutions, and the increased percentage of revenue coming from HMO contracts. The mission of UNC Health Care is to provide high quality patient care, educate health-care professionals, advance health research, and provide community service. It is a public academic medical center operated by and for the people of North Carolina. UNC Health Care includes a 684-bed complex at the UNC campus in Chapel Hill, North Carolina, and 18 satellite clinics. More than 4,000 health-care staff are employed, in addition to 883 physicians and 544 residents.

Background

In response to the market forces mentioned above, the top leadership at UNC Hospitals established the following six strategic quality goals in 1996 and identified key strategies for goal attainment: 1. enhance patient satisfaction and consistently exceed benchmarked average

Table 1. Health-care transition.

From	To
Acute inpatient care	Outpatient care
Fee for service	Managed care; capitation
Separate delivery systems	Integrated care and financing
Quality assurance to satisfy regulators	Total quality to satisfy market
Unaware of costs	Cost conscious

2. enhance staff satisfaction

3. measure, assess, and improve patient outcomes and cost-effectiveness to provide the best value in health-care services

4. establish a responsive environment for all caregivers and network partners

5. elevate the public visibility and image of UNC Hospitals statewide

6. become more managed care ready and responsive.

Through collection of employee relations data, exit surveys, and employee roundtable discussions with the chief operating officer, it was clear the employees were not receiving full communication from their direct supervisors about important institutional changes. Additionally, some employees were dissatisfied with their level of input into decision making, their relationship with their immediate supervisor, and with the overall work environment. The management council, comprising the top 16 executives, believed that a satisfied staff is likely to give exceptional service to patients and other customers, as well as have higher productivity and increased accomplishments. Furthermore, the management council postulated that providing more and better leadership training would improve the leadership skills of supervisors in communicating with staff, empower people to make improvements, and develop the full capability of staff. UNC Hospitals did have in place a supervisory training program, but it was not linked strategically with the current institutional goals.

The Charge

Thus, the management council directed the human resource development department (HRD) to enhance its supervisory training to better link with the new institutional goals. Because HRD is responsible for organizational development in addition to training, the department brought forth a systems perspective based on data from its extensive consulting work within the organization on team building, change management, and strategic planning. In its proposal to the management council, HRD helped to reframe the initial charge of "enhancing a supervisory program" by proposing a leadership development plan and not just a class-based curriculum. Based on data from the extensive needs assessment that HRD conducted, and coupled with the changing pressures occurring in health care as mentioned earlier, the plan was designed to address the full leadership system, and not just a "fix the first-line supervisor approach." Using this definition, there are 500 current leaders. Approximately 70 new leaders are hired or promoted each year.

Development and Implementation

Below is a chronology of how a common vision and action plan was realized.

A. Review of Current Data (March-June 1997)

1. The 360-degree developmental feedback pilot involved 24 supervisors and managers from five departments and data from 178 other staff who completed survey forms. The developmental needs were aggregated and formed the basis for a competency identification survey.

2. Exit Survey Data. Reviewed reasons why people were leaving: key factors included poor morale, ineffective communication between supervisors and staff, and limited advancement opportunities.

3. Employee Roundtable Minutes. Employees are randomly invited in groups of 10-15 to meet with the chief operating officer to discuss issues that are on their minds. Data from these meetings confirmed the other data already mentioned.

B. Create Competency Identification Survey (May 1997)

A survey of 34 competencies was given to people from executive, middle, first-line, and staff positions across the hospital to prioritize. These competencies were adapted from the management competencies models put forth by Personnel Decisions Inc. and Development Dimensions International.

C. Benchmark With Other Institutions (June-July 1997)

Five hospitals were surveyed. The main finding was that most hospitals had some type of management orientation program in which an overview of leadership philosophy and core knowledge was covered, and that other hospitals tended to mandate training for leaders and require more training hours than we did.

D. Obtain Input for the Hospital's Learning Organization (June-July 1997)

Under the leadership of the director of human resources, an informal organization was formed called the Learning Organization. It comprised department directors, educators, and other staff members from across the institution who wanted to discuss creative new learning strategies to meet current hospital challenges.

E. Draft the Plan (September 1997)

The prioritized competencies were then crafted into a UNC Hospitals Leadership Model (figure 1). With these competencies and a set of guiding principles in mind, four overall plan objectives were established:

1. Orient new leaders (for instance, supervisors, managers, and department heads) to health care and the expectations the UNC Hospitals has of them

2. Enable leaders to use resources to efficiently work hospital administrative systems and to effectively manage human resource issues so that staff are treated within the letter and spirit of hospital policies and values

Figure 1. Leadership competency model.

3. Provide tools to diagnose system weaknesses and staff performance problems that can be addressed in partnership with staff
4. Create a work environment that fosters customer responsiveness, teamwork, and staff satisfaction.

F. Present Draft Plan back to Learning Organization (October 1997)

A rough draft of the leadership development plan was presented back to the Learning Organization group for their feedback.

G. Present Plan Proposal to Management Council For Approval (December 1997)

HRD proposed that the courses that were to support the overall leadership plan objectives be part of a required leadership curriculum. In addition, HRD requested that the management council participate in the leadership plan and even co-instruct the management orientation program. Because so much feedback had been solicited throughout the process, which was already based on solid needs assessment data, the proposal easily gained approval. The recommendations were presented in check list format to assure clarity of sign-off on particular items. (Table 2 provides a full description of complete leadership development curriculum.)

Key Strategies and Highlights
360-degree Developmental Feedback Pilot

Our goal in launching the 360-degree developmental feedback pilot was to improve the effectiveness of leaders and to create better teamwork through improved communication between management and staff. Although we noted an increase in communication and teamwork between the different levels of management because the 360-degree feedback was done with in-tact management teams (for instance, a director and her reporting supervisors/managers), the impact on front-line staff was less dramatic than expected.

Though participating leaders were expected to create a development plan that was to be shared with their supervisor, and encouraged to share with their staff, many leaders kept their feedback data internal. After all, the 360-degree feedback was developmental in nature and not used as part of the performance appraisal process. Therefore, leaders had full control of what or how much data they wanted to share. There were some leaders who did choose to share their data and/or their action plan with their staff, and, in those cases, the leaders reported more open communication between themselves and staff, and more staff involvement with decision making.

Table 2. Leadership development program summary.

I. REQUIRED COURSES

Overview Session for Management Orientation

This session is for the supervisors of the leaders who attend the Management Orientation Program.
One of the competencies for leaders at UNC Hospitals is acquiring organizational knowledge about key administrative processes. As a way of helping new leaders acquire this critical knowledge, an Organizational Knowledge Assessment was developed. This assessment consists of a set of open-ended questions on critical knowledge areas. These open-ended questions are designed to promote analytical thinking. The process of new leaders dialoging with their supervisors about the answers to the assessment will encourage the learning of important information. Supervisors of new leaders can also provide additional clarification and linkages to other available resources to create a customized development plan for new leaders. Resource tools such as on-line self study, mentoring, the Hospitals Business Practices Manual, HR coaching sessions, and classes will be available.

Management Orientation Program

The purpose of this program is to help new leaders *(department heads, managers, and supervisors)* get off to a good start, and to serve as a refresher for current leaders. The program provides leaders with the "big picture" view of our financial and market situation. Leadership competencies and expected responsibilities that the institution has of its leaders are stated. Participants develop plans for creating a more productive and satisfying work environment based on input from their supervisor and staff. And to help new leaders enhance their knowledge about administrative processes, an Organizational Knowledge Assessment is used as a tool which encourages dialogue between leaders and their supervisors. Participants also view skits that highlight important human resource policies and procedures and receive a comprehensive overview of the functional human resource areas.

Program Agenda
1. Welcome
2. True/False quiz about health-care business environment
3. UNC Hospitals' leadership expectations (leadership competencies)
4. Analysis of expectations and needs data from supervisor and staff
5. Create a plan and a communication strategy to address departmental needs
6. Organizational Knowledge Assessment overview
7. Human resource services departmental overview
8. Overview of human resource Website
9. Important information on key human resource functional areas: recruitment, position and compensation management, employee records, employee and management services
10. Evaluation and wrap up

Optimizing Staff Performance (Supervisor In Transition)

In this program, action planning begun in the Management Orientation Program to create a more productive and satisfying work environment is continued by having the leaders reassess their staff needs that were identified previously. Practical communication strategies for supporting staff and dealing with individual performance issues are provided and practiced. Leaders learn to work with their staff to diagnose the level of staff competence and commitment and address those issues by using the Situational Leadership Model. Leaders also use group problem-solving techniques to identify strategies for addressing challenges that they currently encounter in their work settings.

continued on page 184

Table 2. Leadership development program summary (continued).

Quality Leadership

The program helps to increase the leader's knowledge of CQI problem-solving methodologies and analytical tools. The Joiner 7-step problem-solving model is used and specific CQI tools such as brainstorming, flow charting, nominal group technique, cause and effect diagramming, and Pareto principle are taught within interactive case study approach. Meeting facilitation skills such as active listening, group facilitation, and constructive feedback are used to provide leaders with a model of how to run effective problem-solving meetings. Leaders also work on an action plan where they are to involve their staff in the improvement of a work process.

EEO Institute

The three-day program is offered by the Office of State Personnel. It provides an understanding of the federal EEO laws and regulations, as well as North Carolina laws and general statutes. Methods to build a repertoire of practical methods to overcome cultural barriers and manage workplace diversity are also covered. Participants also learn to interview effectively in situations involving potential discrimination on the basis of age, sex, ethnic origin, or disability.

II. SUGGESTED COURSES

Leadership and TeamWorking*

The goal of this program is to create sustained increases in the performance of work teams. Participating leaders gain insight into their leadership style and assess the development needs and staff satisfaction of their work teams. Team concepts and skills in team building that are common to high performing teams are discussed and practiced such as: clarifying the team's purpose, negotiating empowerment, building relationships and communication, promoting flexibility, optimizing performance, creating recognition and appreciation, and boosting morale.

Through diagnostic assessments, leaders can identify their team member needs and then implement specific action plans. Experts have shown, and our work here at UNC Hospitals has confirmed, that organizational learning is more effective and sustained when it is done within a work unit and by the leader. Leaders in this program commit to conduct, with the help of human resource development if needed, just-in-time team building training modules. These training modules are customized to support the needs revealed in the various team assessments and can be conducted in one-hour segments. Leaders must agree to meet regularly with their teams until the team goals are achieved. Estimated work site training time is dependent on the individual team needs and can range anywhere from 8 - 20 hours over the course of six months.

New Employee Orientation Overview

Any leader who is interested in what is covered in the "New Employee Orientation Program" is invited to attend this class. The philosophy and format of New Employee Orientation will be covered as well as the forms new employees are requested to complete. The program will also help leaders complement their departmental orientation accordingly.

Human Resources: Employee Relations In-Depth

Participants will be able to gain an in-depth understanding of the required documentation and required elements of the following HR policies: Corrective Action, Attendance and Tardiness, and Grievance and Mediation. Emphasis will also be placed on how to improve the ability to recognize and resolve employee performance issues.

Table 2. Leadership development program summary (continued).

Human Resources: Regulatory Compliance In-Depth

Participants learn to better address issues related to the following laws: the EEO (Equal Opportunity Act), ADA (Americans with Disability Act), and the FMLA (Family Medical Leave Act). The history and purpose of these laws will also be presented as well as how to determine eligibility. Practical examples will be given using a case study approach.

Human Resources: Operations In-Depth

In-depth coverage of recruitment and employment, classification and compensation, and maintenance of accurate employee records. Expectations when forwarding recruitment job classification requests will be discussed as well as how to update employee records through the PARM office.

Accessing HR Documents Online

In response to feedback on evaluation forms, this is a session devoted solely to hands-on training (using both the Hedrick and Hospital computer labs) for employees interested in online access of HR information. Participants receive an overview of the Internet as an information storage and retrieval tool, plus practical training in the use of our HR Intranet Home Page as well as Netscape as an Internet browser and use of Adobe Acrobat as a Netscape plug-in application.

Online Clearance Procedure Training

Participants can improve the efficiency of processing terminations by learning how to download and process HR forms from the Web.

*Adapted from Blanchard Training and Development's TeamWorking program.

Nonetheless, we learned something very important from this process. Participants noted that the most useful element of the developmental feedback process was the interaction and sharing of information among the in-tact management team. Through this dialogue, leaders were able to validate their strengths and developmental needs and learn about the perception of their co-workers. We realized that it was this external sharing of data that actually strengthened relationships and communication, and built trust within the management team.

The Learning Organization Drives New Leadership Model

This informal group was an outgrowth of an official affiliation with an organization known as the Learning Consortium. The consortium is composed of regionally based university and business organizations that have formed strategic partnerships for sharing training resources through collaboration. The consortium provides conferences, retreats, speakers, facilitators, and course offerings.

Because of its broad employee representation, we thought the use of the hospitals' Learning Organization as a group to prioritize the competencies identified in the needs assessment data, and to be a sounding board in developing the guiding principles for the Leadership Development Plan.

The meeting outcome was a prioritized list of leadership competencies and the establishment of five guiding principles. These guiding principles pointed the leadership development curriculum in a new direction that was more aligned with the institution's goals. As table 3 shows, these new directions illuminated a gap in our past approach to leadership development and gave further impetus to cre-

Table 3. A directional shift in the five guiding principles.

Guiding Principle	Past Program Approach	New Direction
Employee as customer	Driven by generic needs. Did not include formal way to get feedback from staff prior to or after the program	Leaders need feedback from staff to foster recognition of their developmental needs and summon commitment to address those needs
Assessment-driven, Individualized development	Standard curriculum; everyone covers the same material	Curriculum needs to be customized to leaders' specific needs
Leader as teacher	Human resource development is the main teacher. Leaders are not expected to formally "teach"	Leaders learn skills just by preparing to teach others, and learnings are more credible when staff see their leader developing their team in a just-in-time purposeful way
Think globally, act locally	Focused mostly on local/departmental level. Little emphasis on global business and financial environment	Leaders need a global perspective on current business challenges and strategic direction, as well as understanding their local departmental environment
Leadership inclusiveness	More stratified classroom experience where curriculum was geared more for front-line supervisors	Need to include people from diverse departments and job classifications in class to break down internal barriers and we/they thinking

ating a new leadership development plan where these principles could be put into action.

Emergence of a New Leadership Model

The insights gained from the 360-degree developmental feedback pilot, combined with the guiding principles and program direction established by the hospitals' Learning Organization, formed the basis for a new approach to the implementation of the Leadership Development Plan. The significance of the model was not so much a difference in the content (competencies, for instance), but in the living of that content. For example, the competency of "foster teamwork" is lived by requiring participating leaders to meet with their managers and staff before a class intervention to obtain perceptions of team and operational performance. After a class, leaders are also expected to meet with staff to share back the analyzed data and partner with them to put an action plan into practice. Often these action plans include working with teams to clarify goals or involve them in the implementing of new initiatives. All of our leadership development programs that make up the required curriculum follow the model illustrated and discussed in the next section.

Leadership Development Implementation Model

As you can see in figure 2, there is the iterative process of leaders collecting data from their external environment, analyzing that data internally and assessing their developmental needs, and then taking action based on that analysis and assessment in the external environment. This structure is based on our learnings and goals for leaders to value what their staff tell them about operations and the work environment. The guiding principles established by the learning organization helped to define the focus for the data collection and consequential action. Leader participants collect data about 1) others' (manager and staff) needs, expectations, and perceived operational strengths and 2) the organizational needs at the global and local level. Then, participants analyze the data and assess their developmental needs by comparing their capabilities versus the demands from the external environment. The participants take the action within three weeks after the class of setting personal development plans and involving others who are doing the operational work. The "others" are usually individual staff or work teams. Leaders may end up providing facilitation, teaching, or coaching as needed to implement their departmental action plan. Leaders are also expected to measure the impact of their actions on the organization.

Figure 2. Leadership development implementation model.

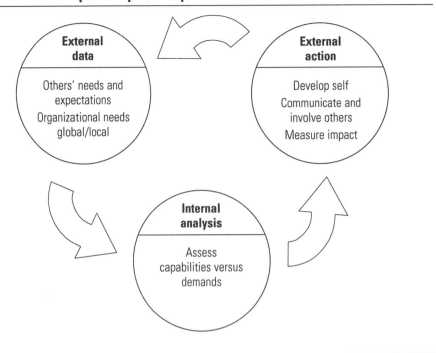

Management Orientation

This full-day program is required for people who are newly hired or promoted into a leadership role (those with responsibility for hiring, coaching, and appraising performance), and suggested for current leaders. The goal is to provide leaders with a global view of our financial and market situation, the leadership expectations the institution has of them, the knowledge and resources needed for administering key policies, and tools to create a more productive and satisfying work environment. Management council members co-facilitate this program with HRD staff (table 4 and table 5).

Overview Session for Management Orientation

This session is for the managers of the leaders who attend the Management Orientation Program. Briefly outlined in table 6, the program gives managers an overview of the objectives and explains their role of "leader as teacher" in the orienting of their new leader. It is really part of the larger management orientation program.

Table 4. Management orientation program.

External Data Components	Internal Analysis	External Action
Before class, leaders have their staff complete a "Staff Feedback Questionnaire" where staff list the top five departmental accomplishments during the past six months that they are most proud of, and list five expectations that staff have for future team accomplishments. Leaders also receive data from their managers on departmental goals and expectations.	Leaders compare the data from their manager and staff, and put together an action plan. Leaders also self-assess their need for additional classes in human resource and other administrative policies.	Leaders are expected to share back their analysis of the data with their staff and managers and begin to involve staff in working on key goals. Leaders also complete an Organizational Knowledge Assessment (a list of 20 key questions on key administrative and human resource policy areas) and discuss the answers with their managers. Assessment becomes a communication and learning tool about key administrative processes. Credit for the class is given only after proof of managers and leaders discussed the answers to the Organizational Knowledge Assessment

Optimizing Staff Performance

In this 8-hour required program, described in table 7, practical communication strategies for supporting staff in dealing with individual performance issues are provided and practiced. Leaders learn to work with their staff to diagnose the level of staff competence and commitment and address those issues by using Blanchard's Situational Leadership Model. Strategies for increasing staff satisfaction are also discussed.

Leadership and TeamWorking

This is a suggested four-day intensive program. The goal is to create sustained increases in the performance of work teams (table 8). Participating leaders gain insight into their leadership style and assess the developmental needs of their work teams. Team concepts and skills in team building that are common to high performing teams are discussed and practiced.

Table 5. Questionnaire formats used for manager/staff feedback.

Management Orientation Pre-Work
Manager Feedback Questionnaire

Leader/Participant _____

Department/Unit_____

In preparation for the upcoming Management Orientation Program, please have a dialogue with your supervisor to answer the following questions and record those comments on this sheet. Please bring the completed sheet with you to the Management Orientation Program.

What are the three most critical objectives that you have of my team/department over the next six months? How will progress on the objectives be evaluated?

What are the ways that we will give and receive feedback to each other as I work on these above objectives?

What are the key relationships that need to be managed with respect to these objectives?

Management Orientation Pre-Work
Staff Feedback Questionnaire

Leader/Participant _____

Department/Unit_____

In preparation for the upcoming Management Orientation Program I am to attend, please answer the following questions and return the completed sheet to me by _____. This information will help us to develop a plan to create a more productive and satisfying work environment.

1. **Please list the top five team/department accomplishments during the last six months that you are most proud of.**
   -
   -
   -
   -
   -

2. **Please list five of your expectations of what our team/department should be working on (i.e., customer satisfaction, work process improvement, work relationships/environment) over the next six months.**
   -
   -
   -
   -
   -

Table 6. Session for managers of the management orientation attendees.

External Data Component	Internal Analysis	External Action
Before the Management Orientation Program, the leaders' managers complete a questionnaire where they list the 5-8 most important expectations that they have for the department over the next six months.	During the session, the managers analyze the values and teachable points that they want to make explicit to their new leaders, as well as ways for the manager to get feedback from the new leader on how the orientation process is going.	After the Management Orientation Program, the manager is to act as "teacher" by discussing the new leader's answers to an Organizational Knowledge Assessment the new leader will receive in Management Orientation, but completes after the class.

Table 7. Optimizing staff performance.

External Data Component	Internal Analysis	External Action
Before the class, staff are asked to complete a 13-question staff satisfaction survey. Survey was developed in-house based on a literature search of satisfaction research.	During class, participants analyze trends from satisfaction survey and assess areas of satisfaction and areas of improvement. Leaders also analyze their personal leadership style.	After class, leaders share satisfaction survey analysis and verify with full staff or team. Leaders involve staff to celebrate what is working well and plan for how to increase staff satisfaction. Leaders are encouraged to repeat survey in six months to monitor effectiveness of intervention.

Table 8. Leadership and TeamWorking.

External Data Component	Internal Analysis	External Action
Before the class, HRD consultants meet with leaders and their managers to sign a contract of understanding about the program requirements to meet with one's staff on a continual basis to conduct just-in-time team training sessions. Participating leaders also have team members complete Blanchard's Team Development Stage Analysis Instrument.	Leaders analyze their team's stage of development and pinpoint specific team strengths and developmental needs. Leaders also take the Personal Profile and Blanchard's Team Leader Behavior Analysis instruments to identify their personality and team leadership style. Leaders practice conducting just-in-time training modules and get intensive feedback from class participants.	Leaders share back results of Team Development Stage Analysis. Leaders work with staff to set team development goals and then teach targeted just-in-time training modules to their intact teams on a continual basis.

Evaluation Model

We adopted Kirkpatricks's 4-level evaluation model, with particular emphasis on levels 2 and 3, the increase in skills and knowledge, and the impact on the department.

For each of the new programs, Management Orientation and Leadership and TeamWorking, we collected initial reaction data, and then did a postprogram follow-up evaluation in which we obtained feedback from participating leaders and their managers. The evaluation data also asked the leaders to comment on their individualized action plans and assess their progress to date.

Findings

As was true for both these new programs, their strength was in the dialogue between the leaders and their managers and between leaders and their staff. The following details the results that occurred from leaders taking subsequent action with full manager and staff team.

Management Orientation Program

Four sessions of the Management Orientation Program have been conducted to date—with a total of 66 participants. Also, four sessions of the overview session for management orientation with 17 participants (direct managers of leaders participating in the management orientation program) have been conducted. Immediate class feedback from all management orientation sessions was very positive. Overall class usefulness was rated as a 4.40 on a 5-point scale with 5 being most useful (see selected comments below). The most consistent suggestions were to have more in-depth human resource administration training, and more tools for creating a motivated and productive work environment. As a result, we expanded management orientation to a full day from its original half day. Some of the feedback:

- "Class was exceptionally well organized, informative, and interesting."
- "Human resource skits were great; helped clarify information."
- "Group discussions, sharing ideas, and tools were very helpful."
- "Meeting division director was helpful; put a face to a name."

A two-month postprogram evaluation revealed that 87 percent of the participants' managers found that the Management Orientation Program did, "to a great extent," better orient the participating leaders to UNC Hospitals. Seventy-four percent of participants indicated that they had increased the extent of their organizational knowledge. The most positive aspect of the Organizational Knowledge

Assessment proved to be the conversation between the participating leaders and their managers. "The Organizational Knowledge Assessment was the best. We worked at linking our department goals to the organizational goals, which provided the new supervisors with a clearer view of our departmental goals," claimed the manager of a program participant. Another manager described how the discussion of the Organizational Knowledge Assessment brought up issues and problem-solving ideas that the manager was initially not aware of.

Leadership and TeamWorking

Twenty-six leaders have participated from 19 different departments. Immediate postclass reaction revealed that 100 percent of the participants indicated they would "absolutely recommend this course to others." On average, the course received a 4.5 for overall usefulness of the course out of a 5 on a 5-point scale for "extremely useful." Some comments were:

- "I really believe that this program will certainly not only build individual work teams, but will help build institutional pride and purpose within the UNC Health Care System."
- "At first I thought four days away from work is a lot. After the first day, I realized no work is too important to avoid something (this workshop) that can improve our lives from this day forward."
- "This has been the best learning experience I have had while employed here. At no point did I get bored."

Most important, over half of the participants took active steps to teach and learn with their department teams on a continual, just-in-time basis on areas of team development that were revealed in the team assessments.

As one would suspect, those leaders who worked with their teams consistently over time showed the most significant improvements in team productivity. The following is a sampling of the outcomes that were achieved as a result of the program as reported in the six month postprogram evaluation:

- Where there had been barriers between food production and tray line assembly teams, the supervisors of those two teams are now working together as a management team; for instance, pulling together to take on additional responsibility for operations during this time of staff shortage; launching a new competency-based task training program for more structured and consistent job training; creating a culture of continual feedback and professional development.

- Employees are following departmental policies and procedures more consistently and there is increased attendance of staff members on weekend shifts because supervisors hold employees more accountable.
- Nurse manager and team members created a new, more consistent orientation protocol for new nurses.
- Team member initiated a special "Nurses Are the Angels On Earth" recognition award for caring service beyond the call of duty.
- Staff initiated on-the-spot group problem-solving to prioritize care and reorganize work in the emergency department.
- Improved working partnership between the leader and her staff so that group problem-solving instead of personal attack has become the norm.

Costs

Because most of the leadership programs were developed in-house, the cost was primarily in development time, and, of course, the time of the participants. The three HRD consultants, along with the associate director and the director of the department, were involved in aspects of the design, development, and conducting of various aspects of the program. The associate director spent approximately 50 percent of her time in the development and design of the program and then another 10 percent in the administration of the program for the past two years. The rest of the staff spent on average 5 percent of their time. The Leadership and TeamWorking program was purchased from Blanchard Training and Development. The average cost of the materials per leader participant is $502, which includes team and individual assessment instruments and resource materials. When leaders conduct the just-in-time training sessions with their teams, another $90 per staff member is factored in because each staff member receives a companion team development workbook.

Conclusions and Recommendations

There were many lessons we learned through this process. Specifically, we learned that treating the needs and expectations of staff as valid data to be acted upon in the external environment helps leaders to live competencies such as creating a customer service environment and building teamwork.

We also learned about the importance of creating vehicles and processes that inculcate the concept of leader as teacher and mentor. As mentioned earlier, part of the management orientation process is for new leaders to collect data about expectations from their manager. Participating leaders receive a feedback questionnaire to give to their manager to complete as part of their pre-work for management orientation. Yet, when we would meet with the leaders' managers to go over the pre-work requirements during the overview session, the managers had invariably not received any requests from their subordinate leaders to complete the feedback questionnaires. This points to the difficulty in trying to have leaders go against the traditional hierarchy of downward communication. In many cases it was essential for the manager to initiate the expectation discussion and model that it was acceptable for the subordinate leader to engage in this type of dialogue.

Another mechanism we used for creating a culture that values leadership development is to request our top leadership to mandate key leadership courses. In a busy 24-hour-a-day critical service operation, it is easy for leaders to resort to crisis management and not make the time for investing in the leadership skills that would avert some of those crises. By the top leadership approving a required leadership curriculum, it sends a message that leadership development is important at all levels of management, and that people take the time to consider human resource data and take action on it. HRD also provides a quarterly report to the management council that tracks the required curriculum completion status of each new leader.

In the Future

Although each of our leadership programs includes some type of staff data, there is no current organizational mechanism to measure staff satisfaction on a consistent basis outside of the educational realm. For the full leadership to view staff feedback as legitimate as patient feedback, it would need to be tracked on a hospital-wide regular basis. As was proven with the Leadership and TeamWorking program, it is the sustained and continual effort to act on staff feedback and treat the employee as customers that brings the biggest gains in increasing staff satisfaction and creating a customer responsive environment.

Additionally, HRD is exploring ways to further integrate leadership elements into current human resource systems. We are working with key departments to identify and use leadership competencies in the hiring and performance appraisal process for leaders.

Finally, HRD is planning to go online with part of the information covered in management orientation. Currently, management orientation is offered only once a quarter to keep up with the demand of new leaders being hired. However, a new leader may have to wait three months before the class is offered. We hope to have an on-line educational component that would allow new leaders to become acquainted with key leadership information within a week after they are hired.

Questions for Discussion

1. What were the important lessons from the past experience with 360-degree developmental feedback pilot?
2. What other strategies could be used to further realize the guiding principles of "employee as customer" and "leader as teacher"?
3. Is measuring staff satisfaction really critical for developing effective leaders and realizing organizational goals?
4. How could you envision using this Leadership Development Implementation Model in your organization?

The Author

Donna L. Kaye is the associate director of the human resource development department at UNC Health Care. She is responsible for the development and implementation of leadership development initiatives, and has been the project leader for the leadership development plan mentioned in this case. She is also involved in consulting with internal leaders to assess specific work team needs and then partnering with leaders to implement the appropriate interventions. Past organizational development experience has been in strategic planning, change management, team building, leadership coaching, and targeted recruitment planning. Kaye earned a bachelor of science degree in consumer economics from Cornell University as well as a postgraduate diploma in training and development from New York University.

Building Depth in New Benches: Nurturing Nontraditional Leaders

Camp RYLA, Rotary International

Sylvia Ryce Cornell

Leadership in organizations is often studied from the perspective of corporate managers who rise to the top or near the top of their organizations. Individuals who manage to transform the culture of moribund companies are usually described and perceived as visionary leaders. Their unique gifts are often described as a calling. For those of us who seek to hone the skills of fast track employees with potential, the focus is placed on winners.

As we develop curriculum and programs to polish these diamonds, is it possible that we often step through rough pieces of coal whose carats are never burnished and cut? It takes patience and a willingness to cut through exterior masks and reveal the gemstones that lie beneath the surface.

Sylvia Ryce Cornell's fascination with developing programs for marginalized populations began during her graduate studies at the University of Houston. Most of the research on leadership development appeared to be centered around corporate executives and other highly placed professionals. As her program designs moved into the areas of youth work, the same hierarchy was evident. Honor students and the presidents of mainstream student groups, such as the student council, were routinely sent to leadership training programs.

A second tier of unrecognized leaders existed within the same pool of students. Young people, often labeled as hopeless troublemakers, exhibited phenomenal characteristics usually attributed to their more socially acceptable peers. The young gang leaders, hip-hop rap artists, and class clowns demonstrated influencing skills, a gift for inclusion and team building, and a high level of creativity. What if these youngsters were taught to embrace these mis-

This case was prepared to serve as a basis for discussion rather than to illustrate either effective or ineffective administrative and management practices.

directed gifts and utilize them in positive actions? They could return to their peer groups as servant leaders and shift the tide of destructive behavior into a wellspring of service.

For purposes of this case study, we will examine teaching the leadership skills to the brightest and best. Starting with this opinion is a catalyst for new directions in youth leadership training.

Young adults have great potential to change the world for good. Leadership development for this underrepresented population must be predicated upon high expectations. As we compile and collate more data about their impact upon their peer groups, funding for proactive activities will be easier to attain.

There are two defining moments in each man's life.
The first comes when he is born.
The second occurs when he discovers why he was born.
—Unknown

Overview of Camp RYLA

The Rotary Youth Leadership Awards (RYLA) were officially established by Rotary International in 1971. RYLA initiatives exist on a worldwide basis in sites as diverse as Europe and South America.

Most programs are centered around a week-long camp, usually referred to as Camp RYLA. Local Rotary Clubs underwrite the expenses of young people (between the ages of 18 and 30) for a series of seminars, lectures, and other activities centered around leadership development and career awareness.

The 57 Rotary Clubs in the greater Houston area sponsored the first annual Camp RYLA on the weekend of February 21-23, 1997. This event, held at Camp Strake Conference Center, a site owned by the Boy Scouts of America, involved approximately 70 young adults from high schools throughout the area. Each RYLA scholar was sponsored by a local Rotary Club.

The success of the first initiative was duplicated on the weekend of February 28–March 1, 1998. Again 70 young adults participated. Each weekend followed the theme of "Leading to Make A Difference."

Six experienced facilitators were recruited from local organizations that focus on the art and science of leadership. These adults led high school sophomores and juniors in workshops designed to provide the tools for an effective leader. The topics covered included goal-setting, effective communication, conflict resolution, and the characteristics of effective leaders.

The campers interacted with these dynamic adults throughout the weekend and learned from peer facilitators from the District Interact Board. Rotary District 5890 is committed to the development of young leaders. These young adults from Interact are leaders in high school service clubs sponsored by local Rotary Clubs. We were especially proud of the fact that each of the youth facilitators for Year Two was a participant from the inaugural Camp RYLA.

The theme of "Leading to Make a Difference" was enhanced by outside speakers who have made an impact upon their communities. Year One speakers included Kwame Thompson, a dynamic young law student from St. Louis, Missouri, who gave the opening keynote address. He had waged an effective campaign to become mayor of a suburban municipality. Local speakers included Richard Franke, marketing director of Junior Achievement of Southeast Texas; David Baxter, principal of a magnet school in Aldine ISD; and Adrian Garcia, an officer with the Mayor's Anti-Gang Office (MAGO).

Year Two speakers were limited to a keynote speaker and a speaker for the Saturday morning general session. This was an adjustment made because of the comments of the first group: that they preferred fewer speakers and more small group interaction.

Structured instruments included a communication style survey and the Campbell Community Survey, a questionnaire designed and scored by David L. Campbell through the Center for Creative Leadership. The results of these instruments gave us empirical data on the attitudes and belief systems of the campers. Each RYLA participant was an outstanding young adult, as evidenced by the numerous community service activities listed on their applications. Each wrote an impressive essay that assisted sponsoring Rotary Clubs in selecting candidates.

We experienced fun-filled and intensive experiences that combined learning, food, social activities, and a youth-designed and -directed closing ceremony on Sunday morning. At the conclusion of the weekend, each group presented a service project that they designed to "make a difference" in their communities.

The groups were creative in their presentation modes. One group, who created an after-care program for latchkey kids, opened with a skit depicting a bored kid coming in from school with nothing to do. Another group created a teen club/activity center, complete with young rappers (a multiracial duo) with a lyric that depicted the need for clean and wholesome activities for youth. They ended their presentation with graphics (pie charts and so on) that demonstrated a statistical decrease in youth crime and teen pregnancy as a result of their program.

Despite the fact that we had a few loners, the weekends were not marred with any obvious cross words or formation of cliques. Even those who included negative comments on the final surveys for single events gave a high evaluation for the entire weekend.

The overwhelming majority, however, expressed enthusiasm, insight, and a sense of camaraderie. This was especially gratifying because most of the 70 campers came in on Friday as complete strangers to the others. The bonding with their facilitators and with each other was most rewarding.

With all of the negative publicity that accompanies the actions of many adolescents, these youngsters are a shining example of what can happen when the brightest and best fuse their talent and ideals. They demonstrated the power of young adults to effect meaningful change within their peer groups and their communities.

Each weekend followed the same basic schedule and format, shown in the Camp RYLA schedule (table 1).

Preparing for a Successful Event

The gestation period for our initial Camp RYLA surpassed that of the average elephant. Rotary District 5890 is a geographically dispersed district that spans six counties around the metropolitan Houston CMSA. Fifty-seven independent Rotary Clubs elect a district-wide corporate governance structure on an annual basis. Our inaugural Camp RYLA occurred after three separate district governors and their appointed program managers attempted to create a program for our area. The fact that these individuals serve on a purely voluntary basis created a second problem—that of adequate funding for personnel, materials, and a site.

We were successful in launching Camp RYLA when the voluntary steering committee was placed under the direction of an executive from Boy Scouts of America. He used his network to secure facilities at Camp Strake, a beautiful conference center and Boy Scout camp located forty miles north of Houston. We were able to use the site at cost and secure the services of year round personnel for site maintenance and meals. Each year's steering committee has included a

Table 1. Camp RYLA Schedule.

Friday Evening

7:00–8:30 p.m.	Icebreakers/Energizers/ Team Building Exercises
8:45 p.m.	Assembly/Overview of Weekend
9:00 p.m.	Opening Keynote
9:30 p.m.–-	Mixer

Saturday

7:30–8:15 a.m.	Breakfast
8:30–8:50 a.m.	Outdoor Exercises/Experiential Games
8:50–10:00 a.m.	Small Groups—Facilitated
	What is A Leader?
	How Do We Communicate?
10:00–10:30 a.m.	Assembly—Has Leadership Changed?
10:40–11:45 a.m.	Small Groups—Facilitated
	Time Management/Delegation
	Basics of Decision Making
	Intro to Goal Setting
12:00–12:45 p.m.	Lunch
12:50–1:15 p.m.	"Leading Despite Adversity"
1:20–2:30 p.m.	Small Groups—Facilitated
	Feedback/Questions on Topics to Date
	Experiential Activities (Team Building)
	Goal Setting
2:40–3:30 p.m.	Assembly
	Making A Difference in My Community
	Sylvia Ryce Cornell
	Community Survey Distribution
	(Weather Permitting) Nature Walk/Journals
3:40–4:30 p.m.	Small Groups—Facilitated
	Goal Setting
	Selection of Group Project
4:40–5:30 p.m.	Project Planning Sessions (Scattered Sites)
	Select Scribes and Spokespersons
5:30–6:00 p.m.	Free Time
6:00–7:00 p.m.	Dinner
7:15–9:00 p.m.	Preparation of Projects
	Group Presentations
	Presentation of Projects
	Method/Mode Set by Group
	Role Play
	Presentation
	Audio-Visual Aids
9:00 p.m.–	Campfire (Weather Permitting)

continued on page 202

Table 1. Camp RYLA Schedule (continued).

Sunday

7:30–8:15 a.m.	Breakfast
8:30–9:00 a.m.	Private Time/Reflections
9:15–10:30 a.m.	Closing Activity
	Prepared by Campers and Interact Board
11:00 a.m.–Noon	Farewell Assembly /
	Future Directions
	Weekend Evaluations
12:15–	Lunch
1:00 p.m.	Farewells/Departures

Sylvia Ryce Cornell
Program Coordinator
Rotary Club of Oyster Creek

Scout executive to serve as the liaison between the RYLA planners and Camp Strake. These individuals were also Rotarians, so the organization was a stakeholder throughout the planning process.

As the program planner for these first events, I was able to tap into my networks of professional consultants from local organizations. The local chapter of ASTD was a source of gifted individuals who donated their professional services at cost. We added facilitators for Year Two from sources as diverse as the local Junior Achievement executives and a retired marine who is an ROTC instructor.

Although the facilitators brought a wealth of information and experience in the art and science of leadership, age factors were an important consideration. Most of them were accustomed to working with adult learners. It was important for them to feel comfortable with adolescents and to take their unique learning styles and developmental stages into consideration.

This potential problem was alleviated and eliminated through two actions. Each adult facilitator was paired with an adolescent co-facilitator. The teams were trained together at a day-long "train-the-trainer session" at least six weeks prior to Camp RYLA. This workshop served a dual purpose: 1) the adults were reminded of adolescent characteristics, and 2) the session was an initial bonding experience between the co-facilitators.

As program designer, I was careful to let each team find its own comfort zone with delivery and separation of tasks. The young adults who were selected as co-facilitators enjoyed a learning experience on two levels. Their adult peers became caring mentors who helped them to hone their presentation and delivery skills, as they learned. The adult facilitators gained the advantage of peer influence as they worked with their small groups. Campers were more comfortable with expressing themselves to another adolescent when problems surfaced.

The beauty of this approach was highlighted by the teen facilitators' initiative in several areas. The first adolescent team established a tradition of putting together gift packets for each camper as a present from their peers. We gave them adequate money to go to Sam's Warehouse and purchase the junk food and candy of choice for teens. They put the packets together with small favors that only another teen could appreciate.

They also worked as camp counselors in the social activities. Each teen facilitator was assigned to a cabin and placed in a position of responsibility at night. This opportunity to bond with no adults around was especially important for the campers and for their young leaders.

The teen facilitators were also given full rein in the design and implementation of the opening mixer and the final commitment project. Each year, a popular young disc jockey came up and took over at the conclusion of the opening ceremony. This young man, an enterprising entrepreneur, shared the story of establishing his own company during his college days. His large selection of urban contemporary music and classics, such as the sock hop, was a great hit for each weekend. Shyness and the discomfort of being surrounded by strangers were dissipated as each camper, the adults, and their teen peer facilitators gyrated to the music. A full supply of snacks, the way to any teen's heart, gave them energy throughout the dance. Adult stamina and dancing skills were put to the test with no long-term damage.

Facilitator Training

The training workshops were enjoyable events that gave the facilitators reminders of their adolescent days, allowed them to become familiar with the structured instruments used during the weekend, and introduced them to the curriculum for the weekend. Each of these instructors, including the teens, was given a large notebook that included the materials given to each RYLA participant.

Instructor notebooks included supplemental materials in team building and adolescent learning styles. The three-ring binder format gave them an opportunity to add materials of their choice for a long-term collection of resources.

Two items from this binder are included (below) as an example of the training session. Each training session started with a questionnaire that the adults completed and shared with each other. These questions spurred memories that had not been considered for years. The questions were also a reminder to each individual that the campers within their small groups were living through these issues as they learned to be leaders.

The exercise was titled, "I Remember When I Was A Teenager . . ." Each participant was asked to complete open-ended statements. Some of the questions included:

When I was a teenager . . .

- My most trusted adult was _____
- I had too little_____ too much_____ facial hair
- My most embarrassing moment came _____
- The one secret that I never told anyone _____
- My favorite song was _____
- My favorite outfit was _____

The adults were further reminded of our tendency toward *adultism* in a section that follows:

> When teens are consistently blamed for failure, labeled as lazy, troublesome, dishonest, and stupid, they become prime targets for undesirable affiliations. Paul Kivel, one of the founders of the Oakland Men's Projects, called this type of behavior from adult role models "adultism." Many of you may recognize the following expressions. Think back to how you felt when you heard them.
>
> - Not now. I don't have time.
> - You're too young to understand.
> - Go to your room.
> - Not until you finish your homework.
> - Clean your plate.
> - I work my fingers to the bone for you.
> - Wait till you have children.
> - When I was your age, I had it a lot harder.
> - Do what I say.
> - Not in my house (class) you don't.
> - Because I said so.
> - Sit up. Sit up straight.
> - Don't you talk back to me.
> - This hurts me more than it hurts you.
> - You get right upstairs and change into something decent.

- Is that the best you can do?
- Pay attention when I'm talking to you.
- I brought you into this world—I can take you out!
- You're stupid.
- Shut up.
- You show me some respect.

Can you add others?

Some of the statements were added to the student's manuals. The facilitators were encouraged to engage their small groups in dialogue about their reactions to those statements and similar comments in their encounters with adults. We sought to explore all facets of communication for these student leaders.

Creating an Identity for RYLA

Although many of the programs sponsored by Rotary International have distinctive logos, we could not find a symbol that represented the RYLA program. Rotarians wear a distinct pin in the shape of a gear wheel. There is a symbol for the Interact Clubs that appears on their pins.

A Rotarian on the original steering committee owned a graphics and printing firm. He and his designers set out to create a distinct logo for our RYLA program that embodied the Rotary images. The resulting symbol was used on all RYLA stationery, the T-shirts worn by campers, and the certificates given to each participant at the end of the camp (figure 1).

The RYLA logo was used each year for the weekend event. We added a second logo during Year Two which incorporated the major

Figure 1. Camp RYLA logo.

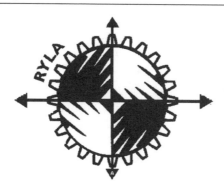

points of learning that we emphasized—head, heart, and feet. More detail about the origins of this symbol, that we dubbed RYLEE (Rotary Youth Leadership Energetic Endeavors), is discussed below.

RYLA Curriculum

Although the same basic curriculum was used for each year's event, modifications existed during the second session. District 5890 was fortunate enough to form a partnership with the John Ben Shepperd Public Leadership Institute for Year One assistance. This program, housed on the Permian Basin Campus of the University of Texas, conducts proprietary leadership seminars across the state of Texas.

With their permission, we amended the program's daylong format to meet our needs for a weekend event. One of their facilitators came to Houston and participated in the train-the-trainer session and assisted in interpreting the curriculum for our program staff. The Institute shipped copies of the student handbook in three-hole punch format about two weeks prior to Camp RYLA 1997. This action provided a substantial savings in reproduction costs. All we had to do was insert the materials in the student binders.

For Year Two, we designed our curriculum from start to finish. The Shepperd Institute curriculum was ideal for our initial needs because it focused on the core qualities of leadership that we needed. Sessions were centered upon communication, goal-setting, the basic attributes of leadership, and using those skills within the leader's community. Based on our learning from Year One evaluations, the steering committee agreed on an expansion of the curriculum to provide more information about project management skills. We were asking the small groups to use their new skills for the design of service projects. One adult observer during the first year noted that the campers in attendance managed to do more with their service projects than many adults on a task force accomplish over a six-month period.

We decided to give even more structure to their efforts through providing the core elements of planning and implementing a project. An advisor to the steering committee, a retired engineer, had served as a project manager all over the world. He provided invaluable assistance in designing this portion of the curriculum and providing the introduction before the small group interactions.

Because our theme, "Leading to Make A Difference," was focused on servant leadership, we sought to incorporate an abstract concept into each aspect of the weekend. Throughout the sessions, campers were taught that they were SCOPEs and encouraged to repeat the slogan: *I am a Successful, Competent, Outgoing, Positive, Enthusiastic leader, and I can make a difference.* This chant increased in volume and intensity as the weekend progressed.

For Year Two, we added a mascot, RYLEE (Rotary Youth Leadership Energetic Endeavors), to the printed material. This character, in the manner of the lightning bolt used to symbolize electricity, exemplified the main tenets of our leadership skills. Campers were introduced to RYLEE in their notebooks. His image and core tenets appeared right after the letter of welcome from the director.

The RYLEE mascot is depicted in table 2, which shows some of the materials we included in each camper's manual.

Communication Style Survey

Camp RYLA was designed as a milestone on a journey toward successful leadership. We used two structured instruments that the campers could add to their tool kits for effective leadership. Neither instrument was threatening or provided any ranking that would contribute to hierarchies within their small groups. They were used for catalytic purposes to emphasize major points of the curriculum—communication and service learning.

Each camper's notebook included a self-scoring instrument published by Human Resource Development Quarterly (HRDQ), *The Communication Style Survey.* The instrument, in booklet form, includes a pull-out questionnaire that examines an individual's communication style.

The group facilitators introduced these surveys right after a discussion of the characteristics of an effective leader. Debriefing included an explanation that understanding one's communication style made it easier to identify the styles of others in interactions with their peers. After scoring the instrument, the participant was able to identify a primary communication style on a quadrant.

Scoring instructions used distinct shapes for each communication style: A triangle ▲ for a "systematic" communication style; a circle ● for a "considerate" communication style; and so on.

It was interesting to note that a large percentage of the campers for each year scored high on the considerate scale. Because one of the trouble spots for that communication style is listed as conflict avoidance, the skills to overcome this tendency were included. Conflict resolution was stressed as a portion of the communication skills.

Table 2. Sample pages from a camper's manual.

Your presence here is the beginning of an experience that we hope you will never forget. When this weekend is over, we are confident that you will become a Leader Who Makes a Difference.

We will focus upon activities that are centered upon effective leaders' heads, hearts, and feet. HEAD skills will be taught through guidance in goal-setting, capturing your dreams, and teaching you to articulate a vision for group projects. HEART skills will focus upon supporting your goals and dreams through the use of motivational techniques and reinforcing your belief that you can "make a difference." What are the FEET skills? The actual implementation of your projects will be reinforced through skills in time management, project planning, and making the goals workable through defining and overcoming any possible barriers to success. We are excited about this weekend. Here's hoping Camp RYLA '98 whets your appetite for an exciting feast of opportunities.

Leading to Make a Difference
Camp RYLA, 1998

Our graphic, RYLEE, personifies the areas of learning that we hope to emphasize. We want to capture your energies and eliminate any boundaries upon your belief that you can create change.

We want each young person who participates in Camp RYLA to leave this site with a renewed sense of dedication to the Rotary theme of "Service Above Self." It is our fervent desire to give each participant tools and techniques to become a "servant leader."

Camp RYLA will include a service project for each of your groups. After we provide the campers with basic leadership tools and pique your desire to create change in your environment(s), you will be expected to design a realistic and meaningful service project for your groups. You will have an opportunity to watch the leaders in your groups soar. These projects will be presented to the entire group before Saturday night's campfire (weather permitting).

We have adequate supplies and materials on hand to give the group the base for visual aids. You will have an opportunity to sell us on the benefits of putting your plans into action.

MEET RYLEE!
Rotary
Youth

Leaders'

Energetic   Endeavors

Campbell Community Survey

The second instrument that we used was contributed and scored by the Center for Creative Leadership's Colorado Springs Branch. David Campbell, the author of the *Campbell Community Survey,* provided adequate instruments each year for us to administer to campers after a discussion on how they could "make a difference" in their schools and communities.

For Year One, we received forty-eight (48) responses that were eligible for scoring. The survey was administered to the entire group before the afternoon break for their nature walks. Although the results yielded valuable information in planning the second event, we sought to get more detailed information about the campers and their reactions for Year Two.

After the lecturette, the campers in the second session returned to their small groups to complete the survey. We coded the instruments and divided them according to individual groups, with a separate set of instruments for the adult facilitators and camp staff. The resulting summary reports gave us baseline information that included a demographic summary.

The feedback report to the center captures some of the campers' comments (table 3). Letters from the adult facilitators are shown in table 4.

For Rotarians with reservations about expanding the outreach efforts for Camp RYLA to inner city youth, we gained some valuable information. The demographic profile for each session was predominantly middle class and upper middle class youth. Although diversity existed through the inclusion of minority groups, those few Asians and African American youth who participated came from largely affluent suburban school districts. A few of the campers from rural areas were avid participants, but they were a minority.

No attempt was made to "dumb down" any of the curriculum. These young leaders were bright individuals who responded well to our high expectations for them.

Key Learnings

As a Leadership Development practitioner, my approach to developing young leaders is admittedly nontraditional. A quest to include more marginalized youth in youth programs must use empirical data. RYLA was designed to test some personal theories and to apply existing research. The research into motivation and its role in teaching adolescents yields conflicting trends and theories within the educational psychology community.

Table 3. Feedback report on Camp RYLA.

Campbell Community Survey
Camp RYLA
Debriefing Questionnaire
Responses
Location Code 10273—Completed by Sylvia Ryce Cornell

1. What was your role in managing the project?

I served as Program Chair for Rotary District 5890's third official attempt to initiate Camp RYLA (Rotary Youth Leadership Awards). As such, I assumed full responsibility for curriculum development, selection and training of facilitators, speakers, and administration of structured instruments. This was the first time that we pulled it off and it was an overwhelming success.

2. What was (were) the reason(s) you decided to have your community participate in this survey? What did you hope to accomplish?

The focus of the camp was the development of leadership skills in a selected group of adolescents from schools throughout the greater Houston area. The theme, "Leading to Make A Difference," was predicated upon the belief that developing servant leadership skills in these young adults would give them the intrinsic motivation to make a positive difference in their neighborhoods and immediate environments. The survey questions were ideally suited to develop reflective analysis of their feelings toward their community. The survey questions were utilized as a catalyst for many productive discussions in the groups. We administered the survey just before the groups began to design a service project.

3. What information in the results was surprising to you? What do you see as positive and negative?

The valleys in the tolerance and geography ranges. This may be attributable to participants' awareness of adult Rotarians' tendency toward conservative attitudes and resistance to change. I consider this to be a positive sign that they are willing to challenge the status quo. It was also intriguing to notice the ethnic differences in key areas such as drugs. We have validation for previous observations about the inaccuracy of stereotypes linking minority youth with social problems such as drugs. The higher sense of belongingness by minority youth was another catalyst for some paradigm shifts on the part of decision makers for Rotary Youth Activities. This is a positive indicator.

4. What was the overall reaction to the results?

Too soon to make an accurate assessment. This data will be quite helpful in promoting more diverse programs for the district. No inner city schools were represented and we have grossly inadequate support for Interact Clubs in areas where they are most needed. The participants were eager to implement some of the service projects that they designed.

5. What concerns do you have about your community after reviewing your report?

Numerous—some are referenced in Item #4. Although we cannot build Rome in one day and upon the basis of one activity, the success of the program and the evidence of reflective attitudes on the part of our future leadership was refreshing. Some comments from the young adults are appended.

Like many traditional organizational structures, some of the older Rotary leaders will fight change with every available tool. I would like to believe that enough progressive leadership is emerging to question and challenge to counter this problem.

6. What do you and/or your community plan to do now that you have taken this survey?

The Interact Clubs in the district are having their second District Assembly in two weeks. The leadership or Board for Interact (high school level Rotary Clubs) was part of the teams that facilitated RYLA groups. Hopefully, RYLA participants will move into new positions of district wide leadership. They have the impetus to form similar initiatives. I have agreed to serve as an "on call" resource for those Campers who want to take it to the next level. (See Note.)

7. What difficulties did you experience in explaining the results to your group?

None. I went into detailed explanations of the reason for answering the questions as openly and as honestly as possible. We established a relationship based upon mutual trust and respect. One of the most rewarding comments on evaluation forms stated that I was an obvious "pioneer" in the area of leadership development. It was surprising that someone of my generation (an obvious euphemism for age :-)) was so in tune with young people of their age group.

The real challenge will be getting the adult leadership to accept the implications of their responses. It will take a high level of diplomacy and no small amount of providing room for "saving face."

continued on page 212

Table 3. Feedback report on Camp RYLA (continued).

8. Please list any specific comments, positive or negative, about the survey itself and the report.

It is an excellent vehicle for getting communities to practice self-reflection and correlating their personal sense of self-worth with their attitudes toward their environments. With Dr. Campbell's permission, I want to publish the results of the experience in an ERIC document that includes selected portions of the data.

Again, these young people were "the cream of the cream." Selection was highly competitive. My original premise for Camp RYLA was to mix this type of young leader with "at-risk" leaders such as "gang-bangers" to redirect the talent of negative leadership. That approach proved to be so controversial, that I elected not to wage that particular battle.

One key facilitator, however, does want to design a similar activity for youth from inner city high schools in the area. He has the support of local politicians and school administrators. If this comes to pass, I would like to incorporate the survey into that activity.

Appendix

Campers were divided into five groups that were led by four ASTD facilitators, and Terrance Collins, a field representative for the John Ben Shepperd Institute. We utilized some of the Shepperd curriculum, augmented by ours, to create a fast-paced, experiential weekend. Our theme, "Leading to Make A Difference," was tested through the development of a service project by each of the groups. These were presented to the other campers on Saturday evening.

The groups were creative in their presentation modes. One group, who created an after care program for latchkey kids, opened with a skit depicting a bored kid coming in from school with nothing to do. Another group created a teen club/activity center, complete with young rappers (a multi-racial duo) with a lyric that depicted the need for clean and wholesome activities for youth. They ended their presentation with graphics (pie charts, etc.) that demonstrated a statistical decrease in youth crime and teen pregnancy as the result of their program.

Some comments from evaluations:

15 yr. old male—"It is great, there is no flaw in anything."

16 yr. old male—"This conference was a confidence builder to me as well as the group as a whole. The time that we spent together will always be in my heart and mind. The conference could have been better if we could have met for a longer duration of time."

16 yr. old female—"I had a really great weekend. I think I have left a better person. I am ready to lead now—because of this weekend I was able to get over my shyness in front of others."

15 yr. old female—"This is one of the greatest experiences I've had the privelege (sic) to enjoy."

16 yr. old male—"Awesome."

16 yr. old male—"The weekend was a great chance to see how other leaders around me are leading in their schools and communities. It has inspired me to continue to stand up for what I believe and what I think I can do for all of those around me."

16 yr. old male—"I had great expectations for this weekend, and I wasn't let down. It is comforting to know that there are so many young leaders that are so enthusiastic and as concerned about their communities as we all should be. Our future looks awesome!"

16 yr. old male—"Everything was well planned and well thought out. This camp was very helpful in discovering leadership traits and discovering helpful hints to many problems. I've been to many leadership camps and this one above all is the best. It provided motivation that will last a lifetime."

17 yr. old female—"The material presented to us over this weekend was phenomenal. I've been to leadership programs before, and this one definitely came out on top. I enjoyed the facilitators. They were awesome! The trust that was placed within us was incredible, especially for me, because I've always had trouble trusting people. You've done an immense service to the world."

Not everyone was totally enthusiastic. Some felt we had too many speakers. Others mentioned the food or a need for more free time. The overwhelming majority, however, expressed enthusiasm, insight, and a sense of camaraderie. This was especially gratifying because most of the seventy campers came in on Friday as complete strangers to the others. The bonding with their facilitators and with each other was most rewarding.

Despite the fact that we had a few loners, the weekend was not marred with any obvious cross words or formation of cliques. Even those who included negative comments on their evaluations ended by saying that for a "first," Camp R.Y.L.A. was a success.

Note: RYLA's impact was definitely felt throughout this District Conference. Of the six elected District Wide Officers, four were RYLA campers. One of these four attained the top position—District Governor. She is a delightful young Asian American female who keeps in touch, as she continues to reach new heights of leadership and achievement.

Table 4. Facilitators' personal observations.

Comments from Selected Rotarians

Anton Money and Robert (Bob) Skilton are long-term Rotarians who worked at my side throughout each camp. Ken Marsh, a fellow ASTD member, served as one of the facilitators at the first Camp RYLA. As a response to his experience with these motivated youngsters, he became a Rotarian and actively promotes activities for youth within his club.

I am admittedly prejudiced about the success of these two events. Therefore, I asked each of them to share their reactions and memories of the weekends. Their responses are shared without any editing or adjustment from me.

—Sylvia Ryce Cornell

Tony Money

When Rotary District 5890 decided to attempt a week-end Rotary Youth Leadership Awards Program for high school sophomores and juniors, they turned to Sylvia to create the curriculum and oversee its implementation. She did this with great success and the effect on the participants was considerable. A few weeks ago, we invited several of our participants to present to our Rotary Club their reactions to the program after nearly a year had elapsed. They all emphasized how effective the program was, particularly with respect to the opportunities afforded them to express themselves and become a part of the driving force of the program.

Sylvia shows considerable aptitude in being able to empathize with young people. She communicates with them easily and gets excellent response from them.

Bob Skilton

It is my pleasure to recall with you, the experiences we had with the first two annual RYLA camps (1997-1998) for Rotary District 5890. For years, the District had been trying to put a RYLA (Rotary Youth Leadership Awards) program together and only through the leadership of District Governor Ed Martin did things get started in the summer of 1996. He appointed Chad Greer chairman of the RYLA Committee, you, program director, and me, registrar.

This was uncharted territory for all of us. Fortunately, you had visited a RYLA Camp in North Carolina, and experienced through your profession what we were trying to accomplish. Chad Greer, being a no nonsense, well structured individual, began putting a program together. We met regularly every month.

It became apparent to me early on that your job was the most important of all—the program—and we all realized as we went along that you had a mental picture of what we needed to make our beginning a successful one. Everyone contributed ideas, including Tony Money, who had joined us by that time, along with Britt Vincent. You were able to recruit all the people needed for the program—speakers, facilitators, a representation from Interact clubs in the district.

We were somewhat overwhelmed at this point, because we were totally dependent on you and your good judgment to put a good group together. By early February, we were all in a state of frenzy. I was covered over with RYLA applications and checks. Tony was trying to get his assignments of bunks properly assigned. Chad was pulling all the loose ends together, but you maintained an air of confidence that none of us believed.

February 21 finally came, and the students began arriving. There was tumult around the registration desk, but finally, all were registered and sent to their dorms and cabins. All was well. They came back to the meeting hall later to hear the first speaker, Kwame Thompson, who got things started very well.

Saturday morning started in the meeting hall with three speakers, all of which were great. The students then broke into six smaller groups, who stayed together the rest of the day. Some of their activities took them outside. The theme for all their activities was leadership and working together. The day ended with a bonfire, singing, and lots of ice cream.

Sunday morning started with awards from the day before, after which all of us held hands and stood in a big circle. One by one, of our own volition, we stepped forward and spoke a few words about what Camp RYLA had meant to us. It was a very touching experience for all of us. There was laughter, tears, and a general feeling of closeness within the whole group. I couldn't have believed this could happen in such a short amount of time if I hadn't been a part of it.

Yes, it was a success. Students wrote back and thanked us for inviting them to come. We could tell that they were leaving with a better knowledge of what leadership is all about. I left that day with a new respect for you, for you had put a program together which had made a difference to some seventy students—and me.

The 1998 Camp RYLA went together much easier, under the direction of Tony Money. You and I held our same responsibilities. The program, for

continued on page 216

Table 4. Facilitators' personal observations (continued).

the most part, was the same, a few less speakers maybe, but it too was a big success. It just goes to prove that in order to have a good program that accomplishes its goal, you must have the right person to put it together. You have that talent, Sylvia, and it comes from your heart.

I feel that Rotary District 5890 has gotten off to a great start these first two years. My hope is that it will continue to be successful in the years ahead.

Ken Marsh

My experience, as a facilitator, with RYLA '97 was very rewarding and inspiring. I had the pleasure of facilitation of a team of nine (9) young adults, who were already nothing less but impressive young leaders by their attitude and demeanor. My role as a facilitator encompassed highly interactive workshop sessions on leadership, communication, and interpersonal relations.

I also observed these young leaders in action as they designed, developed, and demonstrated a community service project. This community service project, the culmination of utilizing all their knowledge, skills, and attitudes learned during the RYLA Camp Retreat, proved to be very impressive and awe-inspiring.

The young leaders demonstrated a strong concern about community service, a creative and innovative approach to community involvement and insight into their strong moral and ethical natures. I was also very impressed with the young leaders' very strong desire to show adults that the majority of youths are not like the ones portrayed on television, in the news, and movies. These young leaders made me, as a participant and observer, proud to have been a part of such a dynamic weekend and feeling hopeful and encouraged about the future.

I looked at three constructs:
- Attribution theory
- Goal theory
- Self-determination theory.

A motivational theory of particular importance for leadership program developers is self-determination theory (Deci and Ryan, 1985). This theory describes students as having three categories of needs: a sense of competence, a sense of relatedness to others, and a sense of autonomy. Competence involves understanding how to— and believing that one can—achieve various outcomes. Relatedness involves developing satisfactory connections to others in one's social group. Autonomy involves initiating and regulating one's own actions. Much of the research in self-determination theory focuses on the last of these three needs.

We attempted to give the campers as much autonomy as possible in the design of the service projects. Facilitators worked hard to sharpen skills within a very brief period of time and then to stand back as each small group brainstormed and designed its own project.

Although attribution theory focuses on the reasons students perceive for their successes and failures in school, goal theory focuses on the reasons or purposes students perceive for achieving (examples are Ames, 1992; Maehr and Midgley, 1991; Midgley, 1993). Although different researchers define the constructs slightly differently, two main goal orientations are generally discussed. These are task goals and ability goals.

A task goal orientation represents the belief that the purpose of achieving is personal improvement and understanding. Students with a task goal orientation focus on their own progress in mastering skills and knowledge, and they define success in those terms; hence, the traits highlighted in the SCOPE slogan: Success, Competence, Outgoing (initiative), Positive, and Enthusiasm as leaders and as individuals.

Goal orientation represents the belief that the purpose of achieving is the actual demonstration of ability (or, alternatively, the concealment of a lack of ability). It is important that student leaders resist the temptation to avoid demonstrating talent and intelligence. Students with an ability goal orientation focus on appearing competent, often in comparison to others, and define success accordingly. Studies of students' goal orientations generally find that the adoption of task goals is associated with more adaptive patterns of learning than is the adoption of ability goals, including the use of more effective cognitive strategies, a willingness to seek help when it is needed, a greater tendency to engage in challenging tasks, and more positive feelings about school and oneself as a learner (Anderman and Maehr, 1994; Ryan, Hicks, and Midgley, 1997).

The final portion of the slogan was repeated throughout the weekend to assist these young adults in internalizing the belief that they *could* make a difference. Complete validation occurred at the end of each session when the students stepped forward to describe the impact of Camp RYLA upon them. Raw emotion surfaced as campers related the joy of discovering that there were many other young people like themselves. Several students admitted that they were apprehensive about being around a lot of "nerds" for an entire weekend. Their fellow campers were bright individuals with a variety of social styles, but uniformly engaging personalities.

Perhaps the most humbling aspect of each year's camp was a renewed discovery that we have just as much to learn from our future leaders as we have to teach. The emotion that surrounded the final ceremony each year was genuine—many campers actually wept. The adults had to swallow huge lumps in their throats.

Throughout each camper's notebook, we interspersed quotes from famous leaders and appropriate motivational poetry. This closing poem by the late educator, Benjamin Elijah Mays, encompasses the power of these two weekends and their validation of our premise that *young people have unlimited capacity to lead.* As we bid each camper goodbye, the adults experienced the emotion that a mother eagle must feel as she watches her eaglets soar out of sight into the sky.

It must be borne in mind that
the tragedy in life doesn't
lie in not reaching your goal.

The tragedy lies in
having no goal to reach.
It isn't a calamity to die with dreams unfulfilled,
but it is a calamity not to dream.

It is not a disaster to be
unable to capture your ideal,
but it is a disaster
to have no ideal to capture.
It is not a disgrace not
to reach the stars,
but it is a disgrace to
have no stars to reach for,
Not failure, but low aim is sin.

—Benjamin Elijah Mays
(Reprinted with permission.)

Questions for Discussion

1. How do we integrate Leadership Development training into more service learning programs and curricula across the country? The service projects that were designed by RYLA participants were ideally

suited to the hands-on environments and case studies that are sought by educators striving to incorporate community service into standard core curriculum.

2. What strategies are available to blend training for the "upper tier" student like the participants in Camp RYLA and at-risk students? Is this an unrealistic expectation given the political and sociocultural realities of sponsoring organizations? Although the need for alternatives to negative activities for the gang leaders and other students is acknowledged, the "fear factor" is a deterrent. Will exposure to students from a violent world pose genuine risks to students from middle class, controlled environments?

3. The RYLA participants were exposed to curricula usually reserved for adults and corporate leaders. How can practitioners create effective programs that raise the bar, while taking adolescent needs into account? When these programs are evaluated, how much of an adjustment should we make for this nontraditional group of leaders?

4. Should leadership training for adolescents be developed as a specific subset within the field of Leadership Development? Would taking such a step increase efficacy of current programming and practice or blur lines between existing curricula in the discipline of education? Service earning is but one example. Should we consider more multidisciplinary approaches?

5. Collaboration and development of coalitions is a popular topic of discussion in many sectors. More and more federal grants consider the presence or absence of partnerships before awarding funding. What other organizations should we consider for human and financial capital to expand leadership training for adolescents? Rotary International is a service organization. Similar service organizations, such as the Red Cross, have existing programs for youth. Should we consider developing standardized curricula that can be applied across all sectors? Would implementing such a partnership limit creative approaches to programming?

The Author

Sylvia Ryce Cornell is an experienced trainer and consultant. Her experience as a librarian and professional trainer gives her a rare ability to bring detailed information and resources to any company project. Cornell combines a master's degree in library science from Atlanta University and a master of science in occupational education from the University of Houston. She has experience in vocational education through her five-year tenure at Houston Community College as industrial education librarian.

Cornell was exposed to model programs throughout the country as she implemented competency-based programs in the libraries that served industrial education programs. This reinforced her conviction that education and business can meet on common ground to prepare a workforce with technical and critical thinking skills. Cornell has made several presentations on quality partnerships between business and industry, diversity, and strategies for reclaiming at-risk youth to major conferences. Her research for three of these presentations was published as ERIC documents. Presentations on quality partnerships between educators and industry were published in 1991 and 1997. "Beyond the Buzzwords: Delivering Diversity Training That Makes A Difference," an ASTD International Presentation, was published in 1994.

Cornell's professional ties include ASTD, the American Vocational Association (AVA), the Society for Intercultural Education, Training, and Research (SIETAR), and the National Council for Occupational Education (NCOE). Professional involvements keep Cornell abreast of relevant issues in the changing landscape of training and development.

Cornell's expertise includes program design and instructional design in the areas of total quality management, diversity, intercultural communication, and leadership development. Her postgraduate work includes course work at the American Productivity and Quality Center and at the Center for Creative Leadership. Cornell designed and implemented several leadership development and motivational programs for local school districts, universities, and service organizations.

She may be reached at: Creative Concepts Unlimited, Customized Training Programs, 6310 W. Ridgecreek Drive, Missouri City, TX 77489-2822; phone: 281.437.0051; voice mail: 713.628.0145; email: creatvcncp@aol.com; Internet: http://members.aol.com/creatvcncp/homepage.htm.

References

NOTE: A search of the ERIC database resulted in more literature designed for the middle grades using motivation as a keyword. The RYLA campers were high school sophomores and juniors. Therefore, the research data here is relevant to our program design.

Ames, C. (1992). Classrooms: Goals, Structures, and Student Motivation. *Journal of Educational Psychology, 84*(3), 261–271. EJ 452 395.

Anderman, E.M., and M.L. Maehr. (1994). "Motivation and Schooling in the Middle Grades." *Review of Educational Research, 64*(2), 287–309. EJ 488 853.

Deci, E.L., and R.M. Ryan. (1985). *Intrinsic Motivation and Self-determination in Human Behavior.* New York: Plenum.

Maehr, M.L., and C. Midgley. (1991). "Enhancing Student Motivation: A School-wide Approach." *Educational Psychologist, 26*(3/4), 399–427.

Midgley, C. (1993). Motivation and Middle Level Schools. In P.R. Pintrich and M.L. Maehr (editors), *Advances in Motivation and Achievement* (Vol. 8), 219–276. Greenwich, CT: JAI Press.

Ryan, A.M., L. Hicks, and C. Midgley. (1997). "Social Goals, Academic Goals, and Avoiding Seeking Help in the Classroom." *Journal of Early Adolescence, 17*(2), 152–171.

Additional Readings

Ames, C., and J. Archer. (1988). "Achievement Goals in the Classroom: Students' Learning Strategies and Motivation Processes." *Journal of Educational Psychology, 80*(3), 260–267. EJ 388 054.

Deci, E.L., R.U. Vallerand, L.G. Pelletier, and R.M. Ryan. (1991). "Motivation and Education: The Self-determination Perspective." *Educational Psychologist, 26*(3/4), 325–346.

Eccles, J.S., and C. Midgley. (1989). Stage/Environment Fit: Developmentally Appropriate Classrooms for Early Adolescents. In R.E. Ames and C. Ames (editors), *Research on Motivation in Education* (Vol. 3), 139–186. New York: Academic.

Graham, S. (1990). Communicating Low Ability in the Classroom: Bad Things Good Teachers Sometimes Do. In S. Graham and V. Folkes (editors), *Attribution Theory: Applications to Achievement, Mental Health, and Interpersonal Conflict*, 17–36. Hillsdale, NJ: Erlbaum.

Midgley, C., and H. Feldlaufer. (1987). "Students' and Teachers' Decision-making Fit Before and After the Transition to Junior High School." *Journal of Early Adolescence, 7*(2), 225–241.

Midgley, C., and T.C. Urdan. (1992). "The Transition to Middle Level Schools: Making It a Good Experience for All Students." *Middle School Journal, 24*(2), 5–14. EJ 454 359.

Weiner, B. (1985). "An Attributional Theory of Achievement Motivation and Emotion." *Psychological Review, 92*(4), 548–573. EJ 324 684.

Initiating a Culture Change Through the Implementation of the Coaching Capability Project in a Utility Organization

Northern States Power Company

Melody McKay

With the energy field facing deregulation, market positioning and competitive advantage are now critical. Northern States Power recognized the need for a change in leadership style to ensure success in a competitive environment. The Coaching Capability project was launched to move the organization from a command and control culture to one that encourages coaching and collaboration. This was achieved through the development of a comprehensive training program, a coaching resource group, and through follow-up evaluation and management support.

Background

Northern States Power (NSP) believes effective coaching skills are critical to the success of the organization in a competitive environment. NSP also believes an investment needs to be made to ensure that all employees have these skills to work in the changing business.

The Coaching Capability process started in July 1995 when the president of NSP Electric, Larry Taylor, became aware, through feedback he had received from employee meetings, of a major disconnect between how the company's leaders saw the organization operating and what the employees were actually experiencing. There was also concern with the results of a culture survey comparing the NSP organization with another utility company with which there was a proposed merger.

This case was prepared to serve as a basis for discussion rather than to illustrate either effective or ineffective administrative and management practices.

The survey results indicated that NSP was seen as having a "command and control" culture, whereas the second utility was thought to have a "collaborative and coaching" culture. A recommendation was made by John Johnson, Changemaking Systems, to move toward more of a coaching and collaborative environment. The NSP Electric leadership team supported the move toward this nontraditional, yet popular, leadership approach. This would support the utility's move into a deregulated, competitive environment.

This information had a direct impact on NSP's 1996 workforce effectiveness goal. The goal was written to support the Coaching Capability project. The goal stated: "Instill a culture aligned with a competitive and collaborative environment and develop appropriate skills to be effective and productive." Steve Caskey, director, Business and Technology Planning, was assigned to achieve this goal for 1996.

Organizational Profile

NSP, headquartered in Minneapolis, Minnesota, is a major U.S. utility with growing domestic and overseas nonregulated operations. NSP and its wholly owned subsidiary, Northern States Power Company—Wisconsin, operate generation, transmission, and distribution facilities providing electricity to about 1.4 million customers in Minnesota, Wisconsin, North Dakota, South Dakota, and Michigan. The two companies also distribute natural gas to more than 440,000 customers in Minnesota, Wisconsin, North Dakota, and Michigan, and provide a variety of energy-related services throughout these service areas.

Key Players

Several individuals were involved in developing and implementing the Coaching Capability project.

Melody McKay, Quality Academy senior organization development consultant, supported NSP Electric in partnership with Linda Berg, human resource (HR) business consultant. Linda served as the key point of contact of all HR services to that business unit.

Melody was responsible for assessing development needs, developing training plans to ensure improvement of employee performance, and consulting on NSP Electric's workforce effectiveness goals to ensure support of strategic direction.

She was asked to participate in the roll-out of a coaching initiative in support of the Electric's workforce effectiveness goal in November 1995. Melody had joined the Quality Academy consulting team five years prior to this assignment and had supported NSP Electric for two years. She accepted this challenge thinking it would involve only some introductory coaching skills training, because Electric had been working with an outside consultant for some time.

Steve Caskey was responsible for facilitating business planning and strategy which involved structural and organizational issues, work-force planning and development, and culture change. He guaranteed his full support for the project.

Steve stated he did not have a clear view as to what this coaching initiative was or should be, but recognized that there needed to be a change in the role of the NSP Electric leader to enable teams to be successful as the organization moved into deregulation. He planned to use the outside consultant who was already working with the Electric leader team and suggested that Melody contact him for support in conducting the skill analysis and moving forward with the project.

John Johnson, Changemaking Systems, had been involved with NSP Electric's strategic direction for 10 years. He is valued for his strategic focus and for the trust that company leaders have in his coaching skills.

John had recommended to the NSP Electric staff that a Coaching Capability process be implemented. He based his recommendations on two things. He looked at the culture survey results focusing on the "command and control" environment feedback and he considered what he had heard and observed throughout the organization over the years during work with NSP Electric.

Melody, John, and Steve discussed the development of an introductory coaching class and it was clear that Melody would be taking a much more active role in the entire effort. The clarification of roles resulted in the following:

John's role:
- executive advisor to the NSP Electric leader staff
- lead a proposed "internal coach group"
- act as a subject matter expert on coaching and give Melody feedback on course content.

Melody's role:
- develop a project plan in partnership with Steve and gain support for the project
- design, develop, implement, and evaluate an introductory coaching class
- initiate the internal coaching group (now referred to as the Coaching Resource Group—CRG) by developing a draft of a job enhancement opportunity bulletin

- participate as a member of the CRG
- illustrate the ties that the Coaching Capability process has to other internal systems in place by developing a systems diagram/chart that would be presented during the introduction of the class.

 Steve's role:
- act as project manager for the coaching initiative and ensure that the products are in alignment with the workforce effectiveness goal.

Issues and Events

NSP Electric had several issues to confront during the implementation of the Coaching Capability process. There was minimal coaching going on within the organization. The managers, supervisors, team leaders, and other key technical individuals had been brought up in a command and control culture. There was no required leadership development program at the time that ensured all leaders were receiving the skills, opportunities, and practice needed to be effective leaders.

A project plan was created for presentation to the NSP Electric leader team. The goal was to provide a course that would ensure all NSP Electric employees (leaders and front-line) had the basic skills of coaching. An assessment would be designed to evaluate the use of these skills. Internal coaches, whose coaching competence was more advanced, would be identified and would be available to work with leaders on improving their coaching skills with their team members and employees. Ongoing skill development was also discussed and an advanced course was proposed for 1997. It was agreed that there would be a follow-up with course participants to reinforce the skills learned and work through coaching scenarios. The project plan deliverables were directly connected to NSP Electric's workforce effectiveness goal in the business plan.

The project was on a very short timeline. The presentation occurred in December 1995 and the projected roll-out of the training and CRG was by March 15, 1996. Part of this urgency was due to the fact that Melody was scheduled for a maternity leave in early April.

The team was given the go-ahead to take initial steps in implementing a culture change from command and control to coaching and collaborative. The benefits of this project were as follows: support a move toward self-directed work teams, implement redesigned work processes, visibly define the desired culture, increase organizational flexibility and adaptability, and improve safety, productivity, and competitiveness.

There were five basic elements to the implementation plan:

- Mandatory (intentionally mandatory, to acknowledge what the culture currently was) 16-hour coaching course for all supervisors and managers, including the president's leadership team which had to be developed.
- Communication of initiative organization-wide with integration into the performance management process.
- A core group of "experienced coaches" needed to be identified to act as coaches of leaders.
- Special training needed to be developed for the selected coaches.
- An advanced coaching course needed to be designed for ongoing development.

It was critical that the leadership team participate in selecting the experienced coaches and that they themselves "walk the talk" and demonstrate the skills that were expected of all leaders. As stated earlier, they were to attend the introductory training to show their support and challenge other leaders to take a hard look at their skills and abilities and examine how the information presented could aid in improving their communication and coaching skills.

Coaching Resource Group

The project team wanted the CRG to act as a resource to others throughout the organization who were running into difficulty with coaching situations. This could include work with leaders, team members, or peers.

John Johnson was convinced that there were some natural coaches within NSP Electric who could fit the bill. The problem was workload; the entire organization was doing more with less. Larry Taylor and his team wanted input as to who should be on this team. The project team convinced the group that it was beneficial to see who was actually interested in participating by letting them apply through the use of a job enhancement bulletin. The project team agreed to talk to the the leadership team using some general questions to see who they would recommend for the group and invite those individuals to sign the enhancement opportunity as well. All agreed that those interested should participate in an interview process.

An NSP Electric job enhancement opportunity bulletin was developed and distributed to all NSP Electric leaders. The bulletin clarified the following issues: 1) the position, 2) responsibilities, 3) qualifications needed, 4) any special requirements (time they would need to commit), and 5) next steps. For this opportunity, the team asked all applicants to also include a letter indicating why they believed they would add value to the resource group. The team was specifically looking for the following skills and abilities for the coaching resource group:

- demonstrated leadership capabilities—respected by others
- excellent communication skills, both written and oral
- knowledge of NSP Electric and its current culture and norms
- demonstrated coaching skills; viewed as a good coach and ability to help another become a better coach
- ability to provide examples of positively contributing to a teamwork environment.

A list of questions were sent out to Larry Taylor and his leadership team to determine who they thought should represent this group. This information was collected and kept with the enhancement opportunity bulletins and was used as support information when looking at the applicant pool.

Interviews were held and twelve people were selected. John Johnson provided training and coaching to this team. The CRG agreed to meet every two weeks. The meetings consisted of: 1) new information/tips from John on coaching; 2) presentation of two "real" case studies that were developed by members of the group where intentions of coaching and alternative techniques are discussed; and 3) action planning on how to integrate this group into the NSP Electric business.

The group was also asked to work with specific leaders on coaching issues. A representative from this group agreed to attend the course and give a brief presentation of the CRG's role. This representative also invited participants to call anyone on the team to discuss issues and talk strategies.

Members of this group contacted the graduates of the course and explained how the group could support and help them move forward in developing their coaching capability.

The CRG members discussed lessons learned in December 1996. They discovered that they were a resource for themselves based on the good mix of experience and background. Each person brought his or her own expertise to the problem-solving setting. The mentoring format did not work out very well. Others in the organization outside the group were reluctant to ask for help. Members stated they used the meetings as a forum to challenge each other's assumptions around current practices and procedures and to gain ideas for handling challenging employee or peer issues.

In January 1997, the CRG concept was expanded by splitting and establishing three new teams. A defined process was used for selection and the core group provided support and acted as resources by being active members on each team. The core group committed to meeting every six months to evaluate and assess the success of the program.

Coaching Course

The CRG members participated in the pilot of the coaching course that was developed in-house and delivered mid-March 1996. This course was called Coaching for Excellence.

The initial target audience for this course was all NSP Electric leaders. An attendee list was put together based on job responsibilities and pay grade. There were approximately 220 leaders.

All designated individuals received a letter from Larry Taylor stating that they were required to attend this course in 1996. Courses were scheduled, two a month, for the remainder of 1996 to accommodate the leader number. Class size was limited to 20 participants.

After all leaders in Electric were trained, the course would be opened up to all Electric employees who were interested in enhancing or building their coaching skills for either movement into a leadership position or to better work with teammates in their current position. Concurrently, the audience would include those from throughout NSP.

There was some concern on Melody's part as to whether the course should be required or not. Larry strongly felt he needed to send the message that all attend, that he saw it important enough for all leaders to receive training on the basics of coaching. Melody, from a delivery standpoint, was not too excited about having busy leaders showing up for class just because they had to. From past experience, she knew that the instructors would take the blame for the requirement and that leaders would quickly forget who had made the course mandatory.

Designating this course as mandatory did have some repercussions. At the beginning of each of the next three classes, leaders let the instructor know that they were not happy about being there and felt insulted that "HR" thought they needed this basic training. Melody met with Larry and they discussed this roadblock. Melody's concern was that it was hampering the learning of the leaders. Some were doing work during the class, others answered pages, and others left the class, never to return.

Larry agreed this was an issue and they decided he would come to the rest of the scheduled classes and talk to the groups about his vision for increasing the capability of his organization and the benefits to them as leaders for actively participating in the course and giving it their full attention. A diagram was also developed (figure 1) illustrating the integration of the course with other NSP initiatives and models. This helped immensely.

Course Design

Melody worked on the course design of the Coaching for Excellence course. Time was of the essence so the analysis phase was abbreviated. In selecting the CRG, the leader staff had already provided some very valuable information defining what they believed the important skills for a coach were. Melody and John analyzed this information along with benchmarking information that had been gathered in 1995 during a leadership study conducted by an NSP intern.

Melody familiarized John with current lesson plans for courses the Quality Academy was already offering that included coaching con-

Figure 1. Big picture.

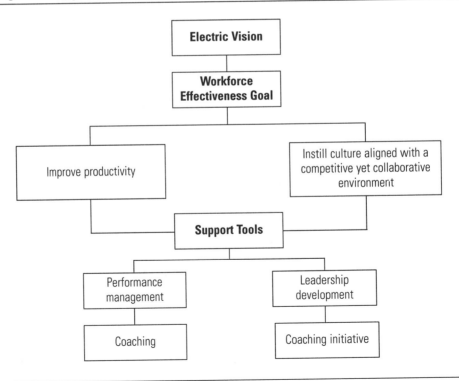

cepts. These courses included: 1) coaching for performance feedback; 2) delegation; 3) performance management; and 4) positive discipline.

Melody, Steve, John, and Linda all agreed that leaders needed to be able to give descriptive regular feedback to individuals, actively listen to concerns, clarify expectations of behavior and job responsibilities, build skills, enhance confidence, encourage flexibility, resolve conflict, and motivate those individuals with whom they were working.

Delivery Method

The course was designed for use in a variety of scheduling structures. The course was flexible enough in its design that it could be presented one module at a time with the introductory information included in the first module, as four four-hour sessions, or as a comprehensive two-day course.

The course information was accessible to any individual who wanted to use it for self-study or review. Based on the busy schedules of the leaders, the project team agreed that there had to be a way leaders could make up a part of the course if they had to miss due to pressing business issues. Copies of all information and videos were kept in the Quality Academy. Leaders could check out the information and videos and were signed off on completion upon return of the videos and a completed exercise guide.

The course was instructor-led, with a detailed, scripted instructor's guide. The participant's guide contained important information needed for reference during and after the course. It included an introduction, course objectives, key points to remember, directions for activities, activities worksheets, and reinforcing activities and references.

The assessments used for the course were kept separate from the participant's guide and were designed on carbonless paper so that the participant could keep one copy and the instructor another for analysis purposes.

Presentation materials for the course consisted of handouts, prepared flip charts, overhead transparencies, and video.

The Course

The course was designed to facilitate learning the essential skills of coaching. The course was built around video, small and large group exercises, and case study analysis. The course goal was defined as follows: provide NSP Electric employees with the basic skills of coaching, including clarifying expectations, building skills, enhancing confidence, encouraging flexibility, resolving conflict, developing motivation, and developing performance feedback skills. The course objectives included the following:

- Given a large group exercise, participants will list the benefits and barriers of coaching.
- Given a six-step process for coaching, leaders and team members will be able to coach each other or peers successfully.
- Given pre-work, self-assessments, exercises, and action planning, participants will gain knowledge and be able to demonstrate the seven foundational coaching skills (listed above).
- Given a lecture and case study exercises, participants will be able to give positive and corrective feedback and receive feedback from team members and peers.

The course outline was as follows:

I. Introduction
- What is coaching?
- Coaching for excellence self-assessment
- Benefits and barriers of coaching
- The leader as coach
- Six-step process for coaching employees
- Feedback pretest

II. Skills of Coaching
- Clarify expectations
- Build skills
- Enhance confidence
- Encourage flexibility
- Resolve conflict
- Develop motivation

III. Feedback
- Why give feedback?
- Types of reinforcement
- What is effective feedback?
- Giving feedback
- Receiving feedback
- Feedback techniques—the BEER and BET processes
- Goal setting

IV. Summary and Evaluation

Evaluation Plan

The course was evaluated using the first three levels of Kirkpatrick's levels of evaluation. The course in its entirety was measured using a scannable document to gather level one reaction/satisfaction from all participants. This document also provided space for written comments. The level one evaluation score for 1996 was 94 percent with a total of 236 NSP Electric leaders evaluating the course.

A pretest and a posttest were also completed for the feedback modules. These were multiple choice tests. The participants were given the pretest at the end of the introduction on day one and given the posttest at the end of day two. Based on statistical results from a *t* test: paired two sample for means, there was a statistically significant change in knowledge for participants.

There was a self-assessment and 360-degree assessment used to gain information on level three of Kirkpatrick's model which looks at behavior change.

One specific example of behavior change follows. A leader at a follow-up session stated that her team had increased productivity by almost three times due to her use of coaching skills with a problem employee. The leader stated that she focused and concentrated on what the issues were in dealing with an employee, and actually observed behaviors that could be documented rather than relying on feedback from other team members. The problem employee resigned from the company once the expected behavior was defined by the leader. Morale increased and communication lines opened up which, in turn, sped up turnaround time on jobs produced which increased customer satisfaction and productivity.

Assessment Process

The leaders were asked to assess themselves, using a 21-question self-assessment worksheet, during the introduction of the class. On the first day of the course they were also given the opportunity to pick up five assessments that they could distribute to their work group for feedback on their coaching skills. The five assessments were accompanied by a memo that the leader could use to communicate the purpose of the assessments to their employees.

These assessments were mailed directly back to Melody and were entered into a database along with the self-assessments. The information was summarized and sent to each participant within one month of course completion.

Six weeks prior to the follow-up session, the leader was mailed: 1) an invitation to attend the follow-up session; 2) the self-assessment instrument; 3) five leader assessments and the accompanying memo.

The leader was asked to fill out the self-assessment and return it to Melody and to distribute the leader assessment with the memo to the same five people they asked for feedback during class.

Summary reports were then run on both the self assessments and the leader assessments. Each participant received a copy of his or her summary information at the follow-up session.

There was an average increase of 19 percent in the self-assessment scores, based on the first three follow-up sessions, and an average increase of 12 percent for the leader assessment scores. These assessments are still an option today with the course for any leaders that attend.

Follow-up sessions

Follow-up sessions were scheduled for approximately six months after the training. Participants were invited back to see their pre- and post-assessment results. They also participated in exercises to reinforce the coaching skills through the use of case study discussion and role play. Goals were revisited and the question was asked, did they do what they said they were going to do when they left the classroom? Some were surprised that they had accomplished their goal, many could not even remember what their goal was.

After the follow-up session, participants were on their own in building their coaching skills and abilities. As stated earlier, unless they were directly involved as a CRG member, they did not take advantage of the mentoring opportunity available. There are no other follow-up statistics or any discussions scheduled with these individuals to ensure they are moving forward in instilling a coaching culture within the teams and work groups.

The coaching resource group has evolved into what is now called the "culture team." This team is actively promoting a change environment through continued support of the coaching initiative and through the use of a culture survey and the implementation of action plans based on survey results.

Four of the original CRG members are still participating and benefiting from each other. Ironically, but not unexpectedly, several members of the original CRG have since been placed in new leadership positions throughout the organization.

Conclusions and Recommendations

This program was successful for a number of reasons. The first being that the results were directly tied to a goal for the organization. The support from the leader team enabled the resources to be freed up for the CRG and for participation in the training and follow-up sessions. The energy of the project team was incredible. John, Steve, Linda, and Melody all saw the benefits of what this initiative could mean to the organization and worked together to eliminate barriers and move forward.

The Coaching for Excellence course is still being offered three years later at NSP as an open enrollment class. Reaction evaluation has remained the same—individuals are very satisfied with the course content. Instructors who were involved during the NSP Electric leader portion agree that when participants attend the course willingly, the course is much easier to teach; there is more interaction, and the group is more positive and willing to discuss issues and solutions. The case discussions add the most value and participants enjoy practicing the new skills in a safe training environment.

The follow-up sessions are still scheduled six months after class and are positively received by the participants.

The workforce effectiveness goal is still present in the business plan and even though it does not distinctly define coaching as the goal, it is implied that these are the skills needed to successfully meet this goal. Coaching has now become normative, in that the leadership competency model centers on it and assumes it.

Reaction from the project team has been positive. Steve stated he sees this as an ongoing development process. He was very surprised as to the level of grass roots support for the training. Steve had expected a lot more apathy and resistance, and instead saw the momentum being driven from both the bottom and the top of the organization. Middle management was not engaged, supportive, or understanding of the process. That however, did not stop progress. It is Steve's perception that most first-level supervisors knew they needed training and wanted it to be able to move the organization forward. Other managers who yearned for the return to command and control were reluctant to jump in and some have since moved into other areas of the company.

Melody has presented this case at a national conference and, although she has since moved into a leadership position within the Quality Academy, still actively promotes the training and the strategies and keeps in touch with the CRG. She believes her promotion was in part due to her actively practicing the skills she was teaching in the class. She is hoping to start a CRG at the site at which she is now located to ensure that leaders there can start safely discussing employee issues and concerns with others and generating solutions to better the work environment.

John is still working with NSP Electric, reinforcing and encouraging culture change from the top of the organization, and Linda states she is very excited about the changes but thinks that leadership has a long way to go to completely adopt the coaching style. Linda, too, has since been promoted into human resource leadership.

It has become clear to many people at NSP that the coaching development initiatives are having a direct impact on culture transformation. Coaching is here to stay as an expectation for any future leaders of the company and its many businesses. The increased awareness and comfort using the coaching behaviors have benefited the leaders and the organization.

Larry Taylor had stated at one of the sessions he spoke to that "coaching is not a program or a 'flavor of the month.' It supports business goals, key performance indicators, and operational measures."

This effort is still considered a high priority based on business strategy and customer input. It will continue to be supported in NSP Electric and made available to other areas in NSP.

Questions for Discussion

1. Is implementing a good coaching training program enough to make the training effective in the organization? Why or why not?
2. What else needs to happen to ensure the continued move toward a coaching and collaborative environment?
3. How critical was management's support to the success of the training effort? to the coaching initiative?
4. What could have helped to make this initiative more successful? Were there any critical aspects missing?

The Author

Melody McKay, manager of Customer Service and Applications Training at NSP, received her masters in education in human resource development at the University of Minnesota. She joined Northern States Power Company in 1989 and has worked as a performance consultant for eight years. Melody has presented nationally on the Coaching Capability process and is currently involved in the design and implementation of a new leadership development process for the company. She may be contacted at NSP, 3115 Centre Pointe Drive, Roseville, MN 55108.

Individual Leadership Development Process

Mobil Oil's North America Marketing and Refining Division

James Stryker

The Individual Leadership Development Process (ILDP) is a process designed to improve business performance by developing leadership behaviors in those people in key positions in Mobil Oil's North America Marketing and Refining (NAM&R) Division. The ILDP begins with assessment, testing, and feedback leading to self-awareness, which is the starting point for individual development. Through a series of planned experiences, an attempt is made to grow leadership competencies and link them to action through people in work locations. This is done by modeling the real social process of applying new leadership tools and behaviors in a simulated environment and following up later in the real business setting through action learning.

Introduction

This paper is an attempt to capture and document the Individual Leadership Development Process (ILDP) as it has been created and evolved over the last five years. The ILDP is a process designed to improve leadership skills and competencies in the North America Marketing and Refining (NAM&R) Division of Mobil Oil. The process starts with feedback and continues through the development and application of leadership competencies at work. The two constructs addressed with literature references are the psychological aspect of testing and 360-degree feedback and the sociological aspect of how the knowledge and competency developed through this process is applied in

This case was prepared to serve as a basis for discussion rather than to illustrate either effective or ineffective administrative and management practices.

real work teams, in business units, using the concept of action learning. The purpose of the paper is to document the ILDP and look at what some of the literature says about these two aspects of it.

History and Problem

A shortage of leadership seemed to be a chronic problem at Mobil Oil in the early 1990s. It was spotlighted in the outcome of a corporate-wide career development study done in 1992. This study highlighted four key points:

1. There were too few leaders at all organization levels.
2. Forty percent of the employees surveyed indicated that they were underutilized, so the workforce contribution needed to be leveraged.
3. The organization tolerated weak performance at many levels.
4. People were developed narrowly and lacked a broad understanding of the business.

Based on these findings, senior executives concluded that leadership development and management practices required significant attention.

The financial situation in the early 1990s leading up to this situation was threatening. Product demand was flat. Competition was intense. Expenses, particularly environmental expenses, were escalating rapidly, and the organization was not making any money. In 1992, NAM&R reported an operating loss and ranked 12 out of 13 oil companies in profitability. It was clear that something had to be done.

In early 1993, a climate survey revealed that employees felt that NAM&R had lost focus. Top down policies were stifling creativity. Customer relationships were adversarial. People were focused only on their own narrow functional units. As Marsick and Watkins wrote, "the workplace has changed irrevocably" (1994, p. 353). They go on to talk about how difficult it is to create a learning capacity in an organization that is undergoing massive change. "Learning organizations grow organically, and each company will create a different configuration" (p. 354). NAM&R decided that despite the chaos, they had to begin to create theirs.

The NAM&R executive leadership team held a meeting—in February 1993—that focused on "leadership." It was decided that NAM&R had to start shifting to the creation of a "high performance organization" if they were to have any chance of surviving. The decision was made to build a leadership model, define it, select for it, and build a development process that would enable the organization to create and maintain a critical mass of effective leaders.

The Leadership Model

NAM&R decided that it was important to start by defining what they meant by leadership. Leadership was defined in terms of three components, which included setting a direction, aligning the organization, and energizing the people.

Definition

The definition of leadership agreed on in 1993 follows:

> Leaders influence and shape events. Their energies are directed towards change and continuous improvement where external factors are one of the clear drivers. They are able to create a compelling vision, align the contribution of a critical mass within their teams, and inspire, energize, and excite others to succeed. They use a combination of intelligent risk-taking, trust, innovation, and sheer drive to build on early successes. They establish clarity, take ownership, and hold themselves accountable for results. They always find a way to win.

Competencies and Behaviors

This definition included approximately seven specific behaviors under each of the three main competencies. One example of each follows in table 1.

Table 1. The three main competencies.

Competency	Behavior
Develop bold visions and strategies (Direction)	See how the organization could be and is able to create excitement about getting there
Challenge others to contribute positively to organizational goals (Alignment)	Develop scorecards, key performance indicators, targets and meet them
Energize entire organizations, working relentlessly to keep people fully utilized and excited about being a contributor (Motivated)	Build trust so that people have the confidence to go for outstanding results

There are many other behaviors under each of the competencies. This definition of leadership was later expanded into a 56-question 360-degree feedback instrument.

Strategic Outlook

By early 1994 the need to develop leaders was recognized as one of five critical strategic themes in NAM&R's corporate strategic outlook presentation. The bullet in the high-level overview read as follows: "Motivated and prepared workforce: Develop leaders." It may not seem like much, but it was the first time that a people initiative made the top five. Historically the themes were financial or operations oriented.

Later in 1994 a "leadership report card" was included in the employee climate survey. There were eight questions included, and the rating scale ranged from A = excellent job to F = failing job. In that survey the leaders of the major business units averaged a C− score. At that point the leadership team recognized that they had to stop planning and actually start to grow the leadership competency. They had to get tougher on demanding it in key jobs, working it into evaluations and rewards, and start thinking about organizational learning and individual development.

The 1995 NAM&R human resource strategy included only five priorities. The five follow; four of them addressed the leadership issue.
1. Complete right person in right job process (RP/RJ).
2. Accelerate leadership development.
3. Set up continuing RP/RJ targets and measure progress.
4. Ruthlessly prioritize use of resources on development/improvement activities.
5. Create optimum labor strategy.

Right Person in Right Job

The whole drive behind the right person in the right job process was to get outstanding leadership performance and realize the full economic potential of the NAM&R business. A simple process, based on data, was designed to slot all managers into one of five categories. These categories were based on a simplified 10-point leadership template. This 10-point template evolved from the original leadership definition and the NAM&R 360-degree feedback instrument. The key to this template was the fact that it required evidence of how, through the demonstration (or lack of) each of the leadership behaviors, the leader made or lost money and strengthened or weakened the organization for the future.

All of the leaders in the organization were evaluated on this scale on a percentage fit basis. Each was compared to a "gold standard" of top leaders. The standard was based on those who came the closest to behaving in accordance with the leadership definition. The percentage fit on this scale ranged from 20 percent, which meant the person rarely showed any evidence of leadership behavior, to 100 percent fit, which meant that one consistently demonstrated all preferred behaviors and achieved outstanding results on at least two occasions in the past three years. The goal for fit against this metric was to have 95 percent of the leaders be an 80 to 100 percent fit. In early 1995, only 60 of 170 leaders met this criteria. The goal was an aggressive one. The initial target was to meet the 95 percent fit number by January 1, 1997. This meant that the organization would have to be very focused on both filling jobs with people who demonstrated leadership and on developing the competencies of those already in positions. This realization led to the creation of the ILDP in mid-1995.

Individual Leadership Development Process
Vision

When the ILDP was being designed there were two overarching deliverables articulated. The first was to continuously fill leadership critical positions with individuals assessed at 80 to 100 percent on leadership characteristics. The second was to deliver into critical leadership positions at the earliest practical point in their careers individuals who, through their leadership skills, would bring the most added value to that role and produce the most outstanding results.

There were also several statements or principles agreed to as a vision to guide the evolution of the ILDP. Those principles follow:

- We identify and agree on critical leadership positions throughout the business.
- To get started, we focus on leadership roles that potentially impact on (a) the most people, and (b) the critical strategic business issues.
- We create some tools for identifying "leadership potential": (a) for early in career people who have limited leading people experience, and (b) for early/mid career people who have significant leading people experience.
- We agree on a process for assessing "significant destination potential" for individuals with high leadership potential.
- We agree on a framework for expressing that "potential" in terms of "target positions."
- We agree to "lock on" to these people and stay committed to developing them and exploring their potential for a valid period of time.

- We agree to accept some set-backs and disappointments.
- We build a set of "competency" targets for each individual based on current "target position" and construct a "gap analysis."
- We then use: (a) behavior skills assessment/development, (b) business/technical/other know-how development, and (c) highly focused job experience planning to close the "gaps."
- We are empowered to heavily influence staffing/career development processes and decisions to give priority to routing/development of these people.
- We do not consider "time in position" as a key factor, rather we see achievement of "learning goals" and associated achievement of results as trigger factors in "timing decisions."
- We fight to suppress invalid paradigms. We seek to experiment.
- We agree that these individuals should input their own needs/wants into the process.
- We agree to "flex" compensation systems to fit development plans.
- We allow for a mechanism that permits both entry/exit to this process in a valid way.
- As "target positions" change we adjust the "gap analysis" and "development plan" accordingly.
- We find a way of presenting all relevant data (gap analysis/plans, and so on) in a concise, useable way.
- We share development planning fully with each individual.
- We are free to use any internal/external expertise or process.
- We accept that each individual's development plan may be different.

The leadership team was hopeful that if they followed these principles NAM&R would start to create an organization that could learn and effectively change continuously. "This means that it empowers its people, encourages collaboration and team learning, promotes open dialogue, and acknowledges the interdependence of individuals, the organization, and the communities in which they reside" (Marsick and Watkins, 1994, p. 354). They wanted an organization in which, as Marsick and Watkins went on to describe, "learning is rewarded, planned for, and supported through a culture open to risk taking, experimentation, and collaboration" (p. 355). The ILDP design team agreed with Hollomon and Coleman (1987) who wrote that "since organizational effectiveness is highly dependent upon the ability of managers to motivate subordinates toward higher productivity, the need for managers to function as leaders is increasingly being emphasized" (p. 16). Hence, the NAM&R strategy was to start this learning process in the leadership team.

Design Overview

This section of the paper will provide a high level overview of the ILDP. Each of the component pieces will be discussed in more detail in subsequent sections. Cashman and Reisberg (1994) wrote about executive development as:

> Most executive development programs begin and end with psychological assessment. Although a valuable tool, it is not enough. A person, no less than an elephant, is not understood from one vantage point. To psychology we must add the perspectives of human development, career management, interpersonal influence, and lifestyle balance. There is also the limitation of working with one expert. When a team of coaches with specialties in different disciplines all work together with one executive, the results can be dramatic. Fragmented information integrates into focused powerful leadership, consistent with the uniqueness of the person. (p. 9)

The design of the ILDP parallels the Cashman and Reisberg description nicely. It starts with an in-depth personal assessment consisting of the NAM&R leadership 360-degree feedback instrument used in conjunction with the Occupational Personality Questionnaire (OPQ), which is a self-report measure of a person's typical ways of behaving. The feedback from both of these measures is delivered in a one-day feedback workshop early in the ILDP. This workshop is delivered by an industrial psychologist from Saville & Holdsworth Ltd. (SHL).

The second part of the ILDP consists of a two-day Coaching and Learning Workshop, which explores both sides of the coach and learner relationship. The participants are both learners, in the sense of participating in developing their own leadership competencies, and they are coaches. In the organization, they are the ones who need to coach their teams. This workshop is delivered by a senior consultant from Innovation Associates.

The third piece of this process is a four-day business skills development session that is conducted around the "case" of a fictional integrated business unit manager whom we call "Bill Butcher." The Bill Butcher case is facilitated by a combination of faculty members from the Impact Planning Group (IPG), combined with one or more industrial psychologists from SHL. The IPG faculty provide the functional knowledge needed by Bill Butcher whereas the SHL team focuses on integrating that knowledge and applying it through people. Arie De Gues (1997, p. 74) talks about the concept of "accelerated learning" through "play" and how important it is to let people experiment with the decision-making process to improve both the speed and quality of decisions. This is one of the main functions of the Bill Butcher Workshop.

The fourth piece of the ILDP involves an in-depth, two-day, experiential workshop called the Ariel Group Workshop. It is facilitated by senior consultants from the Ariel Group Inc. All Ariel Group consultants are theater professionals by trade and training. This session explores the communication and presence skills required of leaders in a way that builds off of the "emotional intelligence" ideas of Goleman (1997).

These four sessions take place over the course of a year. People participate in this process in waves or cohorts of about twenty. The participants are drawn from different business units throughout the United States and Mexico, and each comes with different functional skills and backgrounds. Upon completion of these scheduled sessions participants become involved in some form of action learning with others from their own business unit.

This entire process was designed in conjunction with representatives from each of the companies mentioned above working together. They are referred to as "the faculty." Figure 1 provides an overview of the process.

The sections that follow include more detail designed to show how this process links the psychometric assessment and feedback to application in the social system in the workplace.

360-Degree Feedback

"For 360-degree feedback to be valuable, it needs to be seen in a larger context. What are the developmental implications of these perceptions? How do leaders reconcile the gap between self-perception and others' perceptions to enhance their leadership consistent with who they are?" (Cashman and Reisberg, 1994, p. 9). Most people come into the NAM&R ILDP with 360-degree feedback in hand. What is added to that is the larger perspective. The NAM&R 360-degree process, consistent with the findings of Church and Bracken (1997), is based on the "simple assumption, derived in part from measurement theory, that observations obtained from multiple sources will yield more valid and reliable (and therefore more meaningful and useful) results for the individual" (p. 150). Multiple sources are better than one when it comes to observing behavior, and that really is what 360-degree feedback provides.

Figure 1. Overview of the ILDP.

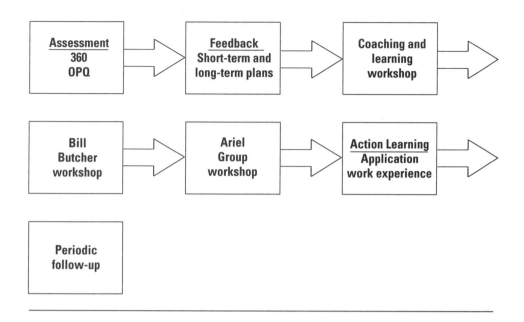

This process uses an iceberg model. Three hundred sixty–degree feedback represents the part of the iceberg that is above the water. It is feedback on behavior that can be seen by others. Leadership development in the ILDP is really about changing these behaviors. Church and Bracken (1997) said that 360-degree feedback can force one "into a cognitive process of reflection that ultimately results in greater levels of awareness of their own actions and the consequences those actions have on others across various levels in and out of the organization" (p. 150). They go on to suggest that the 360-degree method can have a significant impact on these behaviors over time. The ILDP attempts to significantly enhance that impact by delving beneath the water to explore the largest part of the iceberg. That is done with the OPQ. More will be said about that in the next section.

There are a few aspects of 360-degree feedback that deserve some attention. They include the underlying purpose and use of 360, the issue of feedback team selection, the use of written comments, and the use of the 360 to set improvement goals. In a review of the literature on performance appraisal from 1980 through 1984, Reinhardt (1985) said, "Most organizations tie performance appraisal to such personnel decisions as compensation, training and development, and promotion or layoff decisions" (p. 106). None of the literature at that time mentioned 360-degree feedback and most of the concerns seemed to be with having a system that was "legally defensible." The purpose and use of 360-degree feedback in the NAM&R system is very different from that view. The ILDP is for developmental purposes only, and that is articulated very clearly to both raters and participants.

Church and Bracken (1997) make the point that accountability is critical. "In development-only processes, where the ratee is the 'owner' of the feedback with little or no accountability for action, little change should be expected, whereas performance appraisal settings have characteristics that allow for the establishment of accountability mechanisms for all parties involved" (p. 152). Although there is merit to the accountability issue, the ILDP is more closely aligned with the thinking of Waldman, Atwater, and Antonioni (1998). "In theory, the use of 360 degree feedback for evaluative purposes seems logical. An individual held directly accountable for ratings received will be more motivated to take action to make improvements based on feedback. Unfortunately, problems exist that may negate the possible benefits of 360 degree feedback if it is made evaluative" (p. 88). Those problems can include raters changing their ratings and ratees selecting their feedback teams in such a way as to receive only positive feedback.

The ILDP assumption is that leaders are self-motivated and hold themselves accountable for their development. Appraisal systems are not necessary. Changed behavior and improved business results serve as the indicators of progress. Participants in the NAM&R process select their own feedback teams and are encouraged to include a broad representation of people including those with whom they may not have very good relationships. It often turns out that this feedback can create the most insight by providing a contrary view. These views are often articulated in the written comments that are included in the process. Raters are anonymous, but they are asked to provide comments as to what the ratee should start, stop, or continue doing. The NAM&R experience agrees with Waldman et al. who said, "ratees have indicated that the written feedback is more valuable to them than numerical ratings" (1998, p. 92).

It is important that the 360-degree instrument measure the behavior that you really want to encourage. "Even when 360 degree feedback ratings are used strictly for developmental purposes, indi-vi-duals will tend to modify behaviors in many ways to receive more positive ratings. Therefore, it is extremely important that 360 degree surveys reflect those behaviors that the organization values most highly" (Waldman et al., 1998, p. 91). The NAM&R 360-degree instrument is written directly from the leadership definition that the organization worked so hard to gain consensus on. It measures what NAM&R wants to create, and it encourages leaders to set improvement goals toward those behaviors that will drive business performance, both short and long term.

There is one final issue around 360-degree feedback and this development process that is worthy of mention, and that is the use of 360-degree feedback to set improvement goals, the progress against which are then used to rate, rank, and reward individuals. Luis Gomez-Mejia (1990) wrote about the crucial importance of individual-based appraisal and reward programs to business success. He stated, "It is important to identify and recognise outstanding performers so that these individuals do not feel that the fruits of their effort are distributed to fellow employees who do not adhere to similar performance standards" (p. 21). He clearly feels that an appraisal-based reward system is necessary to enhance performance. The ILDP takes a slightly different view. It is the development and demonstration of leadership that is rewarded with more responsible positions, rather than success in an appraisal process being rewarded with reward programs. Development in the ILDP generates more challenging development opportunities that appear to be far more motivating than short-term financial rewards. It should be noted, though, that significant financial rewards do come with the increased challenges.

Occupational Personality Questionnaire (OPQ)

As described in the previous section, 360-degree feedback gives a participant information on his or her actual behavior as perceived by others. To continue the iceberg analysis, this is the part of the iceberg that can be seen above the surface. A process that uses only this type of feedback has some weaknesses. McCauley, Lombardo, and Usher (1989) wrote that, "Most feedback instruments to managers were developed from studying what managers do in their jobs" (p. 390). They go on to talk about the weakness of that approach in terms of assessing development needs and how important it is to go deeper than that in assessing strengths and weaknesses. In line with that thinking, the ILDP attempts to get below the surface and elucidate the supporting structure. For this purpose, the ILDP uses the OPQ instrument from SHL to give leaders feedback on 30 different personality dimensions that are work relevant. NAM&R is concerned with the ways leaders behave, think, and feel, and this instrument provides them feedback on how their personality traits and preferences compare with those of more than 10,000 other middle and senior level U.S. managers. This gives them important information designed to help them understand their 360-degree feedback and effectively translate it into a development plan.

The OPQ reports data through an Expert System. This analysis is in a narrative format and is relatively jargon-free. It gives feedback on specific characteristics such as persuasiveness, control, independence, achievement, and decisiveness. It does this both in data format and in the narrative format describing the individual personality profile in terms of the type of leader, subordinate, and team player the individual tends to be.

During the feedback workshop, the 360-degree feedback and the OPQ data are presented and participants work on integrating the two. The result is a much clearer picture of the entire iceberg. The OPQ helps people to understand their 360-degree feedback and create development plans that are often quite different than they would be from 360 alone. One example is the manager who received feedback that he was a poor delegator. His development plan was to attend a training program on delegation. It was a good training program and he came back an expert in knowing why, when, and how to delegate. He was very surprised when his next 360-degree feedback showed no improvement in this area. He finally began to get a much clearer picture from his OPQ data, which showed he had super high scores in need for controlling, detail consciousness, and achievement. This realization did not make it any more natural for him to delegate, but it did help him to create a plan to overcome his natural inclinations and become relatively good at delegation. It is this broader perspective that provides participants with the start of very useful development plans.

Integration and Application

The Bill Butcher Workshop usually follows the feedback workshop by about six months and is the place where a lot of the information people have received about themselves starts to become very real. The Bill Butcher Workshop creates what Stumpf (1995) called a "live practice field." According to Stumpf, "Behavioral simulations recreate an organizational entity through written materials and implied structures, roles, and functions" (p. 47). Bill Butcher does exactly that. Bill is very real. The case starts at the end of Bill's first week on the job as a new integrated business unit manager. He is on the plane flying home, because his family hasn't moved yet, and he is thinking back over his first week.

Most of Bill's career was spent in one specific function and now he has to deal with a much broader perspective. He is expected to lead an organization that includes all of the functions in the marketing and refining business. His first week is chaos. What began as a well planned orientation to his new business unit disintegrated into one firefight after the next dealing with a range of issues that were quite unfamiliar to Bill. There are 12 sub-cases in this workshop that focus on different aspects of Bill's leadership challenges. These range from dealing with labor relations problems over outsourcing to strategic issues involving unbranded gasoline convenience store competition. Each of these issues challenges Bill's capacity to think and act strategically and to lead his organization.

Stumpf said, "One must be an active observer and player, in active partnership with the organization and its environments, to learn much from events or experiences" (1995, p. 41). In the Bill Butcher case participants actively engage in Bill's issues. Participants are grouped in small teams of four or five. These teams always have a mix of the functional competencies that Bill needs to deal with his problems. These teams are asked to share ideas with each other, discuss Bill's issues, and together recommend solutions. One of the things this session is designed to accomplish is the development by the attendees of a "theory of managing." Argyris (1996) said that "managing means creating intended consequences. In a theory of managing, explanation, generalization, and testing are all in the service of creating managerial actions" (p. 402). Working with these practice situations in a small team to create solutions is a safe way for the participants to get some valuable experience. The goal is that "because simulations carry no risk, managers can explore more creative solutions to problems and provide immediate compelling feedback on decisions" (Matanovich and Cressman, 1996, p. 45).

The facilitators of these sessions coach the participants in the sense that Galwey (1997) writes about it. "Coaching is a way of being, listening, asking, and speaking that draws out and augments characteristics and potential that are already present in a person. An effective coaching relationship creates a safe and challenging environment in which learning can take place" (p. 5). This safe learning environment allows people the space and the reflective time they need to think and talk about these issues. As a secondary benefit the facilitators role model the coaching styles that they would like the participants to use with their own teams.

At the same time that people are working on theories of managing, they are focusing on their own leadership behaviors. They share their OPQ feedback and the behaviors they are trying to develop with their teams. Each session dealing with Bill Butcher's issues ends with the team giving feedback to each team member, specifically focused on the behaviors they are attempting to develop. In a review of studies on feedback systems, Kolb (1995) points out "that although feedback alone is not sufficient to increase performance, feedback plus goals does lead to improved performance" (p. 235). The ILDP, through the Bill Butcher Workshop, allows the participants to set goals, based on their own 360-degree and OPQ feedback, share those goals with a team, practice, and receive ongoing live feedback on their progress. This can be very powerful.

There is another dimension to this development activity. The OPQ feedback provides input as to what kind of team player each individual tends to be and what roles he or she is most effective in. This small team process role models the use of that feedback in a safe setting. The facilitation of a discussion that helps each team member gain a better understanding of all the team members is one of the exercises each of these groups goes through. These exercises really bring the OPQ data to life and get people comfortable in working on their improvement goals which eventually become a part of what they do every day on the job through some type of action learning. Numerous participants have taken this process back to their business units and report significant improvements in the day-to-day functioning of their leadership teams.

Action Learning

"Action learning is a truly unique organizational learning process that requires an instructional mindset usually absent in traditional instructors. Action learning is growing in acceptance around the world. Like the case method, it was designed as a managerial learning process; but if projects and teams are selected appropriately, and designed with teams from the same organization, it offers excellent opportunities for promoting strategic organizational learning" (Keys, 1994, p. 55). In the ILDP, action learning consists of teams of participants, back in their own business units, working together on real business projects. Each of these teams is facilitated by a member of the faculty.

The idea which is described well by Smith and Peters (1997) is that "we can only learn by doing, and then reflecting carefully on what happened, making sense of the lessons and working through how the learning can be built on and used next time around" (p. 65). The faculty member facilitates the team members to focus on their own learning objectives in the context of the real business issues. These are the same objectives that they developed from their 360-degree and OPQ feedback data. At the same time they reinforce the use of the OPQ data to help them function as an effective team. This process ties it all together in the real live social environment of their work. As Smith and Peters (1997) wrote, "It emphasizes personal responsibility for learning, although supportive, but challenging learning partnerships are made available. It requires individuals to resolve significant business, organizational and social problems. By doing so, they can learn and the company 'gets the job done'—a win/win situation for both parties" (p. 65).

Action learning, as the final segment of ILDP, does not really end. It is a process that allows people to learn while doing real work, so it does not ever have to end. A longer-term goal is that some participants will actually start to teach and facilitate other members of the organization and in fact become part of the faculty.

Conclusion

Argyris (1994) summed it up effectively when he wrote, "Today, facing competitive pressures an earlier generation could hardly have imagined, managers need employees who think constantly and creatively about the needs of the organization" (p. 85). This ILDP is the beginning of NAM&R's attempt to develop that capability in the organization. Implicit in this process is the idea that "the key to any educational experience designed to teach senior managers how to reason productively is to connect the program to real business problems" (Argyris, 1991, p. 107). The ILDP attempts to build from a level of individual psychometric feedback to the application of continuous learning in the real, social environment of the team in the business unit.

Remember that from the very beginning this process has been about results. De Gues (1988) captured this idea nicely when he said, "Our exploration into this area is not a luxury. We understand that the only competitive advantage the company of the future will have is its managers' ability to learn faster then their competitors" (p. 74). NAM&R's venture into the ILDP was meant to improve business performance by developing leadership behaviors in those people in key positions in the organization. As of this writing, NAM&R has involved more than 200 leaders in this process and is pleased with the results to date. The process continues to change, as it should, as more is learned through experience.

Results

If you recall, in the 1992-1993 timeframe, the NAM&R financial results were abysmal. They ranked 12 out of 13 oil companies in net profit margin ranking. Only 35 percent of the people in leadership positions demonstrated the behaviors the organization was looking for, and the organization graded the leadership at a C− in an employee climate survey.

In a recent climate survey, completed in November 1997, the leadership grade improved to a B. The last update of the right person right job percentage fit against the leadership template showed an increase from 35 percent to 75 percent of the managers who were an 80 to 100 percent fit. NAM&R generated over $500 million after tax net profit in 1997. This represents over a billion-dollar swing in cash flow versus 1992. What may be the key measure, because the world does change, is the relative competitive ranking. In 1995, 1996, 1997, and for the full year of 1998, NAM&R has ranked number 1 out of the 13 major oil companies in net profit, cents-per-gallon. It would probably not be fair to attribute these results entirely to the leadership development process, but the case could certainly be made that it has been a strong contributor.

The learning is not over for the individual participants. The process is not completed in its design. The business results are not final. They never are. The process will change and grow as the organization learns and grows, and, if that is done more effectively than competition, the impressiveness of NAM&R's results will grow as well.

Implications for Further Work

The idea of participants teaching and facilitating future participants is just starting to be explored in the organization. The idea of learning by teaching seems to hold great potential for the future.

Questions for Discussion

1. Why should management support individual leadership development?

2. How can people find the time to participate in development activities when they are already swamped with work?

3. What is expected of leaders in your organization?
4. How do you determine if someone is a leader in your organization?
5. Who is responsible for learning in your organization?

The Author

James Stryker is the manager of Strategic Business Skills Development for Mobil Oil's North America Marketing and Refining organization, headquartered in Fairfax, Virginia. His expertise includes performance feedback and development, including 360-degree feedback interpretation and use, group facilitation, organizational improvement, and leadership development at all levels from front-line supervision through executive leadership. In his 27 years at Mobil, he has held numerous positions in sales, sales management, administration, financial analysis, and planning, and for the last 12 years he has been involved in every aspect of training and development. For the last four years his primary focus has been on improving the performance of the organization through the design and implementation of the Individual Leadership Development Process. Stryker holds a bachelor's degree in psychology and economics, a masters degree in business administration, and is currently pursuing a Ph.D. in human resource development in the Executive Leadership Program at George Washington University. He can be contacted at the following address: 5701 Windsor Gate Lane, Fairfax, Virginia 22030.

References

Argyris, C. (1991). "Teaching Smart People How to Learn." *Harvard Business Review,* May-June, 99–109.

Argyris, C. (1994). "Good Communication That Blocks Learning." *Harvard Business Review,* July-August, 77–85.

Argyris, C. (1996). "Actionable Knowledge: Design Causality in the Service of Consequential Theory." *Journal of Applied Behavioral Science, 32*(4), 390–406.

Cashman, K., and S. Reisberg. (1994). "Road to Leadership." *Executive Excellence, 11*(12), 9–10.

Church, A.H., and D.W. Bracken. (1997). "Advancing the State of the Art of 360-degree Feedback." *Group & Organization Management, 22*(2), 149–161.

De Geus, A.P. (1988). "Planning as Learning."*Harvard Business Review, 66*(2), 70–74.

De Geus, A.P. (1997). *The Living Company.* Boston: Harvard Business School Press.

Galwey, T. (1997). "The Inner Game of Work: Building Capability in the Workplace." *The Systems Thinker, 8*(6), 1–5.

Goleman, D. (1997). Reprint. *Emotional Intelligence.* New York: Bantam Books. Original edition, New York: Bantam Books, 1995.

Gomez-Mejia, L.R. (1990). "Increasing Productivity: Performance Appraisal and Reward Systems." *Personnel Review, 19*(2), 21–26.

Hollomon, R., and B. Coleman. (1987). "Leadership: The Organizational Imperative." *Mid-South Business Journal, 7*(2), 13–16.

Keys, L. (1994). "Action Learning: Executive Development of Choice for the 1990s." *Journal of Management Development, 13*(8), 50–56.

Kolb, J.A. (1995). "Leader Behaviors Affecting Team Performance." *Journal of Business Communication, 32*(3), 233–248.

Marsick, V.J., and K.E. Watkins. (1994). "The Learning Organization: An Integrative Vision for HRD." *Forum, 5*(4), 353–360.

Matanovich, T.J., and G.E. Cressman. (1996). "Hyper-Learning in a Hyper-World." *Marketing Management, 5*(2), 43–55.

McCauley, C.D., M.M. Lombardo, and C.J. Usher. (1989). "Diagnosing Management Development Needs: An Instrument Based on How Managers Develop." *Journal of Management, 15*(3), 389–403.

Reinhardt, C. (1985). "The State of Performance Appraisal: A Literature Review." *Human Resource Planning, 8*(2), 105–110.

Smith, P.A.C., and V.J. Peters. (1997). "Action Learning Worth a Closer Look." *Ivey Business Quarterly, 62*(1), 63–67.

Stumpf, S. A. (1995). "Applying New Science Theories in Leadership Development Activities." *Journal of Management Development, 14*(5), 39–49.

Waldman, D.A., L.E. Atwater, and D. Antonioni. (1998). "Has 360 Degree Feedback Gone Amok?" *Academy of Management Executive, 12*(2), 86–94.

About the Editor

Franklin C. Ashby is the president of Manchester Training®. With 25 years of experience in training and development, his writings and program designs have been purchased by more than 400 of the *Fortune* 500 companies and translated into 26 languages. Often described as one of America's leading authorities on organizational effectiveness and improvement strategies, Ashby was previously the vice president of instruction and chief educational officer of the world's largest for-profit adult training organization. In this role he was responsible for all matters pertaining to the administration, design, and delivery of all products and services in 77 countries. He also served as the organization's official spokesperson at its headquarter offices in New York.

Ashby has been a featured speaker at dozens of conventions and universities over the years. Recent presentations include a keynote address at the FBI National Academy in Quantico, VA; the keynote address at the Society for Human Resource Management National Leadership Conference in Washington, D.C.; guest lectures at Columbia University and the Columbia Business School; and a lecture tour throughout the United Kingdom.

He is the author of *Revitalizing Your Corporate Culture: Strategies & Tactics for Enlightened Organizations* (Gulf Publishing; 1999).

In addition to a Ph.D. in management and organizational development, Ashby holds an M.A. in adult learning from Columbia University, an M.B.A. in finance and marketing from NYIT, and a B.A. in psychology from Hofstra University.

He and his wife, Rita, and their son, Danny, live on Long Island.

About the Series Editor

Jack Phillips has nearly 30 years of professional experience in human resources and management. He has served as training and development manager at two *Fortune* 500 firms, senior human resources executive at two firms, president of a regional federal savings bank, and management professor at a major state university. In 1992, Phillips founded Performance Resources Organization, an international consulting firm specializing in human resources accountability programs. Phillips consults with his clients in the United States, Canada, England, Italy, Germany, Belgium, South Africa, Mexico, Venezuela, Malaysia, Hong Kong, Indonesia, Australia, New Zealand, and Singapore on issues ranging from measurement and evaluation to productivity and quality enhancement.

A frequent contributor to management literature, Phillips has been author or editor of *HRD Trends Worldwide* (1999), *A New Vision for Human Resources* (1998), *Return on Investment in Training and Performance Improvement Programs* (1997), *Accountability in Human Resource Management* (1996), *Handbook of Training Evaluation and Measurement Methods* (3d edition, 1997), *Measuring Return on Investment* (volume 1, 1994; volume 2, 1997), *Conducting Needs Assessment* (1995), *Recruiting, Training and Retaining New Employees* (1987), and *Improving Supervisors' Effectiveness* (1985), which won an award from the Society for Human Resource Management. Phillips has written more than 100 articles for professional, business, and trade publications.

Phillips holds undergraduate degrees in electrical engineering, physics, and mathematics; a master's degree in decision sciences from Georgia State University; and a doctorate in human resource management from the University of Alabama. In 1987, he won the Yoder-Heneman Personnel Creative Application Award from the Society for Human Resource Management. He is an active member of several professional organizations.

Phillips may be reached at the following address: Performance Resources Organization, Box 380637, Birmingham, AL 35238-0637; phone: 205.678.9700; fax: 205.678.8070; email: roipro@wwisp.com.